Security and Its Challenges in the 21st Century

Innovation and Technology Set

coordinated by
Chantal Ammi

Volume 12

Security and Its Challenges
in the 21st Century

Claudine Guerrier

WILEY

First published 2021 in Great Britain and the United States by ISTE Ltd and John Wiley & Sons, Inc.

ISTE Ltd
27-37 St George's Road
London SW19 4EU
UK

www.iste.co.uk

John Wiley & Sons, Inc.
111 River Street
Hoboken, NJ 07030
USA

www.wiley.com

Library of Congress Control Number: 2021938219

British Library Cataloguing-in-Publication Data
A CIP record for this book is available from the British Library
ISBN 978-1-78630-621-0

Contents

Introduction

"France is [synonymous with] security," said President Emmanuel Macron in a public speech on October 22, 2019. Security appears to have taken precedence in 21st-century media constructs, to the point that practically any country's name could be used in this phrase.

According to *Le Petit Robert*, security is "the absence of danger, i.e., a situation in which someone (or something) is not exposed to critical events or risks".

According to the WHO, security "is a state in which hazards ... leading to physical, psychological or material harm are controlled in order to preserve the health and well-being of individuals and the community". It is therefore necessary to highlight the danger or absence of danger, and the actors involved, whether natural or legal persons.

Legal certainty is not a new concept. During antiquity, Plato and Aristotle insisted on the need to establish powers in order to ensure border security and prevent the outbreak of conflicts. For Plato[1], security meant the use of professional guardians. These guardians were required to obey the orders of the central power, and this model was imposed in ancient Greece.

Thomas Hobbes[2] argued that only exclusive state control, based on an absolute monarchy, can ensure the security of citizens. The State is in a position to oppose all freedoms, except the right to security, which is the source of its legitimacy.

For Max Weber, security is a component of state sovereignty; it has the monopoly of legitimate physical constraint. Democracy involves maintaining a difficult

---

1 *The Republic*; *The Laws*.
2 *Leviathan*.

balance between the right to security and other freedoms that are rather unstable. This is why Weber was in favor of a strong executive.

The problem of what is an admissible form of security has become a topical issue. Article 2 of the European Convention for the Protection of Human Rights and Fundamental Freedoms imposes the right to life as an obligation to maintain law and order. According to Article 1 of the Declaration of the Rights of Man and of the Citizen, equality stems from security.

In the law on everyday security, dated November 15, 2001, "security is a duty for the State, which is responsible throughout the territory of the Republic for the protection of persons, their property and the prerogatives of their citizenship, the defense of their institutions and national interests, the respect of laws, and the maintenance of peace and public order".

Public authorities are not bound by an obligation to produce a specific result, but by a best-endeavors obligation in their security mission. The *Conseil constitutionnel* (Constitutional Council), regarding the law on internal security of October 30, 2017, indicated that this law did not create any rights for individuals and did not generate any new obligations without giving new powers to the administration. While the Constitutional Council recognized the security of persons and property as a principle of constitutional value, it did not recognize a right to security.

However, some victims obtain compensation for damages from special funds or directly from the State. Isn't this a recognition of a right to security?

One administrative judge[3] announced that "the mistakes made by the intelligence services in the surveillance of Mohamed Merah resulted in the failed opportunity to prevent the death of Abel Chennouf". Yet another judgment of February 10, 1982[4] contradicts this conviction. This ruling denied the airline Air-Inter compensation for damage caused by an attack. The highest administrative court noted on this occasion "the difficulty of predicting the nature, date, place and objectives" of a terrorist attack. The *Conseil d'État* (the Council of State) simply placed the onus on the State to mobilize sufficient means to prevent the occurrence of terrorist acts.

This is why the State will be held liable in case of negligence or failure to act, but this assertion does not lead to the conclusion that there is a right to security. Indeed, the *chambre civile de la Cour de cassation* (Civil Chamber of the Court of Cassation)[5] rejects the idea of there being national solidarity in favor of victims of

3 TA of Nîmes, July 12, 2016.
4 EC, February 10, 1982.
5 On September 8, 2005, no. 04-12.277.

criminal offences. The victim, in order to obtain reparation, must demonstrate gross negligence by the State.

The State therefore has no obligation to produce a specific result in matters of security, but an obligation to intervene or not to intervene, except when charged with the mission of safeguarding public order.

If a right to security existed, it would be extremely costly for public authorities. The obligation to provide security is indeed a best-endeavors obligation.

At present, the situation is not clear-cut, since the shortcomings of the State are leading some elected officials to create municipal police forces, sometimes in competition with the national police, and individuals are grouping together to provide security outside of any legal framework. Certain priority missions seem to be reserved for the State, and other missions, presumably, are being transferred to local authorities and private actors in society. The current context is bringing the concept of security into sharp relief.

In the 20th century, the balance between security and privacy was the touchstone of political and legal discourse. Human rights had been officially recognized by the 1948 UN Universal Declaration of Human Rights. These human rights had been the subject of much philosophical debate but had found their roots in the United Kingdom with the Bill of Rights[6] in the United States[7] and, at the time of the French Liberal Revolution, with the Declaration of the Rights of Man and of the Citizen of 1789 in France, which emphasized the right to property and liberty. Let us not forget that this principle of liberty led to the Le Chapelier Law[8], which abolished the right of corporations and groups of individuals to defend particular interests, and to the Allarde Decree which completed the Le Chapelier Law.

However, human rights played an important role after World War II in the 20th century. At that time, these rights were mainly drawn up by Westerners and formed the new basis for the new world order after the failure of Nazism. Human rights ran contrary to the ideas contained in *Mein Kampf*[9], which advocated a hierarchical society based on the concept of races, with inferior races destined to be

---

6 Mary and William, following the civil war and the re-establishment of absolute monarchical power, committed to respecting the rights of their subjects, and a parliamentary monarchy was established.

7 In the United States, human rights are those recognized by the Constitution, by treaties ratified by Congress, and by certain texts adopted by the Senate.

8 In the era of the First Industrial Revolution, the Le Chapelier Law prevented workers from asserting and exercising their rights.

9 By Adolf Hitler.

dominated or even exterminated[10], and the superior race – that of the Aryan man – destined to dominate the world. Echoes of these theories, which are partly also those of Gobineau, are found artistically in representations of Wagner's work and in the film *Metropolis* by Fritz Lang.

The United Nations unites states with an ideal of peace. But beyond the sovereignty of states, the Universal Declaration of Human Rights also outlined the foundations of humanism. This declaration, itself a reference text, emphasizes civil rights, even if the worker is recognized as having the right to decent work. At the level of the Council of Europe, the European Convention for the Protection of Human Rights[11] establishes rights related to the concepts of freedom (freedom of conscience, freedom of opinion, freedom to practice a religion, freedom to start a family[12]) and to physical integrity (prohibition of torture, abolition of the death penalty except in times of war, then abolition of the death penalty[13]). At the UN, the International Covenant on Civil Rights[14] refers to the Universal Declaration of Human Rights and is ratified by many states. Nevertheless, some states that have not ratified the Covenant are far from insignificant in military and economic terms[15]. At the level of the European Union (EU), the recognition of economic and commercial freedoms (free movement of goods and services, free movement of capital) precedes the consideration of human rights, since the European Charter of Human Rights[16] came after the Maastricht Treaty.

The principles of human rights gradually built up a corpus that came to play an essential geopolitical role in the UN, within UN specialized agencies, and outside the UN.

For a long time, the recourse to military coercion, decided by the UN Security Council, and to trade embargoes[17] could only be based on the violation of the territory of a sovereign state: this is what officially justified the UN intervention during the first Iraq war, after the Iraqi army entered Kuwait. Thereafter, the violation of certain human rights could justify intervention. This is what its

---

10 Of Jewish people, for example.

11 Now known as the European Convention for the Protection of Human Rights and Fundamental Freedoms.

12 This reflects the influence of the Christian Democrat movement in the 1950s in Europe (lest we forget that the Christian Democrat Party governed Italy for many years).

13 France therefore only ratified the Convention after the abolition of the death penalty in 1981.

14 1966.

15 One example being the United States.

16 2000.

17 Article 39 of Chapter 7 of the San Francisco Charter.

opponents ironically called "human rightsism". For these states, some of which are powerful (Russia, formerly the USSR, and China), these human rights, which constitute a guarantee for civil populations (use of weapons of mass destruction, violation of the religious rights of certain ethnic groups[18]), are somewhat hypocritical pretexts for advancing one's pawns on the international chessboard. Most Western states, and in particular those that are members of NATO, are favorable to these theories which, in their view, guarantee security for civilian populations. Economic sanctions have been imposed by groups of states against other states on these legal bases on numerous occasions.

In addition, the 1998 Rome Statute, which entered into force in 2002, allows for the prosecution under the International Criminal Court (preceded by the Special Tribunal for the former Yugoslavia and then the Special Tribunal established in 1994 to try crimes committed in Rwanda, in particular genocide) of political and military leaders whose actions would be deemed a violation of the Geneva Convention[19] or constitute crimes against humanity, as defined by the Rome Statute (extermination of a group of people because of their ethnic or religious origin, or rape based on the principle of discrimination).

Naturally, many states have refused to ratify the Rome Statute as it would degrade the concept of security and infringe on state sovereignty. This is the opinion held by the United States, the world's leading military power, which refuses to allow its leaders to be brought to justice, and which has incited its allies to imitate them, with doubtful success[20]. It is also the point of view of Russia and China. This means that the security of civilian populations is not likely to be taken into account when the world's military is involved. In contrast[21], many African military and political leaders are being challenged in The Hague court because their states have ratified the Rome Statute.

Human rights are thus part of the evolution of the concept of security, though an antagonism continues to exist between them.

---

18 During the intervention in the former Yugoslavia, Serbia was accused of violating the rights of Muslim populations, particularly in Bosnia-Herzegovina.

19 On war crimes.

20 France has therefore ratified the Rome Statute.

21 In spite of the OAU's protest.

Security: Actors and Rights

1.1. Numerous actors

We will focus on nation-states and multinationals, but ITEs[1], and even SMEs, play a significant role in the development of security policy, in trade agreements with a military dimension, in cyber-attacks and in the latest technologies, especially artificial intelligence (AI).

1.1.1. *Nation-states*

A nation-state is a concept composed of two notions: a notion of identity (the nation), which designates the grouping of individuals who are supposed to belong to an ethnic group – a set of physical persons linked by a community of philosophical, linguistic and possibly religious beliefs – and a legal notion (the State), a public collectivity that boasts sovereignty that must be respected and possesses administrative institutions that embody the inalienability of the State.

The institutions that chose to maintain or attempt to maintain world peace, that is, the League of Nations after World War I and the UN after World War II, are made up of nation-states. The UN gives one voice to each nation-state, whatever its demographic weight and whatever its influence on the establishment of an international group. This is apparent at the UN General Assembly, where resolutions are not binding, but symbolic. However, this pseudo-equality of nation-states within the UN finds its limits in the Security Council, where certain nation-states have a veto power for resolutions that are binding. Five nation-states are in this privileged situation: the states that emerged victorious from World War II. We are talking about

1 Intermediate-sized companies.

the United Kingdom, the only nation-state to have fought throughout the entire World War II; the United States, which destroyed the second "front" that led it to engage in World War II (Japan, with the atomic bombs of Hiroshima and Nagasaki); Russia, which inherited, at the end of the bipolar world, the seat of the USSR; China; and France. It is the United States, the leading military power, which most frequently, and very logically, has used the veto power.

A reform of the Security Council has been under consideration for several years, whereby new nation-states would have the right of veto: these would be the two nation-states that emerged from World War II defeated, Japan (clashes with China, which has been in permanent rivalry with the Japanese Empire) and Germany, as well as India (clashes with China and Pakistan, which do not want their nuclear-armed enemy to have the right of veto), Brazil and South Africa. The reform, owing to lack of consensus, did not succeed and the UN Security Council continues to function as it is, with possible reversals of alliances. Security is at the heart of the discussions of every Security Council resolution. It should be recalled that the slightest glimmer of a veto power can lead a nation-state to abandon its projects: during the second Iraq war, the speech by the French Prime Minister, Dominique de Villepin, was all that was needed to invoke the right of veto[2].

With the nation-state, either the State pre-exists the nation and is accompanied by the development of a nationalist sentiment, or the individuals grouped in the nation[3] endow themselves with a state. This second case is illustrated quite widely with Germany, which was constituted of Länder, at the time of Bismarck, who created a state from Prussia.

In France, the State was built gradually, with borders that gradually widened[4]. Nationalism flourished in the 18th century, deepening during the Revolutionary and Napoleonic Wars and then during the 1870s and World War I[5].

France is a nation-state with a fairly good balance between the State and the nation, and a strong statist movement, both under the Old Regime and at the end of the 20th century, with the reforms of the National Council of Resistance, the plans[6],

---

2 France would, moreover, have been at least accompanied by China's veto, so that the United States would be forced to renounce launching the war under the comfortable legal banner of the UN in order to engage in the second Iraq war with its faithful allies, in particular the United Kingdom.

3 With ethnicity being one example.

4 For example, Corsica in the 18th century and Nice in the 19th century.

5 A time when Catholics fully joined the nation, committing en masse to defending it and then adhering to the State.

6 Of the Fourth and Fifth Republics.

the semi-public companies until the beginning of the 21st century, and public and private participation for fiber optics, even artificial intelligence.

The EU, with the ideas of some of its forerunners and the underlying philosophy of the Amsterdam Treaty, has a federalist aspect, which is resisted by the nation-states that compose it, and which corresponds, in this resistance to federalism, to the French "*non*" in the referendum on the constitutional treaty in 2005, and to Brexit in the UK. It is true that the United Kingdom only joined the European structure in the 1970s and that France is a founding state of the EEC.

Some nations wish to acquire state(s) and are unable to do so, leading to strong security tensions. This is the case of the Kurdish nation, which is divided between Turkey, Iran, Syria and Iraq. The Kurds have a common language and a common culture. They would like to see a state function recognized, but to no avail. The Kurds have participated in most of the wars that have marred the Middle East. In October 2019, the Turkish Prime Minister, Erdogan, decided to intervene in Syria to establish a "safe zone" between Turkey and Syria. The Kurds tried to obtain autonomy in Syria and Iraq and extended their zone of influence by fighting against supporters of Daesh[7].

Within the EU, Catalonia has the status of a "historical community" and was denied the full status of a "nation" by the Spanish Constitutional Council, even though the decision had previously been approved by the Catalan Parliament, the Catalan people by referendum. In October 2019, a large number of Catalans were protesting against the heavy prison sentences handed down to democratically elected Catalan officials, with the implicit approval of the EU. It therefore appears that the duality of state/nation can in fact generate security breaches!

1.1.2. *Multinationals*

1.1.2.1. *Definitions*

A transnational firm is a commercial company whose head office is located in a so-called "home" country and which has established subsidiaries in one or more foreign countries. Its economic effects are therefore not limited to one nation-state. For Charles-Albert Michalet[8], the multinational character of the firm has four determining features:

---

7 "Ethnicities in Turkey" and "Number of Kurds in Turkey" [Online]. Available at: www.milliyet.com.

8 Michalet, C.-A. (1976). *Le capitalisme mondial*. PUF, Collection Quadrige, Paris.

– the quest for direct access to raw materials[9];

– the possibility of overcoming certain barriers to trade. In the 19th century, and for part of the 20th century, it was necessary to produce in the market where the product was consumed so as not to be affected by import tariffs;

– the search for external opportunities to improve and intensify competitiveness in a relevant market;

– the loss of a technological advantage in a market which leads transnational companies to outsource part of their production abroad, at lower cost, thus increasing profitability and returns on investment.

Charles-Albert Michalet defines a multinational company as a company "most often large in size which, from a national base, has established several subsidiaries in several countries abroad, with a strategy and organization designed on a global scale". Cathal J. Nolan focuses on capital, the flexible technological assets of these companies, which think globally and make decisions based on economies of scale and fiscal policy[10].

René Sandretto[11] defines a multinational company as a firm that is "generally large", whose organization and management are usually centralized, developing their productive activity through subsidiaries in several countries. There are around 80,000 of them, with 8,400,000 subsidiaries. They constitute two-thirds of world trade. The increase is notable, since in 1990 the figure was no more than 37,000.

The majority of multinationals are from the most developed countries. These include Hilton (United States), Bombardier (Canada), Schlumberger (France), Virgin (United Kingdom), Santander (Spain), Fiat (Italy), Nestlé (Switzerland), Ikea (Sweden), ArcelorMittal (Luxembourg), Siemens (Germany), Red Bull (Austria) and Honda (Japan).

In the 21st century, multinationals from emerging countries are gaining positions in the rankings. The most important multinationals from emerging countries are Hutchison Whampoa (Hong Kong), Petronas (Malaysia), Singtel (Singapore) and Samsung (South Korea)[12].

---

9 For example, the hydrocarbon route in the Middle East.

10 Low taxes attract multinational companies, as Ireland demonstrated in the second decade of the 21st century.

11 Professor of Economics at the University Lumière Lyon 2.

12 We must bear in mind that the European Union and Singapore signed a free trade agreement in 2019 and that Singapore is a beacon in the hierarchy of smart cities.

1.1.2.2. *Firms as powerful as states*

According to the United Nations Development Programme[13], in 1999, the American company Ford was comparable to Norway, and Japan's Mitsui and Mitsubishi were comparable to Saudi Arabia and Poland[14]. According to the global Human Development Report[15], 55 of the top 100 global economic players were multinationals. However, these analogies have been challenged by the Swedish economist Johan Norberg, who believes that a comparison between the GDP of a state and the turnover of a multinational is neither rational nor meaningful. GDP takes into account the final value, while turnover reflects what has been produced outside the firm.

In spite of this reservation, multinationals carry a very significant financial and economic weight. In the year 2000, US$208 billion was transferred to developing countries by multinationals compared to just US$53 billion by states. Moreover, these companies tend to amalgamate through mergers and acquisitions.

Multinationals are the relays and, in part, the actors of globalization. Their role has become so eminent that Susan Strange, the author of *The Retreat of the State*, spoke at the beginning of the 21st century of "triangular diplomacy", in other words, relations between governments, businesses and state-owned enterprises. Robert Cox emphasizes that power cannot be reduced to sovereignty, and in particular to the sovereignty of the State; power, in his view, corresponds to a combination of economic and social orders based on modes of production.

In the 21st century, transnationalization is no longer the prerogative of the largest firms, since SMEs often manage to establish themselves in a multinational market. Moreover, multinationals from emerging countries play a significant role in the global economy[16].

1.1.2.3. *Relations between multinationals and states*

Transnationalization is primarily a means for large commercial companies to escape from the single national space of production, from legal, economic, social and political dependence on the State.

---

13 UNDP.

14 And yet Saudi Arabia is a member of the G20.

15 UNDP (1999). Human Development Report [Online]. Available at: http://hdr.undp.org/en/content/human-development-report-1999.

16 See Mittal and Arcelor shortly before the financial crisis of the first decade of the 21st century.

Some economists[17] are of the opinion that a company, even a multinational one, belongs to its region of origin. They believe that the nation influences the ability to make profits in certain industries.

On the contrary, multinational firms are not immune to flexibility. As a result, they are in a position to pose a threat to states. Indeed, multinationals have an economic space that is independent of their home nation-state, which allows them to make the best use of social and environmental standards. The sovereignty of states is then limited by the strategies of multinationals, which play the card of the "lowest social bidder"[18] and the "lowest environmental bidder".

As a result, multinational companies are able to exploit at low cost the natural resources of a nation-state, to locate polluting activities in states that have not committed to respecting caps on pollution and greenhouse gases. Instances of fraud appear, but it is difficult to prove them or file a complaint in court about them, because the illegal activities are frequently set up between two legal orders unable to impose a sanction.

Multinational corporations also resort to corruption sometimes. This may involve bribing state-dependent officials in order to obtain a government contract or capture the State. In this case, corruption is situated far upstream of the decision-making process, whether in Romano-Germanic or common law. Some developing states have created links between the payment of bribes and the securing of public contracts.

Multinationals also use lobbies. The latter are perceived differently depending on the jurisdiction and constitution. In France, for example, a parliamentarian must not allow himself to be influenced by the point of view of a legal entity. This would pose an illegal conflict of interest.

On the contrary, at the level of the EU, lobbies (those of multinational firms, unions, associations) are legal and participate in the development of directives and regulations. Lobbies are well represented at the Commission. When a proposal for a directive or regulation is initiated, during the second stage, before the proposal becomes a draft, multinational firms make their opinion on the proposal known and suggest modifications, which, from their point of view, are improvements to what will become a directive or regulation following adoption by the Council of Ministers and the European Parliament.

---

17 See Stopford, J.M., Strange, S., Henley, J.S. *Rival States, Rival Firms*.
18 That is, few ILO conventions were signed.

Nevertheless, even at the level of the EU, certain measures may represent a sanction for the multinational firm. Competition law is very important at the EU level[19].

If there is suspicion of collusion or abuse of a dominant position, the Commission's Directorate General for Competition conducts an open investigation and sometimes decides on sanctions, which can be severe. For example, in 2008 and 2009, Microsoft was forced to change its policy following heavy European fines[20].

In the majority of cases, in a globalized world, multinationals and states are giving way to cooperation that is more or less harmonious.

The *lex mercatoria*[21] reflects the establishment of a private system of transnational governance. Multinational companies, their lawyers and international arbitrators have introduced national principles of contracts[22], with arbitration rules that determine the procedures to be followed in case of arbitration. States have adapted their laws to this *lex mercatoria*.

States wish to attract investment from multinationals in their territories. For this reason, free zones have been created, with mixed economy companies open to foreign capital. Infrastructures are set up to facilitate the reception of investments and to allow the establishment of subsidiaries.

There is an increase in the financial royalty paid to the host State for the sale of raw materials. Conflicts are rare. The era of nationalizations is (almost) over.

An interdependence between multinationals and States has thus been established. The latter now sign contracts with foreign firms so that they can take charge of the development of numerous activities, in particular innovative activities: this is what is happening in the food-processing, chemical and IT sectors. In the military sector, we

---

19 Articles 85 and 86, then 101 and 102 of the European Union Treaty. Non-exempted agreements and abuses of dominant position are prohibited. If there is a suspicion of a cartel or abuse of a dominant position, the Commission's Directorate General for Competition conducts an investigation and sometimes decides on sanctions, which can be severe. For example, in 2008 and 2009, Microsoft was condemned by the EU Commission.

20 European Commission (2008). Antitrust: Commission imposes € 899 million penalty on Microsoft for non-compliance with March 2004 Decision [Online]. *Europa*, February 27. Available at: https://ec.europa.eu/commission/presscorner/detail/en/IP_08_318.

21 The right of the merchants.

22 With Unidroit, a private law unification body, and OHADA, the Office for the Harmonization of Business Law in Africa.

should not forget the A400M, which has supported, at the EU level, the multinational EADS.

In the 21st century, states wish to maintain good relations with multinationals. In their landmark book, Susan Strange and John Stopford point out: "States are now competing more for ways to create wealth within their territory than for power over a larger territory. Where they used to compete for power as a means of obtaining wealth, they now compete more for wealth as a means of power." And these multinationals are the privileged place for the exchange of capital transfers, and therefore of wealth. Cooperation between multinationals and states is a guarantee of economic security in the market economy.

1.1.2.4. *Legislation governing cooperation between multinationals and states*

In France, the law on the duty of vigilance of parent companies[23] was adopted by the Assemblée nationale (National Assembly) on February 21, 2017 after four years of debate, and applies to French companies or companies established in France with at least 5,000 employees (or 10,000 for subsidiaries of foreign groups). However, the appeal to the Constitutional Council has enabled many provisions of the law to be stripped of their substance. The law, as it stands, obliges the persons concerned to establish a due diligence plan, and the judge has the power to hold the company liable in the event of failure to meet its obligations (pollution, workplace accidents). In Switzerland, a referendum was put to the people on the subject of "Responsible companies to protect human beings and the environment".

Furthermore, "tax havens" introduce a biased notion of the right to competition. According to the United Nations Conference on Trade and Development, "large multinational corporations each have an average of nearly seventy subsidiaries in tax havens ... U.S. multinationals reported $80 billion in profits in Bermuda in 2012, more than the profits reported in Japan, China, Germany and France combined"[24].

The inequality between developed and developing countries is growing, as large states such as the United States can interact with multinational corporations, while developing states are unable to react to the strategy deployed by the multinationals. According to Strange, there is a "growing asymmetry between strong states with structural power and weak states without it".

Multinationals are involved in the exploitation of the periphery (Third World labor, raw materials, land), by the center (senior executives of multinational firms and governments of Western countries and China), with the participation of the

---

23 Law no. 2017-399 of March 27, 2017 relating to the due diligence of parent companies and ordering companies.

24 Argent sale. *Le Monde diplomatique*, April 1, 2018.

center of the periphery (senior executives of subsidiaries, sometimes corrupt governments), and consumers.

Multinationals are at the heart of globalization. The latter encourages a sometimes irrational consumption pattern[25]. The pharmaceutical industry devotes 0.2% of its research to tuberculosis, even though tuberculosis accounts for 18% of diseases worldwide. And a significant proportion of medical manufacturing stems from the mineral and genetic resources of the countries of the South.

Multinationals are perceived in a differentiated way. Some consider multinationals to be a source of wealth, allowing political homogenization and economic interdependence, thus ensuring growth and peace and in turn being an important factor of security. Others consider that multinationals are actors in the exploitation of poor countries for the benefit of a privileged globalized caste. For Noam Chomsky, multinationals are a factor of insecurity, with "private tyrannies" that escape all democratic control[26].

1.1.3. *The GAFAM*

Globalization has been entering the digital age for about two decades now, which has led to specific debates on security.

The terms GAFAM or "Web giants" refer to the 15 or so global Internet players, including Airbnb, Alibaba, Amazon, Apple, Facebook, Google, LinkedIn, Microsoft, Netflix, Twitter, Uber and Yahoo, among others.

These companies have created large user bases and have a considerable turnover, which is divided between dividends and investments. They are constantly innovating in the field of IT.

The acronym GAFAM[27] is formed by the initials of Google, Apple, Facebook, Amazon, Microsoft.

The acronym FANG (for Facebook, Amazon, Netflix, Google) is also frequently used. It is also possible to cite the acronyms NATU for Netflix, Airbnb, Tesla, Uber, and BATX in China for Baidu, Alibaba, Tencent, Xiaomi.

---

25 See powdered milk in sub-Saharan Africa.

26 Baillargeon, N., Barsamian, D. (2002). Entretiens avec Chomsky. *Ecosociété*, 221.

27 Appeared at the beginning of the 21st century under the name GAFA.

These Web giants are international in scope, in terms of both the number of Internet users and data storage (Big Data and cloud computing). Users have been encrypted, but there are:

- 2 billion for Facebook;

- 500 million for Gmail and Twitter;

- 301 million for Yahoo;

- 200 million for LinkedIn;

- 121 million for Amazon.

In terms of request streams, there are 400 million daily messages for Twitter, and more than 18 billion queries per month in the United States for Google. Google introduced MapReduce distributed processing in 2004, released the Android operating system in 2007, and has set a goal to digitize all paper-based books. Facebook offers unlimited space to store photographs. Amazon, Facebook and LinkedIn have created databases called NoSQL, since they challenge the principles of SQL, with:

- DynamoDB for Amazon;

- Cassandra for Facebook;

- Voldemort for LinkedIn.

The power of GAFAM makes it possible to evoke a "digital–industrial" complex[28] through analogy with the military–industrial complex. GAFAM is at the center of security issues in the digital world.

1.2. Rights and security

1.2.1. *The law of armed conflict*

1.2.1.1. *The principles*

Humanity has been waging wars for millennia. The doctrine of "just war" is concerned with the justifications given for resorting to force[29] and the justifications for the use of force[30].

---

28 300 millions d'Américains espionnés par la NSA avec l'appui des majors du numérique [Online]. Available at: https://globalepresse.net/2013/06/08/300-millions-damericains-espionnes-par-la-nsa-avec-lappui-des-majors-du-numerique/.

29 *Jus ad bellum* or the right to war.

30 *Jus in bello* or the right in war.

The role of national and multinational armed forces is primarily preventive and dissuasive. The commitment becomes complete within the framework of a law of armed conflict, legally justified today by a mandate from the UN Security Council. War is an evil that can be justified if it means that a major evil can be avoided.

The United Nations document "A High-level Panel Report on Threats, Challenge and Change" establishes several criteria for the legitimacy of resorting to war:

– the seriousness of the threat: "Does the nature, reality and gravity of the threat to the security of the state or individuals justify the use of military force in the first place? In the case of internal threats, is there a risk of genocide and other mass killings, ethnic cleansing, or serious violations of international humanitarian law, actual or imminent?";

– the legitimacy of the motive: "Legitimate" motives include self-defense, defense of others, resistance to aggression, protection of innocent people from aggressive and brutal regimes, and punishment for serious mistakes that are not punished or redressed;

– the last resort: a state may use force only if it has exhausted all plausible non-violent and/or peaceful alternatives for resolving the conflict in question, including diplomacy;

– proportionality of means: not applying the necessary means above to achieve its objective. The violence involved in the conflict must be proportional to the objective sought. Any state wishing to engage in a war must first compare the good obtained by all parties to the evil that will result for all, including the victims;

– balancing the consequences: a state should only engage in aggression if it believes that there is a possibility of success. The probability of success must be greater than the damage imposed. The objective should be to prevent unnecessary violence and the ultimate goal of armed intervention should be to restore peace;

– legitimate authority and public declaration: the decision to go to war should come from those responsible for appointing and removing governments, that is, the people and their representatives (for the United States), or from governments.

The purpose of the law in war is to ease the lives of wounded soldiers and prisoners in times of war. In this matter, reference should be made to the Geneva Conventions of 1949. The basic principles are as follows:

– prohibition of discrimination: only people who are involved in the war can be used as targets. Other people, "civilians" or "innocent people" must remain safe from attack;

– non-combatant immunity: killing civilians is prohibited except in self-defense and only if necessary.

1.2.1.2. *War in the 21st century*

At the end of the bipolar world and after the dissolution of the Warsaw Pact, conflicts multiplied and intensified. According to Jean Cot[31], one notes "a certain appeasement of tensions and interstate wars with, in return, a multiplication of intrastate conflicts. The brutal easing of tension between East and West seems to be releasing other contained forces, not only in Balkan Europe and in the Caucasus, but everywhere in the world where the two great powers were marking each other".

In the 21st century, civil wars, modern high-intensity conflicts, characterized by the use of armed forces involving all weapons except nuclear weapons[32], and interventions for peace and security have become characteristic of modern warfare. The latter have also developed since the end of the bipolar world. Among the possible interventions are:

– the imposition of economic sanctions, including embargoes. But civilians often suffer more from economic sanctions than state leaders;

– civil intervention, where unarmed intervention in the field of a local conflict is mandated by an intergovernmental or non-governmental organization with the objective of carrying out a mission of observation, intervention or mediation;

– observation missions send observers mandated by an international, national or non-governmental authority to gather information on the ground on the progress of the incriminated facts. The persons informed are the political and diplomatic authorities;

– mediation missions: intervention of a third party who intervenes between the protagonists.

As for the so-called humanitarian interventions, which are increasingly frequent, they have been either praised for having saved the lives of many civilians or criticized for having served as an alibi for nation-states that take advantage of this tragic geo-sequence. The majority of Western states which subscribe to human rights are in favor of these "humanitarian" interventions.

---

31 Cot, J. (2006). *Parier pour la paix*. Charles Lépolld Mayer, Paris. Dossier pour un débat, 153.
32 See the Balkan, Georgian and Iraq wars.

According to Ateliers du sud *et al.*[33]: "NGOs can be subject to manipulation. Thus, in Yugoslavia, certain representatives of humanitarian organizations found themselves not only hostages of the Serbs, but also of the French government, which included them in various negotiations intended to serve, ultimately, electoral objectives. In Cambodia, by working in the refugee camps set up on the Thai border, the NGOs were the instruments of a policy carried out jointly by the Thais, Americans and Chinese, by virtue of their opposition to the Russians and Vietnamese, to maintain these camps. In the Rwandan conflict, they reinforced the positions of militiamen and members of the Armed Forces of Rwanda who were holding the populations in the refugee camps hostage; they thus contributed to the reconstruction of a conflict situation."

From this point of view, the international community, a fundamental notion in humanitarian interventions, is imaginary. It is the nation-states[34] that possess the real decision-making powers. Thus, it is arguably not dedication to the fundamental principles of the Universal Declaration of Human Rights that explains their behavior, but the preservation of their specific interests.

1.2.1.3. *Towards a reform of the UN?*

After the adoption of the San Francisco Charter, conflicts appeared in a bipolar world. The real balance of power was determined by the United States and the USSR, the leading nuclear powers. After the collapse of the bipolar world, the UN faced conflicts in Yugoslavia, Somalia and Rwanda. These were not wars between more or less sovereign states, but intrastate conflicts, civil wars and repressive actions directed by a government against part of the population.

The UN was incapable of dealing with these seemingly inextricable situations. It left Rwanda fraught with massacres. It left Somalia, after the United States abandoned the battlefield. Involved in a mission in Bosnia, it handed over to NATO once the fighting had stopped.

The UN has never had a permanent military force. To intervene, it has called on coalitions of states with more or less convergent interests. These interests are in fact part of a unipolar world.

According to Jean Cot, a reform of the UN would imply giving the Security Council its own means of assessing and controlling UN operations, with the establishment of a military advisory committee, making the UN Department of Peace Operations the real operational headquarters. Above all, it would be

---

33 Ateliers du sud *et al.* (1996). *Journée de travail sur la prévention des conflit.* Charles Léopold Mayer, Paris.

34 And sometimes also multinationals.

appropriate to create a force capable of imposing a halt to fighting on belligerents who do not wish to do so, or to put an end to behavior that is not in conformity with the UN Charter, beginning with the aggression of a power against part of its own population. Jean Cot speaks of a force of modest size to intervene in the intermediate zone between peacekeeping, the domain of the Blue Helmets, and the imposition of peace by force.

With the emergence of non-state actors, the role of citizen associations is bound to develop, especially social networks. The latter have played an undeniable role in social movements opposed to the governments in place[35]. But it is not at all about armed conflicts.

1.2.1.4. *Limitation and conversion of armaments*

Conversion is an ambivalent process that brings together several obstacles[36], including armed forces and economics[37]. Richard Petris, founder of the École de la paix, proposes developments that have little to do with today's world, whether unipolar or multipolar.

Disarmament in industrialized countries is not on the agenda. Programs are being reduced, sometimes abandoned, due to pressure from manufacturers, fear of unemployment and resistance from the military. Disarmament in developing countries is even slower than in industrialized countries, in countries where the military plays a major economic and political role.

1.2.1.5. *Military ethics*

1.2.1.5.1. Case study: Germany

Having involved a large part of the world in World War II, Germany is sensitive to ethics in the military field. After 10 years of allied occupation and control, the Bundeswehr started from the idea that in order to ensure that what happened never happens again, an alliance must be established between the idea of democracy and necessity of military action[38]. The institution of the Parliamentary Commissioner for the Armed Forces is a relatively unique one and has a public law status according to the law. During his or her term of office, the Parliamentary Commissioner for the Armed Forces may not perform any other remunerated functions. The purpose of this

---

35 For example, revolutionary processes in movements dubbed the "Arab Spring" by the media, protests and demonstrations in Algeria in 2019, and demonstrations in Hong Kong against the government allied to China.

36 Reduction of military personnel; closure of bases.

37 Loss of jobs, plant closures, loss of markets, cost of conversion.

38 *Innere Führung*.

incompatibility regime is to guarantee his or her independence. He or she is elected by the Bundestag by secret ballot without prior debate. Candidates are nominated by the Defense Committee or the various parliamentary groups. The candidate who wins a majority of the votes of the Members of the Bundestag is elected.

Any German citizen over 35 years of age is eligible. The Armed Forces Commissioner is elected for a period of five years and may be re-elected.

The Parliamentary Commissioner for the Armed Forces is responsible for "safeguarding fundamental rights and assisting the Bundestag in exercising parliamentary control of the armed forces". He or she is obliged to act at the request of the Bundestag or the Defence Committee to verify certain facts, or when facts come to his attention that suggest that fundamental rights may be violated:

> Its power of control extends to all governmental institutions competent in matters of military defense of the territory, in the first place therefore to the Federal Minister of Defense and his area of competence[39].

Every soldier has the right to address the Parliamentary Commissioner for the Armed Forces personally and directly, without going through the chain of command. A soldier exercising his right to petition may submit to him or her, without any time limit, anything that, in his personal opinion, appears to constitute abuse or unfair treatment.

All soldiers are briefed on the duties and powers of the Parliamentary Commissioner at the beginning of basic training and again after transfer to their troop corps.

The soldier shall not suffer any prejudice in terms of service and shall not be subject to disciplinary sanctions for having referred the matter to the Parliamentary Commissioner for the Armed Forces. The soldier also enjoys the protection of the right of petition.

The other armies do not enjoy the same protective status from an appeal body.

This can be explained by the history of German culture and by the specific role given to the Constitutional Court of Karlsruhe.

---

39 Interparliamentary Journal No. 4 of May 2, 2005 by the German parliamentary assistant trainees for the attention of the congress members of the Friendship Group.

1.2.1.5.2. Hierarchy and armies

The other armies emphasize obedience to hierarchy, which appears as a guarantee for the forces in charge of security.

1.2.2. *Environmental law*

Military law has existed for a long time. In contrast, environmental law is a recent construction. Environmental law bears the mark of the second half of the 20th century and the first half of the 21st century.

In the 1990s, and at the beginning of the 21st century, the environment found its place in international, national and regional concerns. The danger incurred, due to humanity's exploitation of natural and fossil resources, and the result of the technologies put in place by the actors mentioned above, are becoming a growing concern for governance structures, and, progressively, for public opinion on which the various strata of the media classes have exerted an influence.

1.2.2.1. *International environmental law: a set of standards*

These standards are established at the international level by conventions and treaties with the aim of protecting the environment. There are more than 300 international treaties and more than 1,000 bilateral agreements. Among the latter, it is worth drawing attention to the following:

– the declaration adopted by the Stockholm conference on the human environment in June 1972, which states that man has a fundamental right to live in satisfactory conditions and has a duty to protect and improve the environment for current and future generations;

– Article 24 of the Convention of 20 November 1989, which commits States to combat diseases linked to the risks of polluting the natural environment;

– the Convention on the Conservation of European Wildlife and Natural Habitats established in 1979;

– the 2015 Paris agreement, which aims to ensure a global average temperature of no more than 2°C compared to pre-industrial levels.

1.2.2.2. *Taking global goods into account*

This found many echoes in the reports of international organizations, with fears about the transmission of risks to the ecosystem and infectious diseases. In the context of globalization, global public goods are once again based on the concept of a community of interests between nation-states, which draws attention to the risks that the components of the environment are exposed to, regardless of frontiers and particular locations: water, air and forests are at the forefront of these considerations.

Human rights, common goods and public goods are often used indiscriminately, with ambiguous connotations. The UN tends to promote the development of fundamental human rights, education, health and a healthy environment, even if these concepts are also considered commercial goods. The WTO insists on free market access, including that of the environment, while recognizing the need to protect the environment. However, before the DSB[40], environmental concerns always give way in jurisprudence to competition concerns when quantitative restrictions on imports and exports are mentioned. Global public goods, including the environment, can be related to the principles of international solidarity. They can also be inspired, quite differently, by a liberal economic analysis. Global environmental governance seems a distant notion.

1.2.2.3. *Earth Summits and conferences*

In view of this, a look back allows us to forge a focus on the Earth Summits and the conferences of the parties.

1.2.2.3.1. Earth Summits

In 1948, the International Union for Conservation of Nature was created[41], the oldest of the world's global environmental organizations. In France, it is worth mentioning that the National Forestry Office, the Coastal Protection Agency and the National Natural Parks are all members.

In 1966, the UNDP (United Nations Development Programme) was created. The UNDP advocates sustainable development, and also includes environmental issues on its agenda, particularly through the impact of climate change on populations. In the area of "environment and energy", the organization focuses on mobilizing finance to improve environmental management and promote green economies in developing countries, addressing the threats caused by climate change, and improving local resources in order to manage the environment well in the implementation of a development plan. The head office is located in New York City.

In 1972, a report entitled "The Limits to Growth" was published by Meadows and Meadows of the Massachusetts Institute of Technology. This text brought a lawsuit against unlimited growth and the incompatible aspect between the physical

---

40 The Dispute Settlement Body, created in 1995, at the same time as the WTO by the Marrakesh Agreement.
41 World Conservation Union.

limits of the terrestrial ecosystem, the population explosion, the depletion of natural resources and pollution.

From June 5 to 16, 1972, the Stockholm Summit, the United Nations conference on the environment, was held, perceived as the first Earth Summit[42].

1974: Cocoyoc Summit, UNEP/UNCTAD meeting. In the final declaration, the President of Mexico backed the project of the supporters of ecodevelopment. Within the framework of the UN General Assembly, a declaration was made on the establishment of a new international economic order, and the non-aligned countries, in the bipolar world, emphasized the depletion of natural resources.

1982: Nairobi Summit. This was at the origin of the World Charter for Nature adopted by the United Nations (Defrise 1982). This charter had no binding legal force. The preamble states: "Each form of life is unique and must be protected regardless of its value to the human species."

1983: WCED (World Commission on Environment and Development by the UN General Assembly). The objective was to establish evolving missions around the theme of "environment and development": energy, industry, food security, human settlements, international economic relations, assistance in decision-making and international cooperation. The Commission was composed of 21 commissioners from very diverse backgrounds: 6 Western countries, 3 Eastern countries, China and 11 developing countries. The aim was to compensate for the extensive damage suffered by the ecosystem.

1987: publication of the WCED[43] report "Our Common Future".

1988: co-creation of the IPCC (Intergovernmental Panel on Climate Change) by the UNEP and the World Meteorological Organization. The first report[44] enabled the UN General Assembly to draw up a Framework Convention on Climate Change, which came into force in 1994. The second report in 1995 provided the basis for the Kyoto Protocol. The 2001 report emphasized the responsibility of the human species

---

42 Principle Two of the Stockholm Declaration: "The natural resources of the earth, including the air, water, land, flora and fauna, and especially representative samples of natural ecosystems, must be safeguarded for the benefit of present and future generations through careful planning or management, as appropriate." Principle Three: "The capacity of the earth to produce vital renewable resources must be maintained and, wherever practicable, restored or improved."
43 Or the Brundtland Report.
44 1990.

for global warming in the second half of the 20th century. The fourth report of 2007 contextualized international relations after the Kyoto Protocol.

From June 3 to 14, 1992: Earth Summit in Rio. The United Nations Conference on Environment and Development validated the Brundtland Report. The Summit led to the Rio Declaration[45] and was followed by the establishment of three conventions on climate change, biological diversity and desertification.

1997: Kyoto Conference: signature of the Kyoto Protocol on greenhouse gas emissions, ratified in 2004 by Russia, but not ratified by the United States.

2000: Millennium Summit in New York.

2002: World Summit on Sustainable Development in Johannesburg; this came at the intersection of the protection of natural resources and development issues. Civil society became active in such issues.

2005: entry into force of the Kyoto Protocol. A total of 55 countries had to ratify it for the text to come into force, which was done.

2009: Copenhagen Summit[46]. For the United Nations Secretary, this was the first truly global agreement; for other observers, it was a step backwards because it signaled the end of the previous climate regime by closing the door to multilateralism that preceded it. While the Europeans intended to strengthen the Kyoto Protocol, China and the United States, which had not ratified the Kyoto Protocol, supported a less ambitious project on multilateral commitments.

2012: Rio+20, new conference on sustainable development. A report, "The Future We Want", focuses on environmental innovations.

1.2.2.3.2. Conferences of the parties

The United Nations Framework Convention on Climate Change, adopted at the Earth Summit in 1992, introduced multiple conferences of the parties with more or less disappointing results on the limitation of greenhouse gases.

In 1997, during COP 3, the Kyoto Protocol was adopted. The Kyoto Protocol allowed for the quantification of the reduction of greenhouse gas emissions. While developed countries were stakeholders, developing countries and emerging countries

---

45 A total of 27 principles.
46 Corresponds to UNFCCC COP 15.

were exempt on the basis of "common but differentiated responsibility". The main responsibility lay with the developed countries[47]. Although reductions were required only from developed countries, the Protocol provided for reductions to take place in developing countries and countries with economies in transition through two flexibility mechanisms called the Clean Development Mechanism and the Joint Implementation mechanism.

Until the COP 7 in Marrakesh in 2001, negotiations focused on the ways that the Kyoto Protocol could be implemented, with the verification of compliance and possible sanctions. In the event of non-compliance, the use of flexibility mechanisms was permitted. The negotiations did not lead to COP 6 in The Hague in 2000, as opposition arose between the United States and Europe over the flexibility mechanisms, carbon sinks and financing for developing countries.

After this failure, a COP 6bis was organized in 2001 in Bonn. During this COP 6bis, the United States officially announced that it would not ratify the Kyoto Protocol. Since then, the United States has had observer status in the Protocol, as well as being an ex officio member of the Convention, since it has ratified it.

In 2005, a *quorum* was reached. With this entry into force, global warming has not diminished; States' commitments are insufficient in relation to the principles of common goods. Moreover, the Kyoto Protocol only defined a period of application from 2008 to 2012.

In 2014, at the COP 10 in Buenos Aires, a multilateral agreement appeared unthinkable for the period following 2012. Within this framework, the EU was the group of countries most convinced of the need to commit to the fight against climate change and the deleterious effects of CO_2, but there were many divisions within it. Europe seemed to be marginalized at the Warsaw COP in 2013. This conference had its setbacks, coming close to the prospect of a conference without a final agreement and ending with an almost minimalist text in which the States announced "national contributions" at the COP in Paris.

In 2015, the Paris Air Show was held at Le Bourget. All but two states (including the United States) committed not to exceed 1.5° or 2° of warming, and to limit greenhouse gases. Enforcement was very difficult: there were questions about China's commitments; the United States did not feel that it was concerned.

---

47 To limit greenhouse gases.

In reality, the global governance of the fight against global warming has not succeeded in making the Kyoto Protocol, nor, most likely, the Paris Conference, play the leveraging role that it should have played for new commitments by 2050.

On the other hand, civil society is playing a more important role. The general public is aware of the perceived real threat of global warming and the risks of pollution. The rise in temperatures over the last decade, cyclones and other climatic disasters have persuaded citizens of Western countries that their survival is at stake. Media campaigns about the Amazon have influenced voters who, in the European elections in the spring of 2019, voted significantly more than before for green or ecological movements. Some observers are convinced that public opinion is ready to accept a certain decline, which is not certain, but this overall trend is combined with the decline of the growth rate observed in the majority of states. China itself, "the most polluted country in the world", seems ready to take certain measures to change the course it has followed so far. However, the states most committed to the fight against global warming are Australia, Norway, Switzerland, etc., and it should be noted that these countries have a very high Human Development Index (HDI). The increase in life expectancy at birth[48], as well as education partly financed by public funds and not just by loans taken out by students over the course of their professional life that will have to be repaid over a long period time, is symptomatic of this awareness of environmental law, based on state ratification and only partially on global or globalized governance.

On the contrary, the immaturity of the debates on the criteria that should be taken into account to identify the indispensable commitments of each country persists: historical responsibility and the cut-off points for what has preceded it (whether in the past or more recently), the same emission right for each human being, the grandfather clause, and the reduction of emissions at lower cost. The choices relating to these criteria were all explicitly or implicitly present in the Kyoto Protocol, but progress since the ratification of the Kyoto Protocol, since the Paris Conference, has been limited. If the implementation of the Paris COP cannot be compared to the 2009 implementation of the Copenhagen COP, its influence is not certain.

The environment has entered the public and private realm of economic, political and media debates, but international governance has yet to be perfected. Major economic and industrial projects have many difficulties reconciling with environmental law.

This is the case, first and foremost, for the OBOR New Silk Roads project, set up in 2013 and gaining the support of 21 Asian countries in 2014 that invested in the

---

48 See Japan and Norway.

creation of a new bank called the Asian Infrastructure Investment Bank[49]. The project concerns not only Asia, but also Africa and Europe[50].

Previously, the Permanent Court of Arbitration had displeased China[51] by disavowing it and siding with less influential countries such as Manila and the Philippines. Manila was able to demonstrate China's adverse environmental effects on the coral reefs disputed between Manila and China, arguing that China's exploitation of the island was destructive to the island's environment. In the arbitration, the latter was favorable to the other States initially for environmental reasons, then to prevent China from exercising a monopoly on the resources of the China Sea.

1.2.2.3.3. Environmental law and China

Beyond this conflict, environmental issues are at the heart of the implementation of the new Silk Roads. This will be done at a partial cost to the environment.

It is therefore important to be aware of the environmental strategies already in place in this global powerhouse that is China.

According to Marc Lucotte (2019), China has become aware of the environmental impact on its country and its workers. The nation has gradually implemented goals to prevent pollution and protect the environment. However, China remains in a phase of economic growth[52] and the consequences on the environment are increasing in proportion to its development.

In reality, China is undergoing an environmental crisis (Huchet 2016): public health is severely affected as well as land fertility, water and air quality. Indeed, air pollution causes 1.6 million premature deaths per year[53], water shortages are widespread in 440 cities, soil pollution affects the production of food resources and waste sorting is still not widespread. Moreover, the leaders are reducing the scale of this crisis by concealing certain information while the country's population rate, with the abandonment of the one-child policy, continues to grow. China's environmental regulations are not very detailed and are sometimes unclear.

In summary, China is an environmentally costly state. When crossing borders, it will have to respect local standards, that is, those of the country crossed, while respecting international standards that apply to trade and the environment. This will

49 AIIB.

50 See Greece and the port of Piraeus, along with Portugal and Italy.

51 In conflict with Vietnam, the Philippines, Malaysia and Brunei.

52 Even if it is less important than it was 10 years ago.

53 This affects China's HDI for the criterion "life expectancy at birth".

lead to discrepancies in the face of countries with different operating systems and international legislation that is difficult to control. Indeed, in the event of non-compliance with environmental regulations, international arbitration will be required.

The work to complete the Silk Roads project has generated real ecological upheavals, but this remains insufficient. Indeed, China has exploited the environment of the countries spread along the project. China has given priority to its own economic interests while compromising the environmental aspect.

The example of Pakistan is enlightening in this regard. In Pakistan, more than three-quarters of the electricity generated by coal-fired power plants is used by China. The operation of coal-fired power plants requires a large amount of water, and Pakistan could run out of water by 2025 according to environmentalists.

In addition to the danger of water shortage, Pakistan is suffering from serious air pollution because of this project. The Silk Roads project thus requires the use of a large amount of materials, especially sand and limestone, which are necessary for the production of cement and concrete. The latter two represent a major source of greenhouse gases. According to the Tsinghua Center, the 126 countries that have signed agreements with China account for 28% of global greenhouse gas emissions, which contribute to global warming.

In addition, Silk Roads poses a threat to wildlife by increasing wildlife mortality. According to the WWF, 32% of all protected areas in the countries crossed by these roads could be affected, including tigers and pandas. The consequences can be seen in Africa, which has become "China's global factory". Since it lacks natural resources, China exploits oil, gas, wood and minerals from Africa, which generates ecological damage. As a result, fauna and flora are heavily impacted by deforestation and pollution.

China's traditional enemies or non-allies, India, Japan and the United States, are among the few countries not participating in the Chinese project. This is why alternative projects have been created to contend with the New Silk Roads project with the aim of limiting China's economic, commercial and geostrategic influence.

1.2.2.3.4. Environmental law and India

India has outlined its own trade route project: the "Freedom Route" or "Asia–Africa Growth Corridor"[54]. Indian Prime Minister Narendra Modi and Japanese Prime Minister Shinzo Abe are proposing to revitalize old maritime routes linking Africa to the Pacific, thus creating a new Indo-Pacific region. However, this project differs from the one they intend to counteract by focusing their strategy on maritime

---

54 AAGC.

routes, since it forms part of a sustainable development logic and aims to reduce the carbon footprint of trade. India's participation is illustrated by the use of its presence on the African territory to counter relations between China and Africa. Japan, for its part, is offering its expertise in infrastructure construction.

If this Indo-Japanese project puts the environment at the center of its strategy, it is because the new silk routes endanger the application of the Paris agreements. Indeed, according to a study by the Tsinghua Center for Finance and Development, the Chinese project could lead to a global warming of 3°C. This would increase China's gas emissions and constitute a danger for the entire planet, since the country is the leading CO_2 emitter, making up 30% of global emissions.

The international laws most often referred to therefore belong to a different era.

Interceptions

In terms of so-called security interceptions, there has been a transition between the 20th and 21st centuries. The 20th century wanted a balance between privacy and security. The 21st century is concerned with security. This is true in almost all Western countries.

2.1. International interceptions

The United Kingdom had to revise its law, which was not sufficiently protective of privacy, after the Malone[1] ECHR ruling.

2.1.1. *Interceptions in the 20th century*

In the 20th century, the United States and Germany put in place guarantees concerning fundamental rights. The 21st century changed everything.

2.1.1.1. *The United States*

2.1.1.1.1. FISA and computer data

The 1978 FISA[2] included provisions to prohibit measures[3] that make improper use of computer data. These measures were not detailed. However, the law listed procedures that could be ordered by the Attorney General.

---

1 Malone v. United Kingdom, 1984, ECHR, 1985 Act.

2 Foreign Intelligence Surveillance Act.

3 AM 101 (h), FISA.

The information obtained through the FISA system was shrouded in secrecy and was not subject to any lawful exploitation when it concerned US citizens. In criminal matters, this information could be used with the consent of the Attorney General: however, the individual concerned and his lawyer were informed. The defendant was then entitled to appeal to the competent federal court of first instance[4] and to invoke the inadmissibility of the "evidence" gathered by these specific means: he tried to demonstrate that the evidence had not been gathered in a lawful manner and that the surveillance was not in accordance with the law. The decision of the District Court was binding on all federal and state courts of the federation except the courts of appeal. The decision of the District Court was subject to review by appellate courts and the Supreme Court.

2.1.1.1.2. Public control

The Attorney General, who was primarily responsible for the authorization measures, was required to send an annual report to the Federal Courts Administration and Congress on the application of FISA. The report included the total number of applications, renewals and how many applications were denied.

Every six months, the Attorney General also informed the special congressional committees on surveillance activities[5]. These two committees had the right to gather other information on the proviso that such information was essential to the proper performance of their duties. Once a year, the parliamentary committees reported to their respective chambers of law enforcement. These reports sometimes presented observations and proposals.

In the United States, the subject of these measures was not informed. Instead, the concept of "protected persons" and the consideration of certain professional secrets was accepted.

The intercepted conservations could not involve lawyers or priests. Let us not forget that the legal profession is highly valued in the United States and that religion is official in nature. The FBI had to stop the interception as soon as a protected person intervened.

2.1.1.2. *Germany and the G10 Act*[6]

The competent ministers were subject to parliamentary control to the extent that they issued authorizations. The Parliamentary Control Committee[7] of the Federal

---

4 District Court.

5 Article 108(a), FISA.

6 Gesetz 10.

7 PKK/4.

Intelligence Services did not monitor the implementation of the G10, but ministers were obliged to inform the college of deputies of the Bundestag.

Anyone who believed that his or her fundamental rights, including in the area of interception, were being violated could appeal to the Constitutional Court. The Constitutional Court in Karlsruhe accepted appeals even though other legal avenues had not been exhausted.

Law G10 makes no mention of punishment for authorized interceptions. Indeed, the German Penal Code stipulated[8] that an individual who takes an interception measure without authorization is punishable by imprisonment or a fine. Article 3(3) of the Law on Cooperation between the Federation and the Länder stated that this law is applicable to intelligence officers.

2.1.2. *Interceptions in the 21st century*

The United States plays an essential role, but the phenomenon of total security concerns most Western states.

2.1.2.1. *The United States*

Technologies have long existed to regulate intelligence in the United States and abroad. The attacks of September 11, 2001, which received wide media coverage, advanced the use of these technologies.

2.1.2.1.1. The Patriot Act

The Patriot Act was passed unanimously on October 26, 2001[9].

The Patriot Act amended the US law. It increased the ability of police officers to obtain certain types of warrants from the courts to intercept communications and increases the categories of information that such warrants can obtain in certain circumstances. Section 206 of the Patriot Act authorizes the issuance of general warrants[10] under FISA. These warrants are applied for in FISA court and do not require specific identification of the instrument, facility or location subject to surveillance. Rather than requiring officers to obtain a separate FISA warrant for each device they wish to intercept, this provision allows officers to obtain a general

---

8 Article 201 of the German Penal Code.

9 With only one abstention in an atmosphere of exacerbated patriotism.

10 Roving orders.

warrant authorizing them to do so for multiple devices belonging to an individual; section 218 of the Patriot Act allows federal officers to apply for a FISA warrant where obtaining the foreign intelligence is an important reason but not the sole reason, as was the case before the Patriot Act came into force, for obtaining a warrant. Specifically, the law allows intelligence agencies to connect the Carnivore service to an Internet service provider's network to monitor email traffic and keep track of the web browsing of an individual suspected of contact with a foreign power. The NSA, in particular, has established agreements with more than 100 US companies it deems to be reliable.

As for the Terrorist Surveillance Program, this was set up by the Bush administration following the attacks of September 11, 2001 and the adoption of the Patriot Act. Its legality has been called into question because it has not been approved by FISC[11].

2.1.2.1.2. Prism

Known as US-984XN[12], Prism is a US electronic surveillance program that collects information from the Internet and electronic service providers. This program is classified; it falls under the jurisdiction of the National Security Agency and targets people living outside the United States, in conjunction with the Upstream Program. Unlike the Terrorist Surveillance Program, Prism was authorized[13] by an FISC ruling (Protect America Act of 2007, under President George W. Bush). There is therefore a presumption of legality, from the American point of view. Under this system, the NSA has direct access to data hosted by Google, Facebook, YouTube, Microsoft, Yahoo, Skype, AOL, Apple, Paltalk, among others. PRISM is reportedly "the primary source of raw information used to write NSA analytical reports"[14]. Some companies are reluctant to pass on calls from their clients; in general, these companies, when classified information has been disclosed and has been controversial, have indicated that they were not willing to pass on bulk information to the NSA and that, under the US law, they obeyed the rule, stating that the request for information has to be about individuals and comply with the FISA law.

On a geopolitical level, it may seem costly to intercept data from allied representatives, but this is no less part of the balance of power established within the Western bloc; the widely publicized comments of Viviane Reding, EU Justice

---

11 United States Foreign Intelligence Surveillance Court.

12 ZDNet (2013). PRISM: Here's How the NSA Wiretapped the Internet. June 8.

13 *The Washington Post* (2013). NSA Slides Explain the PRISM Data-Collection Program. June 6.

14 See the previous note. Some companies are reluctant to pass on their customers' calls; generally, such companies are reluctant to pass on classified information.

Commissioner in 2013, and Martin Schulz, President of the EU Parliament in 2013[15], form part of the internal communication policy.

2.1.2.2. *American interception law after the Patriot Act*

It is worth mentioning the decree-law of 2002, jurisprudence, and the reform of the FISA law.

2.1.2.2.1. The decree-law of 2002

From 2002 onwards, in the United States, it has no longer been necessary in certain circumstances to seek and obtain judicial authorization to conduct interceptions. In 2002, President Bush signed an Executive Order authorizing the National Security Agency to monitor and intercept inter-country telephone calls and emails transmitted by persons in the United States to persons outside the United States or vice versa, without having to seek prior judicial authorization from the FISA court. The President would have had the authority to issue this Executive Order pursuant to his authority under Article 2 of the US Constitution[16], and pursuant to a joint resolution of both houses of Congress, issued by the Senate, entitled *Authorization for Use of Military Force*[17]. The AUMF resolution authorized the President to use all necessary and appropriate force against states, organizations or persons who, in his opinion, had planned, committed, aided, abetted or harbored the attacks of September 11, 2001, in order to prevent future or potential terrorist acts.

Nevertheless, some groups and individuals have questioned whether the president had the constitutional or congressional authority to issue the 2002 executive order. In particular, they have questioned whether electronic surveillance by the NSA without a warrant under the Executive Order violates the rights of Americans under the Fourth Amendment[18].

Moreover, some observers have questioned the government's claim that the 2002 decree-law was essential on the pretext that warrantless surveillance periods longer than those authorized by FISA are necessary to prevent and combat so-called

---

15 Martin Schulz: "Deeply concerned and shocked by the allegations of espionage by US authorities in EU offices. If these allegations are true, it would be an extremely serious problem that would considerably harm relations between the EU and the United States", quoted in "La NSA espionnait aussi l'Union européenne", *Le Monde*, July 1, 2013.

16 This section specifies the executive powers of the president, including his powers as commander-in-chief of the US armed forces.

17 AUMF, authorization for the use of military force, signed into law by President Bush on September 18, 2001, shortly after the attacks of September 11, 2001.

18 The Fourth Amendment, which dates from 1791, prohibits searches and seizures committed without a legal basis.

terrorist activities. Indeed, while government agencies must generally obtain a court authorization from FISA before conducting warrantless surveillance, FISA provides exceptions to this requirement. The US Attorney General may order electronic surveillance of certain foreign powers without a judicial warrant for up to one year[19]. Electronic surveillance without a judicial warrant is also possible in emergency situations for up to 72 hours[20] and electronic surveillance without a warrant for 15 days following a declaration of war by Congress[21].

On January 17, 2006, two separate lawsuits were launched against the monitoring program without a warrant. The first was initiated by a group of civil liberties organizations led by the American Civil Liberties Union (ACLU) in the Detroit District Court against the NSA. The second was initiated by the Center for Constitutional Rights (CCR) against President Bush, the NSA and the Federal Bureau of Investigation in federal court in Manhattan. According to the ACLU-led group, the NSA's program violated the First Amendment[22], the Fourth Amendment to the Constitution[23] and the constitutional principles of the separation of powers by which the President and Congress are governed. The group called for the program to be declared unconstitutional and for an injunction prohibiting the NSA from continuing its activities in this area. According to the case brought by CCR, information protected by the attorney–client relationship was intercepted in the course of the NSA's warrantless surveillance program. Moreover, the allegations of constitutional violations made in the ACLU case were repeated. Like the ACLU, the CCR sought a declaration of unconstitutionality and an injunction prohibiting the continuation of the program[24].

The debate won over parliamentary circles. When information about the NSA's warrantless oversight program and the executive order authorizing it was made public, various congressional committees voted to investigate the program and the power the president apparently had under the constitution or AUMF resolution to authorize the NSA to conduct warrantless surveillance, even though there was no legislation to change FISA. On January 15, 2006, the Senate Committee of the Judiciary[25] Chairman Arlen Specter announced that his committee would hold hearings on these issues. However, Arlen Specter gave no indication as to the

---

19 50USC 1802.

20 During this 72-hour period, a warrant authorizing such surveillance is sought from the FISA court; see 50USC 1805 (f).

21 50USC 1811.

22 Freedom of expression.

23 Prohibition or supervision of searches.

24 See CCR Files over NSA Domestic Spying Program. Press release of January 17, 2006.

25 SCJ, Senate Committee on Judicial Affairs.

number of hearings or the quality of witnesses. Following on from Senator Specter's statements, the SCJ actually conducted its investigation and was particularly interested in the legality of the program. On February 6, 2006, the SCJ heard from Attorney General Gonzales, who supported the position of the Executive Branch; the President has the authority to authorize the NSA Warrantless Surveillance Program and holds this power by virtue of his powers as Chief Executive Officer, pursuant to Article 2 of the US Constitution and the AUMF Resolution. The SCJ then held two additional hearings on the wartime executive branch and the NSA's oversight authority on February 28 and March 28, 2006.

Jurisprudence

Justice has been pronounced on two occasions. In August 2006, Federal Judge Anna Diggs Taylor, with a seat in Chicago, upheld a complaint filed by lawyers, teachers and journalists who were in frequent contact with the Middle East and believed their communications were being monitored. Believing that President George W. Bush had overstepped his authority by risking the impugned surveillance, Judge Diggs Taylor demanded the immediate termination of the program. An appeal was filed, and her decision was upheld pending a decision by the Court of Appeal. In July 2007, the order to stop "anti-terrorist" interceptions in the United States without a judge's warrant was overturned by a Federal Court of Appeal. This decision left the President free to continue interceptions without a judge's warrant.

2.1.2.2.2. The reform of FISA

The law of August 5, 2007

The law promulgated on August 5, 2007 reformed FISA. The US government could already spy on foreign communications that did not transit through the United States. In 2007, the NSA was enabled to intercept without a warrant telephone calls and emails of foreign nationals transmitted using foreign equipment. Some opponents emphasized the dangers of the drifts, pointing out that it was now possible to intercept Americans communicating with people abroad without criminal or punishable intent. A guarantee exists, however: if an American becomes the main target of interceptions, a warrant is mandatory to continue surveillance. The FISA Court, in this context, no longer plays a significant role, and monitoring by an agency independent of the US government has lived on. It should be noted that this 2007 reform was only valid for six months. It is therefore worth considering the debates that followed at the end of the first decade and the beginning of the second decade of the 21st century.

The law of 2008

In light of the debates that emerged from the previous program and the law of August 5, 2007, which allowed interceptions without a warrant, a law was introduced and passed[26] by the House of Representatives and the Senate on July 10, 2008. This law authorized US intelligence to conduct unauthorized interceptions of electronic communications abroad in cases of espionage or terrorism. The text allowed a 1-year warrant to be obtained for interceptions of foreign groups and individuals. An American citizen could be intercepted if the communication concerned a foreign country. The authorities now had one week, not 72 hours, to obtain a warrant. They must obtain the approval of the special court established by law to intercept an American's conversation abroad, whereas previously the approval of the Attorney General had been sufficient. Thus, the scope for privacy protection was reduced, and for that very reason, a monitoring body was put in place. "The Senate has passed a good bill authorizing intelligence to listen in on a timely basis to the conversations of foreign terrorists in order to defend the freedom of the United States," read a statement released by the White House press office.

The law granted legal immunity to US electronic communication operators accused by the US courts of collaborating with the government and the secret service to carry out illegal interceptions.

In 2008, despite the Federal Court of Appeal decision mentioned above, some 40 recovery motions worth several billion US dollars were filed in connection with telephone interceptions in the United States. The initial draft did not mention legal immunity, but it seemed essential to the executive branch and telecommunication companies. President Bush indicated that he would not wait until the end of the debates to authorize the monitoring of communications[27] of suspected terrorists. In order to justify this stance, the president invoked possible threats to national security[28]. As a result, electronic communication operators were not obliged to pay damages to those who accuse these companies of violating their privacy: "In order to be able to discover … the enemy's plans, we need the cooperation of telecommunications companies … If these companies are subject to lawsuits that could cost them billions of dollars, they will not participate. They won't help us. They will not help protect America." Once the law had been passed, the hypothetical control by the courts was out of reach for all citizens.

---

26 By 69 votes, including that of Mr. Obama, against 28.

27 Telephone conversations and email exchanges.

28 Essential concept in the United States and on the American continent (see Argentina).

The extension of the FISA law until 2017

On September 12, 2012, the US House of Representatives voted[29] to extend the FISA law for five years. The FISA Act was due to expire on December 31, 2012. "Once again, the House of Representatives has passed a law that is so broad and imprecise that, despite its passage 4 years ago, we have little idea how the government is using it," said Michelle Richardson[30]. Richardson added that Americans and their communications were theoretically protected from executive intrusion by the Fourth Amendment to the Constitution. For his part, Senator Ron Wyden said Congress was entitled to information on how many Americans had had their communications intercepted under the authority of the FISA Act. Ron Wyden also denounced the shortcomings of the FISA law in terms of individual liberties.

Furthermore, in 2012, the Electronic Frontier Foundation filed lawsuits in the District of Columbia, claiming that the NSA had failed in its duty to protect US citizens. Despite the actions taken by the ACLU, the Electronic Frontier Foundation, some Senators and members of the House of Representatives, the law was definitively adopted by the Senate in December 2012. Ron Wyden insisted in vain on the prerogatives of the American government provided for in this law, which allows the targeting of any political organization or entity considered as a foreign political organization. This concerned foreign legal and natural persons who are enemies of the United States, as well as foreign persons belonging to allied states of the United States, Canada, countries of the European Union, Australia, etc. Thanks to the FISA law, the US government is in the position to solicit data from large US companies by issuing both a classified warrant that obliges the companies to cooperate with the intelligence services. In the European Union, the Center for Conflict, Freedom and Security Studies published a report[31] in January 2013 that denounced the FISA law and insists on the nuisances and abuses attributable to this law. The Patriot Act and the FISA law are questioned in this report: "Questions of privacy and data protection are raised by the exceptional measures taken in the name of security and the fight against terrorism. It is necessary to underline the particularities of the American system, both because of the Patriot Act and also because of the new FISA law. These aspects have been totally neglected despite their considerable implications for European sovereignty over data and the protection of the rights of its citizens."

---

29 301 votes in favor, 118 votes against, 10 abstentions.

30 The then-legislative advisor to the American Civil Liberties Union.

31 Commissioned by the Committee on Civil Liberties, Justice and Home Affairs (LIBE) of the European Parliament.

It is necessary to take into account the outsourcing generated by the Cloud which is increasingly being used. When the possibilities of the Cloud are combined with the provisions of the Patriot Act and the FISA law, the freedoms of foreigners are potentially threatened. Experts from the Center for the Study of Freedom and Security Conflicts have warned EU politicians and lawyers: "Special attention must be paid to US laws that allow the monitoring of data stored in Clouds by non-U.S. residents. The European Parliament should ask for clarifications on the FISA law, the new situation regarding the Fourth Amendment of the US Constitution, and the Patriot Act (especially Section 215). The European Parliament should consider amending data protection regulations to ensure that appropriate warnings are given regarding personal data (or data vulnerable to political scrutiny) before any data contained in a Cloud is exported to US jurisdictions." In fact, the current balance of power between the United States and the European Union is not conducive to a renegotiation. The United Kingdom adopts virtually all the diplomatic positions of the United States, often participating as an ally in its war efforts; France has not only rejoined the integrated military bodies of NATO, which left in 1966, but has played a leading role among the Western allies in Africa, and more specifically in Libya and Mali. This increased involvement of the United Kingdom and France in the Western military alliance led to close collaboration between intelligence services and, *de facto,* to the pre-eminence of the NSA and the FBI, including in the context of interceptions. It is illusory to think that nation-states wish to question the legal foundations put in place by successive American executives. According to Sophia Helena in 't Velt: "It is clear that the European Commission prefers to look elsewhere. So do national governments, not only because they do not understand what is at stake but also because they are afraid to challenge the American authority."

The Fourth Amendment[32] to the US Constitution, by definition, applies only to US residents, and foreigners are not likely to invoke it for protection. The procedural requirements that must, under FISA, be met by police or intelligence agencies in order to obtain information are not high. The privacy of foreign citizens, even if they are not "terrorists" or "enemies" of the US government, is potentially monitored and the widespread use of the Cloud does not improve the situation.

2.1.2.2.3. The conformity of PRISM to the sources of law

In this context, PRISM seems to be in compliance with the FISA law and the provisions of the Patriot Act, but there remains the question of PRISM's compliance with the Fourth Amendment of the US Constitution.

---

32 Similar to the American constitutional norm that protects the private sphere against state demands.

On August 13, 2013, the G29[33] wrote[34] to the (then) Vice-President of the European Commission, Viviane Reding, to consider and analyze the consequences of the PRISM program on the protection of data belonging to EU citizens.

A US/EU working group was established on access by the US intelligence services to data of European Union citizens; this group includes members of certain data protection authorities, along with European and US legal and technical experts on counterterrorism, but the G29 believes that it is the responsibility of the G29 to independently assess potential violations of European Union law, in particular Directive 95/46, at the source. The main objective of the G29 is to engage in a comparative law analysis to determine the extent to which US legislation is or is not in line with international law and European Union law: this involves examining the nature of the information that has been collected, the conditions of access by US authorities to this information, the controls that exist in the United States and possible remedies for European Union residents. The G29 also intends to identify European surveillance systems comparable to PRISM: "It is indeed important to ensure that European states respect the fundamental right to privacy," the G29 stated in a communiqué issued in August 2013.

In the United States, an internal audit[35] was conducted by the NSA. This audit revealed that the NSA has committed numerous violations of privacy laws since it was given new powers. The NSA reportedly ordered NSA members to falsify reports to the Department of Justice and the office of the Director of National Intelligence and substituted much more general language for small details. The NSA also reportedly concealed the unintentional surveillance of certain US citizens. For example, a significant number of telephone calls from Washington were monitored as a result of a programming error that swapped the prefix for the US capital area (202) with Egypt (20). Data was also captured and stored by an optical cable on US territory, resulting in the capture of communication data from US citizens, which is of course strictly prohibited. It was not until October 2011, months after the program began, that FISC received the information and deemed that what had happened ran contrary to the Constitution.

---

33 The group of European authorities responsible for information technology and civil liberties within the framework of Directive 95/46, the framework directive that preceded the GDPR.

34 Letter sent on August 13, 2013 by G29 President Jacob Kohnstamm to Commissioner Viviane Reding, with a copy to Cecilia Malmström, another European Commissioner, Martin Schulz, President of the European Parliament, and Juan Fernando Lopeez Aguilar, President of the LIBE Committee of the European Parliament.

35 From May 2012.

According to the NSA, "when we make a mistake ... we report it internally and to federal supervisors and get to the bottom of it." Activities are, apparently, continuously audited and "supervised internally and externally"[36]; malfunctions, according to DeLong[37], are "errors, not deliberate violations" and the error rate is reportedly "0.0005%". In addition, when interviewed by Reuters on August 20, 2013, the NSA stated that its mission "focuses on fighting foreign enemies who want to harm the country" and "we defend the United States against such threats while working hard to protect the private lives of Americans. It is not one or the other. It's both."

In contrast, Senators Ron Wyden and Mark Udall[38] said in a statement: "We have said that the violations of laws and regulations are more serious than what is recognized, and we think that Americans need to know that this confirmation is only the tip of the iceberg."

The NSA is controlled by Congress and FISC, which has the mission of overseeing the NSA surveillance programs. The reports received by Congress are not complete: if parliamentarians want to see uncensored reports, and if they have defense clearance, they are obliged to gain secure access to the documents; even parliamentarians with defense clearance are not allowed to take notes.

As for FISC, it does not always have exhaustive information. The President[39] of FISC stated, "FISC is obliged to rely on the accuracy of the information provided to it," insisting on the lack of investigative power vested in his organization. The Senate held hearings on US citizens in 2013. "I continue to be concerned that we are not receiving a candid response from the NSA," said the Chairman of the Senate Judiciary Committee[40].

So, in the United States, the weight is deliberately put on security.

American law influences the European Union countries in the field of interception.

Most EU states, starting with the United Kingdom, adopted laws in the 21st century that facilitated security interception and intelligence capabilities.

---

36 NSA cited by AFP on August 16, 2013.

37 The then-director of the NSA's internal control department.

38 From the Intelligence Commission.

39 At that time, Reggie Walton.

40 Patrick Leahy.

Even in Sweden, after a long political battle inside and outside the Parliament, a security law on interceptions was passed in 2008.

2.2. Interceptions in France

Interceptions in the judicial field are only justified if they can be used as evidence for crimes and misdemeanors. Interceptions therefore form part of the public realm of justice[41].

Security interceptions are, even more so than judicial interceptions, an exception to the principle of inviolability of correspondence, which until 1994 had constitutional value. In fact, judicial interceptions are integrated into the judicial system. Security interceptions, formerly called administrative interceptions, were natural interceptions, ordered by state services, according to their needs. They did not fall within the scope of public law, although they were ordered by public persons. In civil society, they were part of a dark, not to mention totalitarian, vision of the State: the "black cabinets" were replaced by interceptions by the Executive. George Orwell's *1984* was not far off. Weren't the rights that the State had taken for itself abusive?

This is what public opinion feared: its fear was relayed by many newspapers, satirical or otherwise[42]. The theme of "ears" reaps substantial benefits for the press. Ears in popular culture[43] are sympathetic[44] or threatening[45], depending on how they are portrayed. Episodes of the Cold War took away the exotic charm of the

---

41 The administration of justice is exercised on the basis of the principle of equality. The judiciary is the judicial authority instituted by the separation of powers (see Article 64 of the 1958 Constitution).

42 *Le Canard enchaîné, Hara-Kiri, Minute, Charlie-Hebdo.*

43 The ear symbolizes interceptions/listening. Hearing has taken the place of sight: the interception of telephone correspondence has taken the place of the interception of written correspondence, at a time when the Gutenberg Galaxy seems doomed. See Pontoux, J.-M., Dupuis, J. (1996). *Les Oreilles du Président.* Fayard.

44 In this case, the intelligence officer, a pleonasm of the "good ear", is a valiant knight who defends the values of Western civilization. See the popular children's book, *Langelot* by Lieutenant X (Vladimir Volkoff), where an intelligence agent barely of age combines humor, wit and athletic ability; *James Bond* by Ian Fleming adapted for the screen in many cult films. James Bond does not have Langelot's sense of humor: he is a phallic symbol, a lover of good food and the pleasures dispensed by consumer society; *Chapeaux melon et bottes de cuir* (first series of episodes, constantly rerun) is a sophisticated and somewhat lyrical evocation of the inventions of pop art.

45 See *Topaz* by Alfred Hitchcock.

interception/eavesdropping process[46]. In fact, civil society perceived security interceptions/tapping as a violation of human rights.

2.2.1. *The 1991 law*

The government was very aware of this data, which is why, in the law of July 10, 1991, the explanatory memorandum states that "only the search for information relevant to France's internal and external security and the prevention of breaches of state security can justify administrative authorization to intercept certain telephone conversations".

The traditional motives are national security, prevention of terrorism, prevention of crime and organized delinquency, and the protection of France's fundamental economic and scientific interests.

2.2.1.1. *National security*

National security is a traditional concept, but the term did not appear as such in French law. The concept is borrowed from article 8 of the European Convention, which covers national defense along with other attacks on the security and authority of the State. Discussions in the Sénat (French Senate) on this term of national security have been bitter. It is true that the terms are used in the European Convention for the Protection of Human Rights, but national security, in the bill, is not defined. This lack of definition was somewhat questionable.

Indeed, European Union law defines almost all concepts, but French law does not always imitate it, even if it obeys regulations and transposes directives.

Jacques Thyraud noted the difficulty in defining the notions of State security and public safety. He did not want the concept of national security to be introduced to the French legal corpus[47]. The rapporteur Marcel Rudloff pointed out that Jacques Thyraud's reasoning is correct, but that national security finds its place in a sector that is not judicial[48]. Jacques Thyraud withdrew his amendment and was skeptical.

---

46 Prior to and following Arthur Koestler's *Zéro et l'infini*, the countless "testimonies on the Soviet bloc" have consistently alluded to interceptions that prevent any real communication between opponents. In Solzhenitsyn's *In the First Circle*, one of the heroes, a researcher, works on voice identification.

47 Amendment no. 27 presented by Jacques Thyraud. The words "national security" were replaced by the words "State security", JO Sénat, sitting of June 25, 1991.

48 Marcel Rudloff: "Since this is a new concept that will be put into effect by a non-judicial commission, it is not wrong to use another expression reserved for criminal proceedings", JO Sénat, session of June 25, 1991.

The State cannot remain unarmed in the face of threats or crimes. The terms "national security" may be vague: it would be up to the control commission to clarify the concept.

2.2.1.2. *Prevention of terrorism*

The prevention of terrorism is the subject of a consensus. Some members of parliament want it to fall within the area of incrimination and not that of prevention. But since France has been subject to many attacks, the need to prevent assassinations organized for political reasons seems imperative.

At best, some human rights defenders outside of parliament point out that the State, under the guise of preventing terrorism, may be led to carry out security interceptions against intellectuals who support causes that supporters of violence are campaigning for. The Penal Code introduced a specific criminalization of terrorism[49].

2.2.1.3. *The prevention of crime, organized delinquency and the reconstitution or maintenance of dissolved groups*

The prevention of crime or delinquency is also part of the legal grounds for security interceptions. This includes drug trafficking, organized crime, trafficking in arms, ammunition, explosive products and nuclear materials, counterfeiting, serious financial crime, human trafficking and theft of works of art.

The Assemblée nationale is divided. Some parliamentarians noted that all aspects mentioned are misdemeanors or crimes prosecuted under the Penal Code. Why bring judicial matters into the administrative domain?

It is true that Article 8 of the European Convention for the Protection of Human Rights recognizes, in the delimitation of the grounds for security interceptions, drug trafficking and the fight against pimping. However, trafficking in persons is not synonymous with pimping, even if trafficking in persons is often aimed at pimping. The trafficking in question may be commercial in nature, but not necessarily sexual, with the exploitation of human beings reduced to the state of slaves, forced to perform forced labor, without benefiting from any rights or protection that would increase, even slightly, the cost of labor.

As for large-scale banditry, trafficking in arms, ammunition, explosive products and nuclear materials, counterfeiting, serious financial delinquency, theft of works and objects of art, these are not covered by Article 8 of the European Convention for the Protection of Human Rights. This is what justifies, for the authors of the law, the recourse to prevention. However, insofar as incriminating evidence exists, two types

---

49 See Penal Code, articles L421.1–L421.5.

of interceptions coexist: administrative interceptions (prevention) and judicial interceptions, when the offence appears to have been committed.

2.2.1.4. *The reconstitution or maintenance of dissolved groups*

The reconstitution or maintenance of dissolved groups is provided for by the law. The motive seems a little obsolete. It is political in nature since it targets extreme left-wing or extreme right-wing movements, or supporters of autonomist, independentist causes. The enemies of freedom certainly have rights that they would not grant to others, but society believes that it must defend the republican institutions. The defense of public liberties to the detriment of threatening small groups seems to justify this motive. This is in any case the opinion of Charles Lederman, who recalls *La Cagoule* and other prewar militias[50].

2.2.1.5. *The protection of France's fundamental economic and scientific interests*

This is an innovative concept. Does the public interest in protecting economic and scientific interests reflect a hint of state intervention? Surely not. This interest exists in all States[51]. The latter have the duty to fight against nebulae that do not correspond to any of the known legal entities. The concept may seem vague[52]. The idea encompasses various offences (criminal acts) and legal practices. Two amendments have been proposed, one to the Assemblée nationale by Jean-Jacques Hyest, the other by the government[53]. Both were inspired by the draft reform of the Penal Code, which introduced the notion of essential elements of its economic and scientific potential. In fact, the work on the bill on legal interception and on the new Penal Code were almost concurrent. This explains the interferences and the community of formulations.

---

50 Charles Lederman: "The notion of reconstitution or maintenance of dissolved groups, in application of the law of 10 January 1936 on combat groups and private militias seems understandable to us", JO Sénat, session of June 25, 1991.

51 Including the most liberal states: the United States and the United Kingdom, which seek to preserve the economic and scientific heritage of their companies.

52 François d'Aubert: "It's a catch-all formula, almost an alibi, and I don't really see what it can correspond to very precisely. For example, yesterday, during the IAG's visit, I jokingly asked one of our interlocutors whether this text would allow for increased surveillance of Japanese companies. Not understanding the irony, he answered: 'Absolutely'." First session of June 13, 1991.

53 Amendment No. 86 was introduced by the Government, which reads as follows: "In Article 3, replace the words 'of the fundamental economic and scientific interests of France' with the words 'of the essential elements of France's economic and scientific potential'", second sitting of June 13, 1991.

The protection of France's fundamental interests concerns various electronic communication techniques: in the economic and scientific fields, the telephone, if it is still used, is supplemented by fax and email. As technologies evolve, other categories of transmissions will be interested. Several profiles of people are tacitly targeted, including business people and bank account holders.

Tax eavesdropping was discussed[54] during the debate in the Assemblée nationale. The Keeper of the Seals wanted reassurance that security interceptions would not be able to intervene in the course of investigations undertaken in the area of tax control, and that, in customs matters, they would be limited to the fight against drug trafficking and the laundering of money derived from this trafficking.

Is there a risk that banking secrecy[55] could be undermined? Almost all inter-bank transfers pass through a network fed by bank computers, and stock market orders are cleared in Paris by a similar system. This phenomenon is more related to computing than to telecommunications, but the links between computing and telecommunications are so inseparable that the question arises.

Some economic and union leaders may be suspected[56]. The government considered these suspicions to be paranoia. Democratic executives that recognize freedom of enterprise and trade union freedom would not allow themselves to be led astray in ways that would make economic or trade union leaders potential enemies. Moreover, the control body ensures that motives are not diverted from the spirit of the law, which respects the general principles of law and individual liberties.

2.2.2. The law of March 9, 2004

Following the law of 1991, the law of March 9, 2004 was adopted, which authorized certain judicial interceptions at the information stage[57].

---

54 See François d'Aubert, Assemblée nationale, First Session, June 13, 1991.

55 On banking secrecy: "Banking secrecy preserves information of a confidential nature, the content of the balance sheet or the movement of the account" (Paris, October 1931, JCP, 1932, 119).

56 Charles Lederman: "Such a provision may lead to the wiretapping of all engineers in our country. I even have the impression that all business leaders could be suspected of intelligence with the enemy and put under wiretap. Thus, we might experience, for example, the union leaders of this or that French factory being tapped on the telephone, on the grounds that it is necessary to safeguard France's economic potential...", JO Sénat, session of June 25, 1991.

57 Mandate of the liberty and custody judge. At that time, security interceptions were requested for a period of four months, renewable, by the services under the Ministry of Defense and Interior.

At that time, security interceptions were requested for a period of four months, renewable, by the services under the Ministry of Defense, the Ministry of the Interior and the Ministry of Customs, and were authorized by the Prime Minister, after the opinion of the *Commission nationale de contrôle des interceptions de sécurité* (French National Commission for the Control of Security Interceptions) (CNCIS), created at the request of the ECHR, following the condemnation of France[58]. The Prime Minister, head of the administration, could overrule an unfavorable opinion of the CNCIS, which was not able to issue injunctions to the Prime Minister. The files were handled by close collaborators of the Prime Minister and signed by the Prime Minister, who was politically and legally responsible for security interception.

2.2.3. *The 2015 Intelligence Act*

The Intelligence Act established an expanded regime for the use of interceptions and metadata. It was still a derogation from the principle of "secrecy of correspondence", governed at the international level by the Universal Declaration of Human Rights, and at the European level, as far as the Council of Europe was concerned, by the European Convention for the Protection of Human Rights, and as far as the European Union was concerned, by the European Charter of Fundamental Rights[59].

2.2.3.1. *The result: broadening of the purposes or motives of the information*

While some of the reasons that may justify the use of information techniques are broadly in line with the reasons of the 1991 law (prevention of terrorism, prevention of organized crime and delinquency, actions aimed at maintaining or reconstituting dissolved groups), others are new or constitute resulting evolutions of old reasons.

2.2.3.1.1. A notable evolution of former reasons for the 1991 law

France's "major economic and scientific interests" were no longer "essential interests". The purpose was broader. It included economic and industrial surveillance as a whole. Some fears about interceptions concerning the country's economic, trade union and scientific personalities, which had already emerged in the debates in the Assemblée nationale and Sénat in 1991, would increase in parliamentary circles in 2015. Some deputies argued that the list was too extensive[60]. "One might think that nuclear power represents a major economic interest for the nation; in this case, following the logic of this text, any protest against nuclear

---

58 Kruslin v. France, ECHR.

59 Article 7.

60 Michel Pouzol, PS congressman.

power could be monitored with the means provided for in this bill.... We demand the deletion of this paragraph." Defense Minister Jean-Yves Le Drian defended this paragraph, in reference to the United Kingdom, which has assigned their "economic well-being" to the activities of British intelligence services[61]. Pierre Lellouche is also clear on this: "The Americans have systematically used the intelligence services for everything that concerns commissions, for instance. We have seen a whole series of actions, organized by the CIA, which subsequently led to legal action.... Thus, in this economic competition, naivety is the worst attitude. It is absolutely essential to strengthen the economic intelligence that our country needs."[62]

"National independence, territorial integrity and national defense" were substituted for "national security". "National defense" is integrated into "national security", the concept of which seemed to have been abandoned. National independence and territorial integrity may seemed to have been approaching another purpose, related to foreign policy, but they may also justify the surveillance of independentists or separatists.

2.2.3.2. New and much debated motives

2.2.3.2.1. Protecting France's interests and international commitments

Article L811-3, section 2, touches on "the essential interests of foreign policy, the execution of France's European and international commitments and the prevention of all forms of foreign interference"[63]. This motive is considered by some deputies to be too imprecise with regard to the importance of the interests. The rapporteur opposed the amendments to delete this motive[64].

---

61 Michel Pouzol, Assemblée nationale, second session of April 13, 2015.

62 Pierre Lellouche, UMP congressman, Assemblée nationale, second session of April 13, 2015.

63 France left the integrated military bodies of NATO in 1966 and rejoined the integrated military bodies of NATO at the end of the first decade of the 21st century: President Nicolas Sarkozy made the announcement before Congress in Washington on November 7, 2007. A motion of no confidence was defeated in the Assemblée nationale on April 8, 2008, and a vote of confidence took place on March 17, 2009. Reinstatement became effective at the NATO summit on April 3 and 4, 2009.

64 Philippe Nauche, draftsman of the opinion: "I am opposed to these deletion amendments.... It is a question of the fundamental missions of our intelligence services, and these missions ... do not date from this bill; they appear in the founding decrees of these services. They allow the Government, the executive, to assess the current international situation in an autonomous manner; they also allow us to take an interest in subjects in the making in order to assess the evolution of the situation. In order to have a good level of information to enable the executive

In order to understand the implications of this motive, it is important to recall a few contextual elements.

France has been a member of the Atlantic Alliance since it was established, but for several decades, while remaining integrated into NATO, it pursued an independent policy: it did not systematically follow the inflections of the pre-eminent American power, opposing the second intervention of the American-British coalition in Iraq. However, since the beginning of the 21st century, contacts between France and NATO's integrated military bodies multiplied and French reintegration appeared to be a logical outcome.

As a founding country of the EEC, France played an important role within the European Union, often in tandem with Germany, as the United Kingdom remained outside both the continent and the euro area. The Lisbon Treaty envisaged a common foreign policy, which did not happen. However, the European Union's High Representative for Foreign Affairs and Security Policy, Federica Mogherini[65], played a significant diplomatic role. The European Union has at times implemented economic and geopolitical positions: this was the case with the economic sanctions against Russia during the conflict between Ukraine and Russia, where the European Union took Ukraine's side.

However, the main military powers of the European Union before Brexit, the United Kingdom and France[66], played their own game, sometimes agreeing with the stance of the European Union, but not systematically. Generally, the United Kingdom and France moved on the chessboard in accordance with the objectives of NATO and the United States, despite the mediatized disengagement of the United States.

It is notably in relation to these French commitments that the "Foreign Affairs" purpose of the European Union is situated. The question of intercepting foreign persons arose in France and an amendment of the Joint Commission that would have left the field open to services appeared shortly before the final adoption of the law. Provoking a strong reaction in civil society, it was finally withdrawn by a government amendment shortly before the vote.

2.2.3.2.2. Attacks on the republican form of the institutions

This new purpose has led to much criticism because of the vague and imprecise nature of the "republican form". In the 19th century, the "republican" form was

---

to make choices, open sources are not enough", Assemblée nationale, second session of April 13, 2015.

65 Succeeding Catherine Ashton on December 1, 2014.

66 Who have engaged in military cooperation.

opposed to the "royalist" form. This prism is outdated. On several occasions, the term "republican" has intervened in recent laws, and in very different areas of law. For example, the 2008 law on the conditions of union representativeness retained "adherence to the republican values of representative unions" and "the republican values of representative unions". In the absence of case law on the subject, the concept of "republican values" seemed to undermine legal certainty. In the law on Intelligence, the SRC group, believing that "the prevention of public violence likely to seriously undermine the public peace" provided for in the initial text could be understood in a broader way, introduced an amendment that provides for "attacks on the republican form of institutions", on the one hand, and "collective violence likely to undermine national security", on the other hand. The amendment was adopted[67]. At a constitutional level, it is based on the last paragraph of Article 89 of the 1958 Constitution, which states that the republican form of government cannot be revised.

In addition, the European Convention for the Protection of Human Rights and Fundamental Freedoms protects minority opinions – opinions that are hardly consistent with commonly held opinions. Does this mean that protecting the republican form of institutions would be consistent with the right to intercept not only the communications of autonomists, but also the communications of persons who do not share the opinions represented in the Assemblée nationale and the Sénat? This is what gives rise to fears and reservations among some parliamentarians and jurists[68].

Justification by the legislator is easy: adherence to the republican form of institutions would make it impossible for "a republican Prime Minister" to authorize such interceptions. However, on this subject, the Constitutional Council, in its decision of July 23, 2015, stated, "The legislator has precisely circumscribed the aims pursued and has not retained criteria that are out of line with the objective pursued by these administrative police measures, and the same applies to the aims defined in a) of 5) referring to the criminal offences of Chapter II of Title I of Book IV of the Penal Code."

---

67 It was justified as follows by Françoise Descamps-Crosnier, SRC congresswoman: "By adopting this much more restrictive wording … we are targeting the most dangerous groups in order to prevent an action that would jeopardize the safety of our fellow citizens", Assemblée nationale, second session of April 13, 2015.

68 Marion Maréchal, National Front congresswoman: "As the text is currently being drafted, we are fearful of a certain number of abuses. I am thinking in particular of the field of action of Intelligence, which will be extended to the prevention of attacks on the republican form of institutions.... Forgive my concern, but when all or almost all of the political class and the government explain that the National Front is not a republican party, understand that this extremely broad formulation may cause me some form of concern", Assemblée nationale, second session of April 13, 2015.

2.2.3.2.3. Collective violence that seriously undermines public peace

This purpose was also discussed. What does the legislator mean by "collective violence"? Are these assaults which are offences subject to the Penal Code? Can the term refer to authorized demonstrations that have "degenerated"? How can we measure and quantify a "serious breach of the public peace"[69]? These remarks are not taken into account by the law commissions and the majority of parliamentarians. In its decision of July 23, 2015, the Constitutional Council stated, "Of those defined in c) of 5) referring to criminal incriminations defined in articles 431-1 to 431-10 of the Penal Code."

2.2.3.2.4. Prevention of the proliferation of weapons of mass destruction

As a nuclear power, France has ratified the Treaty on the Non-Proliferation of Nuclear Weapons[70]. It has also adopted positions in conformity with its Western allies on the Iranian geopolitical issue and on condemning the use of chemical weapons, particularly in Syria, where France has presented an even more critical view than that of some of its allies. Indeed, in full accordance with NATO and its Chicago Summit[71], the national and Atlantic Alliance strategies state that the proliferation of nuclear and other weapons of mass destruction could have consequences for global prosperity.

It is in this context that, after discussion, this purpose was adopted by the Intelligence Act.

For the majority of the political class, the aims seemed to be in line with the objectives envisaged to legally and legitimately undermine the "secrecy of correspondence" and the privacy of the persons targeted by the intelligence, in a perspective of "defense", as well as of "promotion of the fundamental interests of the Nation".

---

69 Aurélie Filipetti, Member of Parliament, argued: "The scope seems too broad to us with regard to the infringements on individual liberties and privacy that are brought about by these intelligence techniques…. The expression of collective violence likely to undermine national security seems to me much too broad and imprecise." Minister Bernard Cazeneuve stated: "Certain forms of violent radicalism undermine the foundations of the Republic and its values: faced with them, we must take preventive measures", Assemblée nationale, second session of April 13, 2015.

70 Treaty on the Non-Proliferation of Nuclear Weapons signed on July 1, 1968, entered into force on March 5, 1970 for an initial period of 25 years.

71 Held in May 2012.

2.2.3.3. *An evolution of the authorization and control procedure*

2.2.3.3.1. Requests for authorization in the 2015 law

The new Article L246-2 of the Internal Security Code stipulated that information and documents are requested by the designated and duly authorized officers of the departments attached to the ministers in charge of internal security, defense, the economy and the budget. The Ministries of Economy and Budget were not previously in charge of the process of requests for security interceptions, but they were able to access technical connection data from a 2010 CNCIS case law: the CNCIS held that detailed invoicing and identifications were part of the preparatory phase of the interception. These provisions came into force on January 1, 2015.

The Intelligence Act thus adopted the provisions of the Military Programming Act with regard to the status of ministers who are entitled to submit interception requests.

Article L121-2 also deals with the status of ministerial delegates, it being understood that the techniques are exclusively implemented by individually designated and authorized agents.

The Ministers of Defense and the Interior, in charge of Customs, the Economy and the Budget, delegate this task of processing the request for authorization individually to "direct employees entitled to secretly defend the nation"[72].

The request outlines:

– the techniques to be implemented;

– the department in charge of implementing the technique(s);

– the purpose(s) pursued;

– the reason(s) for the measures;

– the period of validity of the authorization;

– the person(s), place(s) or vehicle(s) concerned;

– the authorization to proceed with the implementation of an intelligence system.

Authorization is the prerogative of the Prime Minister. The authorization to implement the techniques can only be issued by the Prime Minister, following the decision of the Constitutional Council of July 23, 2015. On this point, there is a continuity with the law of July 10, 1991.

---

72 Article L821-2 in Chapter 1 "of the implementation authorization".

The Prime Minister is a guarantor as well as a decision-maker who cannot be granted injunctions[73]. Insofar as ministers propose written and reasoned requests, it seems consistent that the Prime Minister, who issues the authorization, should be subject to the same procedure. If the Prime Minister is empowered to authorize, it is less as head of government[74] than as the holder of regulatory power[75]. In the hierarchy of regulatory norms, it is the Prime Minister's decrees that take precedence over other regulatory norms.

Taking the past into account with regard to the present implies a formalism that reassures the citizen. As early as 1991, the Law Commission of the Assemblée nationale considered that the Prime Minister's decision had to be written and motivated. The risk of arbitrariness was thus avoided.

2.2.3.3.2. The period of validity of the authorization

The period of validity of the authorization is set at a maximum of four months.

Amendment No. 67 proposed by Éric Ciotti and Charles de la Verpillière aimed to facilitate the work of the intelligence services in logistical terms[76].

Amendment No. 136, as corrected, proposed a renewal period of two months[77]. The government demonstrated[78] that in its opinion, the four-month period was

---

73 It is impossible to issue an injunction to the head of administration, as the prohibition of injunction is one of the basic principles of administrative law. See note Blevet under EC, January 10, 1964, "Minister of Agriculture v. Simonet".

74 The head of government directs the politics of the nation. His role in this area is general. It is not an individual one.

75 Article 37 of the Constitution. What is not a matter for the law (Article 34) is a matter for the regulations.

76 Charles de La Verpillière, UMP congressman: "Experience, particularly the attack of September 11, 2001, shows that attacks and acts of terrorism often require very taxing logistics and very substantial preparation. It may therefore be necessary for surveillance to last more than four months, sometimes at least six or even more. It is true that the authorization is renewable. We propose to extend the authorization to six months, knowing that this in no way weakens the guarantees and controls surrounding the implementation of these interception and surveillance techniques", Assemblée nationale, second session of April 14, 2015.

77 Hervé Morin, UDI congressman: "The four-month period corresponds to the one given since 1991. Except that in 1991, we were talking about telephone tapping, and today we are talking about means of interception that can be extremely intrusive. When we are on algorithms or metadata, we are no longer simply talking about phone tapping! The duration of the renewal of the authorization must therefore be reduced to two months ... The services are able to anticipate and ensure that there is continuity in the means", Assemblée nationale, second session of April 14, 2015.

relevant and had shown its relevance in the past. According to the Keeper of the Seals, Christiane Taubira, the four-month period satisfied the principles of necessity and proportionality. The two amendments were therefore postponed and the former four-month renewable period was maintained.

2.2.3.3.3. The opinions of the Control Commission

The CNCIS

CNCIS notices were given in advance, except in cases of emergency or extreme urgency. In 2003, without revising the 1991 law, and at the request of the CNCIS president, the prior notice regime was extended to cases of emergency and extreme urgency. This was made possible by improved responsiveness. The control of motives had become generalized.

In 2013, in article 20 of the Military Programming Law, interceptions related to geolocation and connection data were included. Contrary to the provisions of the 1991 law, the CNCIS's opinion is given, not *a priori,* but *a posteriori*.

Monitoring and advice from the CNCTR

The question arises as to whether the CNCTR's advice[79], and therefore control, will be effective before or after the interceptions. Debates have been held on this point both in the Assemblée nationale and in the Sénat.

The congressman Jean-Jacques Candelier insisted in particular on the absence of a time limit to act and on the limitation of control by the defense secretary[80].

The question arose as to whether silence constitutes consent, in the event that the time limit for transmitting an opinion, whether favorable or unfavorable, is exceeded. An amendment was tabled on this subject to make it necessary for the

---

78 Jean-Jacques Urvoas, rapporteur: "Under current law, authorizations to implement a security interception last four months and are renewable for four months. Since 1991, no observation has been made that this period is either too long or too short. It seemed to us to be a point of reference. Moreover, in judicial matters, the same techniques are also authorized for four months. It therefore seemed to us quite consistent that the time limits should be identical in the judicial and administrative orders", Assemblée nationale, second session of April 14, 2015.

79 The *Commission nationale de contrôle des techniques de renseignement* took over from the CNCIS.

80 Jean-Jacques Condelier, PF congressman: "The control carried out *a posteriori* by the CNCTR does not appear to be sufficient", Assemblée nationale, first session of April 13, 2015.

opinion to be delivered[81], but not adopted, on the grounds of efficiency[82]. Article L821-1 stipulates that the implementation of intelligence techniques is subject to the prior authorization of the Prime Minister after advice from the CNCTR. The CNCTR's opinion is not required for "operational urgency" and has given rise to censorship by the Constitutional Council[83]. References to the CNCIS were rejected; these were amendment no. 93, presented by the EELV group, and amendment no. 50, presented by members of the CRC group[84].

Exceptions were made for certain protected professions. The question arose as to the definition of these protected occupations. Thus, amendment no. 94, which envisaged protecting surgeons and midwives, was not accepted. On the other hand, with regard to journalists, lawyers, members of parliament, and magistrates, the CNCTR would have to give its opinion in plenary session[85].

---

81 Amendment no. 8, Lionel Tardy, LR: "It is worthwhile to dwell for a moment on paragraph 35. As much as I am seduced by the principle of 'silence equals agreement' in the relations between the administration and the citizens, even if it includes an incalculable number of exceptions, as much as I am very skeptical about the application of this principle to this procedure ... a CNCTR that would be nothing more than a registry office would be useless", Assemblée nationale, second session of April 14, 2015.

82 Bernard Cazeneuve, PS: "The CNCTR is a high administrative authority that gives an advisory opinion. If the government was unable to act in the absence of an opinion being given, this would mean that this high administrative authority, if it took a long time to give this opinion, could block the operation of the system. This is why, in the scheme as it is designed, the government can act even if the advisory commission's opinion has not been given. This does not prevent the advisory commission from controlling, even if the operation is initiated, the conditions under which it was initiated. It is therefore a consultative authority, to which no time limit is imposed, and the government is not obliged to wait for its opinion before acting: all this does not mean that the control does not exist, but that it can, even when the operation has been launched, be carried out by the High Authority", Assemblée nationale, second session of April 14, 2015.

83 Esther Benbassa, EELV Senator: "Even in cases of absolute urgency, we want prior notice from the CNCTR, which would then have one hour to make its decision. Let us not get rid of this essential guarantee", Sénat, June 4, 2015.

84 Jean-Pierre Bosino, CRC Senator: "The CNCTR must be able to fulfil its mission, even in an emergency. Today, the CNCIS can give an opinion day and night, within two hours. Still, human resources are needed. It should not be possible to derogate from the opinion of the supervisory authority", Sénat, June 4, 2015.

85 Christiane Taubira, Keeper of the Seals of France: "It is not the professionals who are protected, but the secrets they hold, useful to democracy and the rule of law: secrecy of sources, secrecy of the investigation, secrecy of national defense. The CNCTR will ensure that the principles of necessity and proportionality are respected", Sénat, June 4, 2015.

On the other hand, for the legal profession, it did not provide for information, the hearing of the President of the Bar and the authorization of the President of the High Court[86]. Lawyers, since the law of July 10, 1991, have consistently sought specific status in the context of interceptions, in order to fully ensure the rights of the defense, but despite their repeated requests, they have not been heard.

A conditional control of the Council of State

Collaboration with the Council of State was established, which was a new element of the Intelligence Act. However, it requires a mandatory prior administrative appeal to the CNCTR. The Council of State could also be approached by any person who wished to verify that no intelligence techniques were regularly used.

When an administrative court or a judicial authority is seized of a procedure or a dispute whose solution depends on the examination of the regularity of one or more techniques for gathering information, it could, of its own motion or at the request of one of the parties, refer the matter to the Council of State for a preliminary ruling. In this case, the Council of State rules within one month.

In addition, the Council of State became competent to hear[87] requests relating to the implementation of Article 41 of Law No. 78-17 of January 6, 1978 relating to files and liberties, for processing and parts of processing relating to State security.

While the CNCTR is not quite a counter-power, it does seem to be taking over at the level of requests for authorizations from the CNCIS.

The CNCTR must also respect national defense secrecy when it decides to refer a case to the public prosecutor, even if the agents who would testify before the CNCTR are not in a position to reveal elements protected for national defense purposes.

Was Cécile Cukierman, CRCE, mistaken when she declared[88], "This bill lays the last stone of the 'punitive society' imagined by Michel Foucault, in his lecture at the Collège de France from 1972–1973, where the individual is followed in all his steps, to see whether he is normal or abnormal?"

---

86 Rectified amendment no. 75 presented by the PRG: "In cases where the implementation of information-gathering techniques mentioned in Title V of the present book concerns a lawyer, the CNCTR must inform and hear the president of the bar of the jurisdiction in which the latter practices and obtain the authorization of the president of the tribunal de grande instance", Sénat, June 4, 2015.

91 Under the conditions provided for in Chapter III of Title VII of the Code of Administrative Justice.

88 Sénat, June 4, 2015.

Nevertheless, perhaps she is not entirely wrong. Indeed, the recording of content also leads to the recording of metadata. The intelligence services, without the approval of the judge, can, since the law on intelligence, capture, fix, transmit the words and images held in confidence, that is, the information data that pass through or are contained in a system. International surveillance measures for interceptions from or to foreign countries are provided for.

At operators, access providers and hosting providers, it is possible to suck up documents and information, as well as install black boxes, and anonymity can be lifted with the authorization of the Prime Minister. The IMSI-catcher, a fake relay antenna, is able to capture data transmitted between the electronic device and the true relay antenna. According to the CNIL, this should make it possible to take, in a certain geographical localization, the entire contents of the correspondences. The CNIL and the Conseil du Numérique (Digital Council) have reservations about the law relating to intelligence.

2.2.4. Reform of the code of criminal procedure

"The State that claims to eradicate all insecurity, even potential insecurity, is caught in a spiral of exception, suspicion and oppression that can go as far as the more or less complete disappearance of liberties,"[89] explains Mireille Delmas-Marty, a law professor who has long been reflecting on the national and international aspects of human rights, particularly in the context of a "dangerous world", to return to one of her best-known titles.

Delmas-Marty made known, notably on France-Culture, in December 2015 and January 2016, certain reservations about the proposed reform of the Code of Criminal Procedure in 2016, stating that this law does not provide any legal security. In its opinion on the bill, the National Consultative Commission on Human Rights denounced "the continuation of a policy of ad hoc 'patch-up' ... preferred to the conduct of a comprehensive reflection on the architecture of criminal procedure and internal security, which is nevertheless eagerly awaited"[90].

The Magistrates' Union[91] challenges a procedure that "is part of the tangle of four texts, reform of the constitution, extension of the state of emergency, modification of this regime and modification of the penal procedure".

---

89 Delmas-Marty, M. (2010). *Libertés et sûreté dans un monde dangereux*. Le Seuil, Paris, 141.
90 Notice of June 4, 2016, No. 69.
91 Hearing by the Commission des lois (French law commission) published on February 12, 2016.

The attacks that took place on French territory in January and November 2015, which received a lot of media coverage through public opinion relays, enabled the government to move forward with projects that had been under consideration for two or three years; the law on information was easily adopted and the draft reform of criminal procedure put forward by Minister Christiane Taubira was considerably supplemented by numerous criminal measures aimed at fighting terrorism, delinquency and organized crime. After Christiane Taubira's resignation, the text was carried out by the new Minister of Justice, Jean-Jacques Urvoas.

This anti-terrorism law[92] has many components. The Council of State approved the plan as a whole, holding that a certain desire for balance appears in the draft submitted to it: it includes a relative facilitation of certain interceptions, as well as several guarantees. For the Conseil d'État, the imperatives of security must not impinge on respect for individual and collective freedoms. The Council of State explicitly relies on article 66 of the Constitution of the Fifth Republic for the judicial authority, guardian of individual liberties, article 2 of the Declaration of the Rights of Man and of the Citizen of 1789[93], article 8 of the European Convention for the Protection of Human Rights and Fundamental Freedoms, and articles 2 and 4 of the Declaration of the Rights of Man of 1789 for the freedom to come and go. However, it will be very difficult to reconcile these requirements.

While it approved the plan as a whole, the Council of State had some reservations about the impact study: it made two requests for corrective referrals, at the initiative of rapporteurs, but was not fully satisfied with the work carried out in this context. In particular, there is a lack of data that would allow a better appreciation of the usefulness of certain measures, comparative law studies, with references to foreign or European illustrations,[94] and a complete state of the law. The reservation also applies to a certain extent to the explanatory memorandum: the Council of State calls for a richer analysis[95].

2.2.4.1. An expansion of interception possibilities after the Intelligence Act

This is the case of public address or video surveillance of a place or a home or the use of cell phone surveillance devices, known as an IMSI-catcher. Until now, sound or video surveillance was governed by the Perben II law.

---

92 Bill to strengthen the fight against organized crime and its financing, efficiency and guarantees of criminal procedure.

93 Four natural rights: freedom, property, security, resistance to oppression.

94 The Council of State even uses the expression "lacunaire" to qualify the rule of law.

95 This would make it possible to "better apprehend, by placing them in a historical perspective, the new balances resulting from the text between the administrative police and the judicial police, on the one hand, and between the public prosecutor's office, the examining magistrate, and the judge of liberties and detention, on the other hand", Conseil d'État, opinion of January 28, 2016.

The article of the Code of Criminal Procedure referred to was article 706.96; it is supplemented by article 706-96-1 and concerns the motives for delinquency and organized crime.

These captures are possible during an organized crime investigation. The new article stipulated, at the request of the public prosecutor, that the judge of liberties and detention can authorize them for a period of one month and that they are renewable once.

The investigating judge may authorize the introduction into a private place or vehicle, including without the knowledge or consent of the owner or lawful occupant, of a device for capturing images and sounds. In the case of a dwelling place, the introduction of a technical device at night must be authorized by the liberty and custody judge, seized by the investigating judge. The premises of media companies, lawyers, doctors, notaries and bailiffs are excluded from this device. The decision is taken for a maximum period of two months and cannot exceed two years.

2.2.4.2. IMSI-catchers

The use of IMSI-catchers for administrative interceptions was introduced in the Intelligence Act. IMSI-catchers, false base stations, can in particular capture the connection data transmitted between the electronic device cell phone and the real base station.

In the judicial field, the use of IMSI-catchers can be made on the basis of the new articles 706-95-4 to 706-95-10 of the Code of Criminal Procedure, which applies to all offences corresponding to organized crime and not only terrorist offences.

In the administrative field, it is the judge of liberties and detention, within the framework of an investigation, who is able to authorize, at the request of the public prosecutor, this interception. The judge authorizes the use of a technical device that identifies the terminal and the subscription number. The authorization is delivered for one month and is renewable once. In case of emergency, it is the public prosecutor who delivers this authorization, confirmed by the judge of liberties and detention within 24 hours.

Within the framework of an investigation, the duration of the authorization delivered by the examining magistrate is two months, renewable once. In the case of interception of correspondence sent or received by terminal equipment, the duration of the authorization given by the liberty or detention judge or the examining magistrate is 48 hours, renewable once. The order is reasoned and is not subject to appeal.

Many criticisms are made of the IMSI-catcher procedures, and attempts to develop a framework are made but rejected.

The IMSI-catcher is an indiscriminate interception method; it allows for the collection of multiple pieces of information on persons unrelated to the case at hand. Numerous amendments aimed at regulating these devices and limiting possible abuses have been tabled during parliamentary discussions. However, they were not adopted, as they were considered by the government to be inappropriate to the objectives of the law.

Thus, before the Assemblée nationale, an amendment was rejected[96] that would tightly regulate the purposes of the IMSI-catcher, which should be limited to the research and recording of offences for which its use has been authorized by the liberty and detention judge or by the investigating judge[97], and exclude offences that could be discovered by this means. An amendment was also rejected[98] that would provide guarantees for the collection of data decided on as a matter of urgency with the authorization of the public prosecutor. The data would have been centralized, preserved and destroyed by the judicial interception platform. The government undertook to offer technical guarantees for the centralization, corresponding to a financial commitment of 2–4 million dollars[99].

Finally, for some MPs, the IMSI-catcher technique is incompatible with the protection of certain professions, lawyers, magistrates, journalists, parliamentarians[100]. Indeed, the dummy relay antenna constituted by the IMSI-catcher collects connection data from all terminals located in a predefined geographical area. It is therefore impossible to exclude certain data under the pretext of protecting certain individuals because of their functions in society, as Alain Tournet, Member of Parliament[101], states in his amendment 135[102]: "The specific nature of the professions in question, particularly with regard to independence and professional secrecy, does not allow recourse to such a system, which is prejudicial to the rights of the defense." These amendments were rejected, without a real solution to this conflict being evoked. Other amendments were adopted.

---

96 No. 361, Assemblée nationale, First Session, March 3, 2016.

97 However, under this amendment, incidental proceedings would not be null and void.

98 No. 363, Assemblée nationale, First Session, March 3, 2016.

99 Referee of the Cour des comptes, April 25, 2016.

100 See Amendment no. 135, Assemblée nationale, First Session, March 3, 2016.

101 GGRD.

102 Assemblée nationale, Amendment no. 135, first sitting of March 3, 2016.

The first step is to specify the conditions for authorizing the use of IMSI-catchers[103]: the authorization decision is written and legitimate, the system is implemented for a limited period of time, one month renewable once during the preliminary investigation and two months renewable twice during the judicial inquiry.

A double judicial supervision implies the intervention of a judicial police officer who draws up a report of the data collection operations.

And the procedures for centralizing, storing and destroying the data collected, set by a decree of the Conseil d'Etat, issued after a reasoned opinion has been given and published by the CNIL; the data is collected by the national platform for judicial interception[104]; it is destroyed at the end of the limitation period for public action.

IMSI-catchers have been discussed extensively both at the time of the Intelligence Act and in the current legislation. Some amendments have emphasized the dichotomy between the IMSI-catcher technique and the basic principles of individual and collective freedoms. This assertion is conceivable, because the lack of differentiation between natural persons that corresponds to this device renders the respect of privacy illusory.

2.2.4.3. *Protected personalities in the field of interception*

Interceptions concerning deputies and senators, magistrates and lawyers are only possible if there are serious, "plausible" grounds for suspecting that one of these individuals has participated, either as perpetrator or as accomplice, in the commission of a crime. Interceptions of protected personalities can only be decided by a reasoned decision of the liberty and detention judge seized by a reasoned order of the investigating judge. The order of the investigating judge and the decision of the liberty and detention judge constitute a double guarantee, which did not formerly exist. The Council of State approves this double examination, which was previously admitted on two occasions for geolocation[105] and within the framework of the bill strengthening the protection of the secrecy of journalists' sources[106]. The Council of State considers that these provisions reinforce the principle of the separation of powers[107], the independence of the judiciary, and deliberate secrecy. In addition, any nullity relating to the proceedings may be sanctioned by the examining magistrate's chamber.

---

103 No. 362, Assemblée nationale, First Session, March 3, 2016.

104 "The system will be applicable as of January 1, 2017. The PNIJ will concentrate the judicial interceptions and the data collected by the use of the IMSI-catcher, that is, the reverse directory", Jean-Jacques Urvoas, Assemblée nationale, first session of March 3, 2016.

105 Article 230-34 of the Code of Criminal Procedure.

106 Law 2010-1 of January 4, 2010.

107 Article 16 of the Declaration of the Rights of Man and of the Citizen.

2.2.4.4. *The national platform for judicial interception*

Since the beginning of its implementation, the *plateforme nationale des interceptions judiciaires* (National Platform for Judicial Interception or PNIJ) has attracted criticism. The law enshrines this platform, dedicating to it Chapter VI of the Code of Criminal Procedure. Despite a real need to improve the interception system, the PNIJ has experienced some dysfunctions: it was the subject of a redesign in 2005; the contract for its design and implementation began in 2011 and ended at the end of 2016. The *Cour des comptes* (Court of Audit) regretted that the platform was hosted, not by the State, but by a commercial company, Thales[108]: "The State preferred to choose a high degree of dependence" by "ignoring the possibilities of inter-ministerial cooperation for the hosting and operation of this system". The Court of Auditors emphasized the benefits of pooling administrative and judicial interception services. Article L230-45 of the Code of Criminal Procedure also stipulates that the main mission of this PNIJ is to centralize the execution of requisitions and interception requests. A decree in the Council of State, issued after a public and reasoned opinion from the CNIL, is the Gordian knot of article 88 of the law. The latter does not develop the role of the PNIJ, undoubtedly because of the political and financial uncertainties that have marked the very progressive implementation of this platform.

With these laws, the executive has at its disposal a wide range of means to diligently monitor natural persons. As for the PNIJ, it is born into multiple uncertainties in legal terms. Will the mutualization of judicial and administrative interceptions bear fruit? Operations will no longer be subject to a fee-for-service payment. The Court of Auditors[109] insists on the need to respect the "principles of independence of the judiciary, primacy of the judicial authority, secrecy of investigation and instruction, and protection of the secrecy of national defense". Yet will these principles prevail?

These laws supplement earlier laws that had already reduced the scope of the area reserved for the secrecy of correspondence. The most recent texts continue a movement towards a panoptic that seems to become a little more real every day.

---

108 Cour des Comptes, April 21, 2016: "In particular, we were unable to determine with certainty the reasons that led the Ministry of the Interior to refuse to install the platform in one of its secure computer sites, even though studies conducted previously had made recommendations to that effect."

113 Quoted in Marc Rees, "PNIJ quand la Cour des comptes étrille les choix du gouvernement", NextINpact, April 25, 2016.

3

Geolocation and Video Protection

Geolocation and video protection are types of monitoring technologies. Their importance is well recognized in the 21st century, but they began to appear in the 20th century. Since 1980, machines have been mobile and have participated in traceability. This is what seems evident in the "profiling of populations"[1] that highlights the outlines of post-Orwellian surveillance. The technical means of capturing sounds and images have given rise to countless legal studies.

3.1. International standards for both geolocation and video protection/ video surveillance

3.1.1. *Comparative legal issues in the era of geolocalization*

In many Western states, the use of electronic means, beacons, infrared devices, satellite images and GPS for geolocation purposes has been integrated into the legal corpus.

Geolocation procedures are subject to clear and precise legal provisions. In the United Kingdom, the use of geolocation devices depends on the administrative area. In France, geolocation is a matter for both the administrative[2] and judicial fields.

In other countries, geolocalization forms part of legal proceedings. Authorities competent to issue geolocation authorizations may be an administrative authority (the United Kingdom), the public prosecutor's office (the Netherlands) or a judge (Canada). The competent authorities are judicial in the Netherlands (public prosecutor's office), Canada (judge) and Germany. In the United Kingdom, only the

---

1 Mattelart, A., Vitalis, A. (2014). *Le profilage des populations*. La Découverte.
2 Article 20 of the Military Programming Law.

Home Secretary[3] has the power to issue intrusive surveillance warrants. A specialized court, the Investigatory Powers Tribunal, created by RIPA, has jurisdiction in cases brought against intrusive surveillance proceedings. France is influenced by British and German references.

The technical means used to capture voices, sounds and images have given rise to an important case law within the ECHR, the European Court of Human Rights of the Council of Europe. The latter is a legal entity that brings together some 40 states of the European continent, including Turkey and Russia. Natural persons can bring an individual application before the ECHR[4].

The first jurisprudence of the ECHR, for technical means, is applied to interception by electronic communications.

Jurisprudence subsequently is applied to "technical means" that seek to capture images and sounds. This concerned a judgment on a closed-circuit television system in 2003 and another judgment, also in 2003, relating to video surveillance. Here, too, the Council of Europe was reflecting on a possible violation of the right to privacy.

The jurisprudence of the ECHR is also interested in geolocalization, with the Uzun v. Germany[5] judgment.

The following facts should be noted in this regard: In the spring of 1993, the Ministry for the Protection of the Constitution of North Rhine-Westphalia set up long-term surveillance of Mr. Uzun, suspected of involvement in crimes committed by the anti-imperialist cell, heir to the "Rote Armee Fraktion", which participated in the ideological legend of the RFA in the 1970s. In October 1995, the Attorney General at the Federal Court of Justice launched an investigation into Uzun and an alleged accomplice, S. Surveillance was stepped up and the Federal Office of the Judicial Police installed two transmitters in S.'s car, which were used indiscriminately by Uzun and S. The latter took steps to evade investigation. For this reason, the Federal Office of the Criminal Investigation Department set up a geolocation system. Uzun and S. were arrested on February 25, 1996. On September 1, 1999, the Düsseldorf Court of Appeals sentenced Uzun to 13 years in prison for attempted murder and bombings. Uzun appealed to the Supreme Court of Appeals, complaining, among other things, that evidence obtained through allegedly illegal surveillance had been used in the trial.

---

3 Secretary of State.

4 When domestic remedies against a violation of the European Convention for the Protection of Human Rights and Fundamental Freedoms have been exhausted.

5 ECHR, Uzun v. Germany judgment, September 2, 2010.

The Federal Court of Justice dismissed the challenge to legality on the grounds that it lacked merit. According to the Federal Court, because of the serious offences that were suspected, the use of GPS constituted a proportionate interference with the exercise of the right to privacy – an interference which was therefore justified.

Uzun took his case to the Federal Constitutional Court, arguing that his surveillance from October 1995 to February 1996 violated his right to privacy. The case was dismissed.

Having exhausted domestic remedies, Uzun referred the matter to the ECHR. There was no question that by carrying out surveillance by means of geolocalization, the investigating authorities had collected, stored and recorded personal data which made it possible to identify individuals and which have been the subject of highly protective texts, both within the Council of Europe and within the European Union.

Questions of accessibility and predictability of the legal basis for interference arose. Uzun argued that the interference was not necessary in a democratic society because the applicable law did not sufficiently protect it from arbitrary intrusion by state authorities. According to the ECHR, it cannot be claimed that the applicant was subjected to full and complete surveillance.

In addition, the enquiry covered very serious offences. The ECHR found that the surveillance of Uzun by GPS was proportionate to the legitimate aims pursued and therefore "necessary in a democratic society". Geolocation, in this context, is not contrary to individual liberties and privacy.

This is the first in-depth reflection on the scope of geolocation. The context was not favorable for Uzun, who was considered a "terrorist". The answer would have been different in a context where a "democratic society" was not at stake.

And, in the years that followed, the context would not have been even less favorable, as Islamist terrorist attacks occurred in the United Kingdom, France, Spain, Tunisia and other countries. And let's not forget the intervention in Afghanistan, with the participation of the American, British and French armies, to stymie the Taliban's advance and maintain the government put in place by the Western Allies.

3.1.2. *Belgian legislation on geolocation*

The opinion of the Belgian Commission for the Protection of Privacy was a bill aimed at regulating the surveillance of employees by the use of the monitoring system associated with the GPS navigation system on service cars. This opinion was grounded on the bases laid down by the law of December 8, 1992 on the protection of privacy with respect to the processing of personal data[6], Directive 2002/58/EC of July 12, 2002 on the protection of privacy in the electronic communications sector (before GDPR) and the law of June 13, 2005 on electronic communications[7].

This text invites employers to follow specific provisions when using an employee geolocation system. It is not a law, but a reference in case a conflict arises between an employee and his employer. Failure to comply with the conditions mentioned in notice no. 12/2005 is not condemnable in itself but may be retained to the detriment of the employer in the event of a legal dispute.

3.1.2.1. *Notice no. 12/2005 of September 7, 2005*

Opinion no. 12/2005 considers four principles that are binding on the employer[8]:

– a ban on geolocating employees outside working hours: geolocating an employee outside of the company's recorded working hours constitutes an invasion of privacy. Any employee geolocation system used by a company must offer the possibility of being easily deactivated by the employee outside of working hours;

– confidentiality of the information collected: the recording of location data prohibits any person other than the user from processing the information collected or even from reading it without the user's consent to the authority in charge of collecting the data;

– respect for the purposes of the geolocation tool: the collection of employee location data may only exist for specific, explicit, legitimate purposes that justify its installation and use, and may not be subsequently processed in a manner incompatible with these purposes. In other words, the employer must be able to justify the purpose of setting up such a system and not deviate from this purpose during the actual use of the equipment. Disputes will be found in favor of the geolocalized employee if the information collected is used for another purpose;

– respect of the proportionality of the monitoring methods: the monitoring methods used to locate the employees of a commercial company must be proportional to the purpose of use defined when the system was installed.

Thus, in the case of a tracking system installed to monitor the performance of missions entrusted to employees, this monitoring can only be carried out on a

---

6 See Article 29.

7 Belgian Institute for Postal Services and Telecommunications, law of June 13, 2005 on electronic communications. Available at: www.ibpt.be/ShowDoc.Aspx.

8 "Mobile token, Géolocalisation du personnel et respect de la vie privée, en Belgique, que dit la loi?" 2012, pp. 2 and 3.

one-off basis and justified either by indications of suspected abuse on the part of certain employees, or by a context where the monitoring is carried out to protect the safety of employees. In general, permanent monitoring with systematic reading of the data recorded by the location system is considered disproportionate. If the geolocation system is used to improve employee travel[9], monitoring measures are justified provided that individuals are not monitored continuously.

3.1.2.2. *The law of December 8, 1992*

The law of December 8, 1992 on the protection of privacy with respect to the processing of personal data states that any computer system that collects data in Belgium must be declared to the Privacy Commission.

3.1.3. *Video surveillance/video protection*

3.1.3.1. *A question of effectiveness?*

Moving image cameras became widespread in Western countries, then in all developed countries in the 1990s. Cameras could be attached to a fixed or moving object. Nowadays, video cameras are mobile. Some software programs are able to count the number of vehicles passing a camera's field of vision, read license plates or even perform real-time facial recognition.

The first video surveillance system was initiated during World War II in Germany, with Siemens AG observing the launch of the V2 rockets in 1942. In Georges Orwell's *1984*, Big Brother is able to identify the actions of the population thanks to cameras installed throughout the city.

In the United Kingdom video surveillance experienced its first boom. Cameras were introduced in the early 1990s when Great Britain was faced with the IRA attacks. After the London truck bombings, the British government decided on an "all-camera surveillance" strategy. Subsequently, video surveillance became the main tool in the fight against crime and delinquency[10]. Every investigation now involves CCTV images.

In 2005, the British government concluded that this policy could not be evaluated. In 2008, Scotland Yard admitted that the policy was ineffective. At the 2008 Security Document World Conference in London, a representative of Scotland Yard spoke of an "utter fiasco".

---

9 Sellers, sales representatives, technicians.

10 There are approximately 6 million CCTV cameras in the UK.

In fact, video surveillance would not reduce delinquency but would see crime take place in unmonitored areas instead.

In the United States, which frequently uses video surveillance, the Department of Justice proposed its assessment in 2005. The conclusions of this report concur with those of Scotland Yard: video surveillance systems have little influence on crime rates.

In France, a report was commissioned in 2009 by the Ministry of the Interior and entrusted to three inspection bodies, including the police and gendarmerie, to "prove the effectiveness of surveillance cameras". Two sociologists, Eric Heilmann and Tanguy Le Goff, dispute the relevance of this report.

The debate is not definitively settled, but the question of the effectiveness/ineffectiveness of video surveillance in the fight against crime remains a topical issue.

3.1.3.2. *The Council of Europe and video surveillance/video protection*

3.1.3.2.1. ECHR: Antovic and Mirkovic v. Montenegro[11], the facts

Antovic and Mirkovic are two Montenegrin research fellows and professors at a university of mathematics.

To protect individuals and property, and monitor teaching, the dean of the faculty took the decision to install video surveillance cameras in the lecture halls. The members of the university were informed of the installation of this device. Ms. Antovic and Mr. Mirkovic complained and referred the matter to the Personal Data Protection Agency to oppose the installation of this kind of device, stating that there were other systems to monitor the protection of persons and property.

The Agency's board was of the opinion that there was no valid reason to implement video surveillance as there was no apparent danger to persons or property. Furthermore, the board held that the surveillance measure did not comply with the protection of personal data. The cameras were therefore removed. However, the teachers sought legal redress on the basis of Article 8 of the European Convention for the Protection of Human Rights and Fundamental Freedoms. They felt that their privacy had been invaded. The Montenegrin courts rejected this claim because they did not consider that privacy was an issue in this case and because the data collected on the cameras did not constitute personal data.

---

11 Antovic and Mirkovic v. Montenegro, November 2017.

Having exhausted domestic remedies, the Montenegrin nationals filed an individual application before the ECHR. The ECHR rejected the argument of the Montenegrin courts, pointing out that the concept of privacy can apply even if the place concerned is a workplace. In its previous case law, the ECHR had already stated that private life can include professional activities[12]. In fact, lecture halls constituted a workplace for these research fellows. The ECHR recalled that the function of university professors is not confined to teaching; they create a relationship with their students through exchanges and by interacting with them so "that university amphitheaters are the workplaces of teachers. It is where they not only teach students, but also interact with them, thus developing mutual relations and constructing their social identity". The judge recalled previous case law in which it was held that secret video surveillance at work constituted an intrusion into the private life of the person concerned.

She considered that this decision should be applied even if employees have been notified of the implementation of the system. The Court concluded that there had been an interference in the rights of the employees due to the video surveillance, as no reason had been provided capable of justifying such a monitoring system in an amphitheater. There had thus been a violation of Article 8 of the European Convention for the Protection of Human Rights and Fundamental Freedoms. It seems that this decision is justified in view of the protection of privacy: everyone must be able to have their privacy safeguarded, even in the workplace. For the Court, a simple precaution to protect people and property does not justify the implementation of an intrusive measure.

3.1.3.2.2. ECHR: Lopez Ribalda and others v. Spain

The case of Lopez Ribalda and others v. Spain is also illuminating[13].

The facts

The nationals were two Spanish saleswomen, who worked at the company canteen as cashiers. After finding irregularities in the stock and daily sales figures, the employer decided to set up a video surveillance system in the store. He warned the employees about the installation but did not indicate that while some cameras were visible, others were hidden. Instances of theft occurred again, and the applicants were summoned to interviews during which a video of the deeds they had committed was shown to them. Disciplinary dismissal followed, as the employees had committed a serious misdemeanor with the intention of harming their employer. After their dismissal, the saleswomen took their case to the labor court[14]. The decision

---

12 Ms. Halford v. United Kingdom, 1997.
13 Lopez Ribalda and Others v. Spain, ECHR, January 9, 2018.
14 See ILO Convention 158.

in the first instance confirmed the decision of the store manager. The appeal decision confirmed the decision of the first instance. According to these judges, the evidence obtained by the hidden cameras was legal evidence obtained in a legal manner. The employer's failure to inform employees of the hidden cameras was justified by the existence of the reasonable suspicions of theft. The courts considered that the existence of hidden cameras was the only way for the company and the company manager to protect the legitimate interests of the commercial company without harming the interests of the employees. This acknowledged breach was therefore fully justified.

The law

Having exhausted domestic remedies, the Spanish nationals filed an individual petition before the ECHR. The ECHR had to determine whether or not the mechanism implemented by the employer was lawful. The Court considered that there are provisions in Spanish domestic law concerning the matter of video surveillance. It indicated that the installation of the system constituted permanent surveillance since the employees were monitored for several weeks throughout the conduct of their professional service. This raised the issue of the proportionality of the measure adopted by the employer. In fact, a balance had to be found between the legitimate interests of the company and the protection of the employees' private life. According to the ECHR, the employer did not take into account the principle of proportionality. The court held that it would have been possible to protect the employer's rights without resorting to such intrusive methods. And the employees had not been kept informed of the extent of the measure implemented. Moreover, the Spanish law on the protection of personal data had not been honored.

The ECHR concluded that there was not a fair balance between the rights and interests at stake. This contravened the decisions taken by national courts as stated in Recital 70. This decision may seem harsh for the employer since the instances of theft against the commercial company employing the cashiers were proven, and if they were proven, it was thanks to the hidden camera system. But it seems vital to the ECHR to recall the importance of privacy at work. The Court wished to curb the temptation to place employees under video surveillance.

This decision may make the ECHR appear very attached to individual liberties. But it should be recalled that the ECHR has already admitted the legitimacy of the use of video surveillance.

3.1.3.2.3. The Köpke case

The Köpke case is very informative in this regard[15]. In this case, an employee was dismissed for theft after her employer discovered this fact, which was damaging for the company, using video surveillance and hidden cameras. The Köpke and Ribalda cases are very similar in nature. But the conclusions of the ECHR were different. In the Köpke case, the ECHR concluded that the test of proportionality between the defense of the legitimate interests of the company and the protection of the employee's private life had been carried out correctly and that no evidence could be held against the employer. It stressed that the video surveillance had spatial and temporal limits; therefore, the surveillance had not been continuous. This is why the ECHR considered that there was no violation of the employee's privacy. In this case, the most important thing is indeed the test of proportionality. Any measure that interferes with privacy must be justified by legitimate reasons that are perceived as important. A mere precautionary measure is not enough, as demonstrated by the Ribalda case law.

Video surveillance, at the level of the Council of Europe, which brings together all the countries of the European continent, with the exception of Belarus[16], is considered likely to infringe on the privacy of individuals. Vigilance should be exercised when the video surveillance system is implemented in a work environment.

In States that do not belong to the Council of Europe, the degree of requirement is far from being the same, and video surveillance is quite widespread in legal terms.

3.2. France

Video surveillance, also known as video protection in France since the LOPPSI 2 of March 14, 2011, has become the favored vehicle of social control. Video surveillance has played a prominent role in the United Kingdom for decades. In France, video surveillance, then video protection, became widespread in the 21st century.

3.2.1. *The legislative and regulatory framework*

In legal terms, video surveillance was first regulated by the law of January 6, 1978 and the law of January 21, 1995[17], and supplemented by the law of August 6, 2004, then replaced, after GDPR, by the law of May 2018[18].

---

15 Köpke v. Germany, ECHR, October 5, 2010.
16 Which, among other things, has not abolished the death penalty.
17 Law no. 95673.
18 Law 2018-493 of June 20, 2018.

The law of January 21, 1995 is related to security and was amended by the law of January 23, 2006; it gave rise to the implementing decree of October 17, 1996[19], amended by the decree of July 28, 2006. A circular from the Ministry of the Interior came into force on October 22, 1996. The scope of application was first limited to the security of goods and people, and subsequently to the fight against terrorism. Moreover, article 10.1 of the law of January 21, 1995 states: "Visual video surveillance recordings … that are used in automated processing or contained in files structured according to criteria that make it possible to identify, directly or indirectly, natural persons … are subject to the law 78-17 of 6 January 1978."

The natural persons concerned by these provisions can include, in particular, employees who are employed by companies that use video protection installations to ensure the security of persons and property and who are likely to be subject to surveillance.

Employees are required to be informed of the implementation of a video protection system in their workplace. They must also be informed of the quality of the recipients of the recorded images and the terms of access rights. The principle of loyalty inherent in social law, which excludes any means of proof that is collected without the employee's knowledge, naturally applies to the field of protection[20]. When the company reaches the workforce threshold that leads to the creation of a works council[21], the latter is "informed and consulted beforehand"[22]. In fact, the Cour de Cassation (French Court of Appeal) does not consider means that would not have been known to the employee: "The employer may not implement a control system that has not been brought to the employee's prior knowledge"; "the use of clandestine surveillance procedures … is exempt."

Supervision is of course conditioned by the principle of proportionality. As early as 1980, the Ministry of Labor made it known that if the purpose of video surveillance is to monitor professional activity, this objective would be considered an infringement of individual liberties by the courts, which subsequently complied with this point of view.

Currently, video protection is used in many companies: just like biometrics, it is an instrument of control. Moreover, just like the cell phone provided by a company, it is a human resource management tool. A balance must be struck between the

19 Decree no. 96-926.

20 Cour de Cassation, ch. soc., November 20, 1991, 88-43 120; Cour de Cassation, ch. soc., May 22, 1995, 93-44 078; Cour de Cassation, ch. soc., March 14, 2000, 98-42090.

21 Nowadays, this would be a Social and Economic Committee (CSE).

22 Article L432-2, paragraph one of the Labor Code.

power of management[23], which allows a certain degree of surveillance, and respect for freedoms.

In this context, it is necessary to determine how the obligation to provide information and the principle of proportionality are applied[24].

3.2.2. *The case law just before the LOPPSI 2 and the Jean-Marc Philippe establishments*

When the bill was being drafted, the CNIL – which has been empowered to impose sanctions since the amendment of August 6, 2004 – and the courts no longer hesitated to rule on video surveillance disputes involving employees.

3.2.2.1. *The facts*

The Jean-Marc Philippe company is a ready-to-wear limited company. On December 13, 2007, a complaint was filed with the CNIL: the plaintiff insisted in particular on the fact that the cameras were continuously filming the premises, open or not to the public, including the rooms reserved for staff. On February 11, 2008[25], the CNIL decided to carry out an on-site inspection. On February 15, 2008, a delegation of the CNIL went to the head office. After two hours of investigation, the delegation was forced to interrupt its mission: the Managing Director of the company, who was not aware of the audit, opposed the continuation of this operation. An order dated March 6, 2008, issued by the President of the Tribunal de Grande Instance de Paris, allowed the CNIL delegation to resume its monitoring, which was carried out without hindrance on this occasion.

The CNIL delegation noted that a video surveillance system was installed in the stores and at the head office. The images were recorded continuously on a digital medium. At the head office, 11 cameras filmed both places open to the public[26] and spaces allocated to staff where goods were not stored. Company managers, the CEO and the MD were able to connect to a remote server, via the Internet, by entering the IP address of the server, their account identifier and their password to view the images. The latter were also accessible from two supervision stations. The security

---

23 Waquet, P. (2000). Les libertés dans l'entreprise. *RJS*, 5, p. 335: "At least at the time and place of work, the employee no longer does what he wants, but he must accomplish the task assigned to him: his indiscipline or failure to do so may be sanctioned."

24 Casaux-Labrunée, L. (2008). "Now placed at the head of the Labor Code.... This principle confirms its vocation to be generally applicable in domestic law." *Droit social,* November 11, p. 1032.

25 Decision no. 2008-023 C.

26 Store, access door.

measures were not very effective: the supervision software was accessible without a password at the supervision station; moreover, two servers were free to access as long as the access door and session were not locked. The delegation noted that the video surveillance software was set up to keep the images for seven days.

Several conclusions emerged. There had been no prior declaration to the CNIL, nor were there any prefectural decrees authorizing the implementation of the video surveillance system. The persons concerned were not informed: there was a sign referring to the law of January 21, 1995 and the decree of October 17, 1996, but this sign was located behind the counter on the first floor of the store in a not very visible way. In the employment contracts concluded after the installation of the video surveillance system, the following sentence had been inserted: "The employee is informed that a video surveillance system is installed at all the company's sites." No information amendment was provided for the employment contracts concluded before the installation of the video surveillance system.

3.2.2.2. *The law*

3.2.2.2.1. The formal notice of May 29, 2008

In view of the aforementioned facts, the CNIL, in its decision of May 2008[27], issued a formal notice to the Company to take various measures within one month. The purpose was to proceed with the completion of prior formalities, to ensure that the purpose of video surveillance was to fight against theft, and not to place employees under constant surveillance; cameras, the presence of which was not justified by a legitimate purpose, were removed. It requested the company to communicate to the CNIL all the measures taken within the J.-M. Philippe company to enforce the right to information in terms of personal data, and to implement the guarantees required by the security and confidentiality of processing so that only authorized persons could access the supervision software and computer servers. The formal notice was served on August 1, 2008.

3.2.2.2.2. The company's response to the CNIL

Following the due diligence inspection by the CNIL on April 10, 2008, the company proceeded to declare the video surveillance system recorded on July 1, 2008[28].

In a letter dated August 29, 2008, the company informed the CNIL that it had informed its former staff of the presence of video surveillance cameras in writing.

---

27 Deliberation no. 2008-155 of May 29, 2008.
28 Received on July 16, 2008.

3.2.2.2.3. The CNIL's sanction report of March 12, 2009

The CNIL notified the company of a report proposing a sanction of at least 15,000 euros. It insisted on the fact that the company had not complied with the CNIL's formal notice of May 29, 2008, except for the prior formalities.

3.2.2.2.4. The decision of the CNIL's restricted committee of April 16, 2009

During the CNIL's restricted committee of April 16, 2009, the company produced written observations and presented oral observations on this report. Several in-depth analyses were carried out.

3.2.2.2.5. The lack of proportionality with regard to the video surveillance of employees

In its deliberation no. 2008-155 of May 29, 2008, the CNIL provided the company with formal notice to take the necessary measures to ensure that the implementation of the video surveillance system was strictly limited to the objective of fighting theft and did not result in placing employees under constant surveillance, which would involve removing cameras, the presence of which was not justified by a security imperative of the premises.

However, the company did not take any measures to limit video surveillance of employees. The company argued that the presence of all the cameras was arguably justified by the "handling of goods" and by "the free circulation of the general public and staff". This means that in theory only the administrative offices "where employees who occupy a permanent position and who are not in constant contact with the merchandise are installed" would not be exposed to video surveillance. The CNIL therefore emphasized the principle of proportionality. When a video surveillance device is able to target members of staff, the number, location, orientation, rate of operation of the cameras and the nature of the tasks carried out by the people concerned are to be taken into account upon installation of the system. According to the screenshots taken by the CNIL delegation on an inspection visit, contrary to the company's assertions, offices and workstations were filmed continuously, and employees were under the permanent surveillance by the employer. This surveillance "therefore appears excessive and the video surveillance system is not, therefore, strictly limited to the objective of fighting theft and leads to placing the persons concerned under surveillance that is disproportionate to the objective pursued". This led the CNIL to conclude that the company had not complied with the CNIL's formal notice and had not complied with the provisions of sections 1 and 2 of Article 6 of Law 78-17 of January 6, 1978 as amended.

3.2.2.2.6. The obligation to inform individuals

The data controller must inform the persons concerned by the processing, in particular of the purpose, their right of access, rectification and opposition. In its deliberation no. 2008-155 of May 29, 2008, the CNIL gave formal notice to the company to take all measures in this regard, as the information provided was considered unsatisfactory. Indeed, the purposes pursued, the recipients of the images and the precise terms and conditions for exercising the right of access available to the persons concerned were not indicated. The formal notice was not followed up on this point.

However, the formal notice was followed by action in terms of there being a breach of data security obligations: the company isolated the registration server in a room equipped with a locking system, access to which was reserved exclusively for authorized managers. The viewing of the images was only accessible to the company's legal representative after a password had been entered.

For these reasons, the CNIL set the amount of the financial penalty at 6,000 euros, that is, 5,000 euros less than the amount proposed by the initial report. Nevertheless, this was intended to serve as a warning, in particular, for the lack of proportionality when it comes to the continuous supervision of employees. This practice was unambiguously condemned.

3.2.2.2.7. The judgment of the tribunal de grande instance de Paris

The refusal of the company's CEO to allow the CNIL to carry out an on-site inspection led the independent administrative authority to refer the matter to the public prosecutor[29] for the crime of obstruction. The tribunal de grande instance de Paris upheld the offense of obstruction and handed down a sentence of 5,000 euros, 4,000 of which were suspended.

While drafting the LOPPSI 2, the CNIL was therefore prepared to protect employees against video surveillance that was disproportionate to the objective pursued. According to a press release[30] by the CNIL, "the deployment of a surveillance system, even if it meets a security requirement, should not lead to a generalized and permanent surveillance of the personnel, especially in places where there is no risk of theft".

However, the Cour de Cassation does not neglect to take into account legal analyses presented by companies[31]. This appears in particular in the decision of the

---

29 Article 40 of the Code of Criminal Procedure.

30 As of September 22, 2009.

31 Cour de Cassation, ch. soc. not published in the Bulletin, February 2, 2011, 10-14263.

Cour de Cassation of February 2, 2011, on the lawfulness of evidence by means of video surveillance. A barman, hired on August 1, 1995 by the company Amneville loisirs, was fired for serious misconduct. Video surveillance cameras existed, and recordings were used as evidence. The case was first judged by the industrial tribunal, formerly the Metz Court of Appeals[32]. A discussion therefore took place on the law of evidence. The purpose is the security of goods and persons; the question arose as to whether the purpose was different in this case, that is, the supervision of employees' work. By neglecting to carry out this research, the Court of Appeal arguably deprived its decision of a legal basis[33]. Moreover, insofar as the employee retains his/her right to privacy in the workplace, the employer must, if he/she supervises employees, use only means that are proportionate in relation to privacy and individual liberties. "By simply stating that the cameras did not infringe on the privacy of employees when it had itself noted that these cameras were operating permanently, thus suggesting that the infringement of privacy was not only established, but also, and above all, excessive." The Court of Appeal would have violated article 1121-1 of the Labor Code. This was not the reasoning followed by the Cour de Cassation. The latter argued that the entire staff of the brewery and of the casino bar were aware of the presence of video surveillance cameras in continuous operation; consequently, the disputed video recordings constituted a lawful means of proof.

This dichotomy between purpose and lawfulness of evidence in terms of video surveillance would not continue to create further case law. The issue of the possible reversal of purpose was not definitively settled. However, in February 2011, shortly before the constitutionality review of the LOPPSI 2, this confirmation ruling of the Cour de Cassation was favorable to companies wishing to be able to permanently monitor their employees without having to worry about the purpose. This corresponds to part of the French doctrine which considers that the respect of privacy should not be used against employers: "Should the employer really have to suffer all the consequences of the introduction of the employee's private life in the company, often at the sole initiative of the employee? Is it fair to accept that the employee may deliberately bring his private life into the company with the risks that this entails of confrontation with his professional life, and that in the event of a conflict, he may claim against the employer the right to respect for his private life that he himself has taken the risk of exposing? There is something 'wrong' in the reasoning, which judges could perhaps rectify by developing a jurisprudence similar to that which marks the boundary between private life and professional life in matters of commuting accidents: tolerate only those digressions made mandatory by the 'essential necessities of daily life'."[34] But another doctrinal standard insists on

---

32 Cour d'appel de Metz, chambre sociale, January 13, 2010.

33 With regard to Articles L 1224-1 of the French Labor Code.

34 Casaux-Labrunée, L. (2008). *Droit social*, 11, November, p. 1041.

the freedoms that are due to employees, especially when it comes to information technologies, and especially video surveillance.

And it is possible to note a certain ambivalence between the point of view expressed by the CNIL and that expressed by the Cour de Cassation.

3.2.3. *The entry into force of the LOPPSI 2*

This text marks a turning point in video surveillance law, known as video protection. The change of term corresponded to a broadening of the missions. Video protection devices could now be installed to combat drug trafficking and illicit commercial transactions.

During the debate on LOPPSI 2, a number of parliamentarians called for the CNIL to be involved in the decision-making process in order to preserve individual freedoms. From that point onwards, the CNIL has been able to exercise control to ensure that the video protection system is used in accordance with the law of January 6, 1978 amended by the law of August 6, 2004. When the CNIL finds a breach of these provisions, it is entitled to give formal notice to the person in charge of a system to stop it. If the person responsible does not comply with the formal notice, the CNIL may issue a public warning. When these measures do not succeed in putting an end to the observed breach, the CNIL may impose sanctions and request the State representative remove the video protection device.

3.2.4. *Jurisprudence after LOPPSI 2*

3.2.4.1. *Océatech Equipement*

The case law following the entry into force of the LOPPSI 2 is illustrated in particular by the "Océatech Equipement" case. It should be noted that LOPPSI 2 came into force on March 14, 2011.

3.2.4.1.1. The facts

Océatech Equipement specializes in the supply of equipment to healthcare professionals, has a staff force comprising fewer than 11 employees and is based in Toulouse.

On July 27, 2011, the CNIL received a complaint from an employee who drew the attention of the supervisory authority to the installation of a video surveillance system that was to be located on the company's premises, which would allow the employer to monitor employees and listen to their conversations.

Pursuant to Decision No. 2011-268C of October 7, 2011 of the President of the CNIL, a delegation of the CNIL carried out an audit on October 12, 2011 at the company's headquarters. Seven cameras filmed places restricted to the public, and one camera filmed places open to the public: this camera, which was located in the manager's office, had in its field of vision a private road that served the company and other companies, a road whose access was subject to free movement[35] during the day.

The manager accessed real-time image viewing and recordings via a terminal server connection. The real-time images, unlike the recordings, were sounded. Recordings could be manually triggered at any time. In addition, recordings were programmed to be triggered by motion detection during off-peak hours[36] for a duration of 45 seconds.

The video surveillance system was declared to the CNIL on September 13, 2011[37], with the aim of ensuring the "security of goods and people". Moreover, in two letters sent to employees on July 5, 2011, following a reminder of the grievances that had arisen between the two people, a different purpose appeared: "In order to determine the responsibilities of each person, an audio and video recording system will be set up forthwith." In the statement of September 13, 2011, the duration indicated is one month. The delegation of the CNIL noted, during the on-site inspection carried out on October 12, 2011, the presence of 4,076 video files, but automated purges of recordings were not provided for.

The company did not request, as it should have done, prefectural authorization before installing the cameras.

The information panels relating to the video protection installation, visible during the inspection, were located on the entrance door outside the premises and in the technicians' workshop; they did not mention the rights to reject, access and rectify the data collected[38].

3.2.4.1.2. The law

Analysis and qualification of the facts

Failure to define a specific purpose

There are two incompatible purposes: "the security of persons and property" and "the determination of the responsibilities of each person", which is an effective

---

35 Access was closed to the public by electric gate only at night.

36 Monday to Friday between 7:00 p.m. and 8:00 a.m., Saturday and Sunday all day long.

37 File No. 1531538.

38 These mentions were required by article 32 of the law of January 6, 1978.

purpose. This effective purpose corresponds to the number and orientation of the cameras and the possibility of listening to the sound, which were noted during the inspection; in particular, the cameras located above the employees' spheres of work were able to view, at all times, the screens of the employees' computers and the employees themselves; it was also possible to listen to the sound.

This dichotomy between official purpose and declared effective purpose is contrary to paragraph 2 of Article 6 of Law 78-17 of January 6, 1978, according to which data shall not be subject to further processing in a manner incompatible with the purposes for which it was declared.

A misuse of purpose

According to article 226-21 of the Penal Code: "The fact, by any person holding personal data during their recording, filing, transmission or any other form of processing, of diverting this information from its purpose, as defined by the legislative provision, the regulatory act or the decision of the CNIL authorizing the automated processing, or declarations prior to the implementation of this treatment, is punishable by 5 years' imprisonment and a fine of 30,000 euros." The misappropriation of purpose is frequent but can be severely punished.

Constant monitoring of employees: a lack of proportion

The video protection installation placed the employees under the constant and permanent surveillance of the employer. Following and prior to the LOPPSI 2, this constitutes a breach of paragraph 3 of article 6 of the law of January 6, 1978, which stipulates that the personal data collected must be adequate, relevant and not excessive in relation to the purposes.

In addition, labor law was also pronounced. According to article 1121-1 of the Labor Code: "No one may place restrictions on the rights of individuals and individual and collective freedoms that are not justified by the nature of the task to be performed or proportionate to the purpose sought."

Closely supervised employee monitoring

A failure to define the length of time data is kept

The declaration mentions a duration of one month, but there is no self-purging of the recordings. The situation does not comply with the law: it constitutes a violation of paragraph 5 of article 6 of the law of January 6, 1978 according to which personal data is kept in a form that allows the identification of the persons concerned for a period that does not exceed the period necessary for the purposes for which it is collected and processed.

The breaches constituted violations of Article 226-20 of the Penal Code, which punishes the retention of personal data beyond the period provided for by law or regulation with five years' imprisonment and a fine of 300,000 euros, with exceptions for historical, statistical and scientific research.

A failure to disclose information

The information signs and the employment contracts consulted by the members of the CNIL delegation during the inspection and the internal regulations did not provide sufficient information for:

– customers: they were not informed about the identity of the data controller, about the purpose of the processing for which the data is intended, nor about the right to object, access or rectify the data, as previously mentioned[39]; or

– employees: they were not informed, either in their employment contract or in the internal regulations on the right to object, access or rectify the data, as previously mentioned.

In this matter, there is a breach of the law of January 6, 1978, and a breach of the Penal Code.

Article 32 of the law of January 6, 1978, which was not respected by the company Océatech Equipement, obliges the data controller to provide the persons from whom personal data is collected with information on the data controller, the purpose, the recipients, the rights of access, rectification and, possibly, opposition.

According to article R625-10, paragraph 1, of the Penal Code, "a person responsible for the automated processing of personal data is punishable by a fine for a level 5 offence in the following cases: 1) failure to inform the person from whom personal data is collected: a) of the identity of the person responsible for the processing and, if necessary, of that of his representative; b) of the purpose pursued by the processing for which the data are intended; e) of the recipients or categories of recipients of the data; and f) of their right to object, query, access or rectify (the data collected)."

Qualification under the law of January 21, 1995

The company did not request prefectural authorization before installing the video protection; it had therefore violated the obligations of III of article 10 of the law of January 21, 1995 according to which the installation of a video protection system is subject to a prefectural authorization, following the opinion of a departmental

---

39 See articles 38–40 of the law of January 6, 1978 as amended by the law of August 6, 2004.

commission[40]; the prefectural authorization mentions the useful precautions; it is also likely to violate VI of article 10 of the law of January 21, 1995: this paragraph relates to offences which occur when a video protection system is installed or maintained without authorization, when video protection recordings are made without authorization and when images are used for purposes other than those for which they were intended. This lack of authorization is punishable by three years of imprisonment and a fine of 45,000 euros.

The formal notice issued against Océatech Equipement

The CNIL gave the company Océatech Equipement notice, within six weeks from the notification of the decision, to ensure that the installation implemented was exclusively limited to the official purpose of the processing – the security of goods and persons – and was not dedicated to any other purpose. The company was also to ensure that the employees were no longer subject to constant and permanent monitoring, in accordance with the principles of adequacy, relevance and proportionality of data. The formal notice required an automated purge of the recordings to be set up, in line with the one-month duration that appears in the declaration of September 13, 2011. It required compliance with respect to the purpose pursued by the processing, to the right to object, access and rectify, with modification of the information signs visible by customers, visitors, employees, with necessary changes to the employment contracts and the internal regulations. In addition, the CNIL gave formal notice, on the basis of the law of January 21, 1995, to Océatech Equipement to apply for prefectural authorization in order to comply with the regulations concerning outward-facing cameras.

At the end of the six-week period, if the company had not complied with the formal notice, the CNIL was to appoint a rapporteur who would have the powers to ask the restricted committee to pronounce a sanction[41] and would ask the State representative in the department to order the suspension or removal of the video protection system. The CNIL decided to make this formal notice public because of "the nature and seriousness of the breaches committed".

Océatech Equipement took this formal notice into account. It modified the device and, in particular, removed certain cameras in order to meet the purpose officially declared to the CNIL: the protection of property and persons. It defined a period for which the images could be stored in accordance with the law and provided individual information to employees. As the configuration of the premises did not allow employees to be filmed at their workstations, the company undertook to stop recording images and sounds from the cameras during employees' working

---

40 Presided over by a magistrate of the bench or an honorary magistrate.
41 See article 45 of the law of January 6, 1978.

hours. The CNIL also noted that these actions were carried out swiftly[42]. The compliance was noted, and the CNIL decided not to follow up the matter and proclaimed the formal notice against the company Océatech Equipement closed.

Case law confirms the CNIL's desire to prevent the constant surveillance of the persons concerned. And this has been taken into account by the Cour de Cassation.

The LOPPSI 2, through its video protection component, has become common practice. The CNIL pronounces more and more controls and sanctions.

3.2.4.2. *Arcades des Champs-Élysées*

In 2013, it is worth mentioning the deliberation on January 3, 2013 of the home owners' association Arcades des Champs-Élysées.

3.2.4.2.1. The facts

Arcades des Champs-Élysées was managing a mixed-use residential and commercial building on the Champs-Élysées. On February 23, 2012, the CNIL heard of a complaint from several security guards whose task was to monitor the building of the association. These security guards were employees of the company Byblos, an agency specializing in security operations, and were working under a service contract that had been concluded with the association. This complaint involved the installation of a video protection device located in the premises of the building's security post, which could infringe on the privacy of the people working in the premises by carrying out permanent surveillance of the people employed in security. The association indicated that the video protection installation was intended for the security of persons and property and had reportedly been put in place in 2010 following complaints from the residents of the building who had noticed the absenteeism of the surveillance officers. This installation was carried out on the suggestion of the service provider with the agreement of the association.

The device consisted of a single camera positioned to effectively visualize the agents' workstation; it was teamed with a recorder that saved images for a guaranteed period of 30 days. The images were accessible to the management of the surveillance company, the association and the surveillance team leader. In addition, the building as a whole was equipped with a video surveillance system consisting of 57 cameras, the monitors of which were located at the security post.

---

42 "Dans des délais exemplaires", CNIL, June 11, 2012, decision to close the formal notice against the company Océatech Equipement.

3.2.4.2.2. The law

Formal notice

On July 19, 2012[43], the CNIL gave notice to the association to remove the camera filming the security post. This formal notice was not followed by action: the association made known that in its view, the device did not infringe on the privacy of employees and that it was necessary and proportionate to the protection of persons and property.

One month later, the president of the CNIL[44] asked the Secretary General to carry out an inspection of the association. During this inspection[45], which notably made it possible to determine that the disputed video protection system was still in place, the conclusions were obvious: on October 1, 2012, a rapporteur was designated[46].

At the end of the investigation, the rapporteur considered that there had been a breach of several obligations of the law of January 6, 1978 and had the association notified in person, delivering a written report listing the breaches of the law that had appeared to have occurred. The report proposed that the restricted committee pronounce a pecuniary sanction against the association. The date of the session of the restricted committee was fixed for November 8, 2012 and the association received a summons: it was specified that it had one month to make known its written observations. The association forwarded its written observations by mail, which were received on October 31, 2012, and its oral observations were made at the restricted committee session on November 8, 2012.

At the end of the procedure, the restricted panel adopted a decision that took into account the points of law discussed.

The quality of the data controller

Pursuant to the law of January 6, 1978 amended by the law of August 6, 2004, "the person responsible for processing personal data is, unless expressly designated by the legislative or regulatory provisions relating to such processing, the person, public authority, service or body that determines its purposes and means." With regard to the processing of the Arcades des Champs-Elysées housing association, the quality of the person in charge was established by drawing on several elements. First of all, the video protection system was installed at the security post of the Arcades des

---

43 Deliberation of the restricted committee of the CNIL no. 2012-475 of January 3, 2013.

44 Isabelle Falque-Pierrotin.

45 As of September 4, 2012.

46 Emmanuel de Givry, statutory auditor and deputy vice-president, on the basis of the law of January 6, 1978 as amended by the law of August 6, 2004.

Champs-Élysées building and was occupied by employees of Byblos, a security service provider and subcontractor of the building's co-owner-management association. In addition, the costs incurred by the installation of the video protection system were borne by the association, which had agreed to having the system installed. As well, despite a change in the service provider, the camera was not removed, and the new service provider did not have physical control of the system. Finally, the association indicated to the CNIL that it was solely in charge of security; it had carried out the procedure for declaring the processing to the CNIL and had informed the persons concerned by posting a notice. It is therefore the system that must be considered the association's data controller.

Proportionality and surveillance of security employees through video protection

According to decision 2012-023 of July 19, 2012, in its formal notice, the president of the CNIL considered that the video protection installation in question should, under the terms of article L1121-1 of the Labor Code[47], be perceived as disproportionate since the processing placed the security guards present in the building's security post under permanent surveillance.

The question of proportionality arose again before the restricted committee. The finding established that the premises were equipped with a video protection camera oriented in such a way that it could film the employees present in the premises when they were at their posts. The camera filmed continuously on weekends and during the week between 6 p.m. and 8 a.m., but the camera only filmed the rest of the time when motion was detected. The finding also established that the images captured by the camera were recorded. Access to the recordings from the security station was determined by a password. The recipients of the data were the management of the security company, the home owners' association, and the security team leader.

According to the declaration of the processing to the CNIL established by the association on August 30, 2012[48], the declared purpose was the security of people and property. According to the association's lawyer, the security of people and property justified the permanent surveillance of the employees of the security post. Indeed, this continuous monitoring supplemented the performance of monitoring tasks by the agents and in particular combatted absenteeism which was likely to affect the security of persons and property.

---

47 "No one may place restrictions on the rights of individuals and individual and collective freedoms that are not justified by the nature of the task to be performed or proportionate to the end sought."

48 The number assigned to the processing declaration is 1612174.

The association went further: it even went so far as to question the existence of a right to privacy in the workplace, recognized since the Halford decision within the countries of the Council of Europe. This was based on two facts: the employees complained rather late about the presence of the disputed camera; moreover, the contract with the first service provider had been terminated. As a result, the causes of the complaint were not to be found in the invasion of employees' privacy, but in an internal conflict within the employing company. From then on, new security guards were in place and accepted the presence of the camera. This acceptance, this consent, provided a basis of legality and legitimacy to the presence of the cameras and their recordings.

This reasoning was not supported by the restricted committee of the CNIL. The association's written and oral observations showed that the purpose of the disputed treatment was to ensure the security not of the agents filmed continuously during their presence in the room made available to them, but of the building's occupants. The objective of security did not give rise to criticism but could in no way justify putting employees whose mission was to ensure security under constant surveillance, unless the necessity could be demonstrated. However, the reasons justifying such surveillance could only be based on the specific situation or the precise risk[49] to which the persons under surveillance were exposed and not in order to ensure the security of third parties or their property: the security of the building's occupants was ensured by the network of cameras located in the body of the building and not in the premises assigned to the security guards.

Moreover, the decision of January 3, 2013 states: "It is of little importance that the employees have not previously complained about the installation of the camera and that the new security agents accept the principle as long as the continuous nature of the surveillance resulting from the disputed processing is not justified by a need for the security of persons and property but results from the desire to control the activity of the employees." Acceptance by the employees therefore plays no role in the legal or illegal nature of the use of a video protection device. The concept of acceptance was highlighted by the association. The former security guards of the subcontracting service provider did not accept the video protection system: they had demonstrated this by filing a complaint. The new security guards from the association's provider accepted the installation; the association had checked with its subcontractor to make sure that the employees agreed. No doubt, it relied on the notion, implicit or explicit, of a psychological contract[50]. Yet, the agreement of will on the part of the employees was not taken into account by the data controller. The only point that was taken into account was the adequate and necessary security: the security of goods and persons. In this case, and in this context, the objective of

---

49 See the monitoring theory in human resources management.

50 Management of organizations.

security of goods and persons did not apply and the constant surveillance of employees via video protection had no legal basis.

The constant surveillance of employees via video protection is therefore closely circumscribed. It is an exception to the rule. Only the security of goods and persons, duly proven, justifies the intrusive surveillance that a video protection device constitutes for employees. The notion of proportionality is examined with great care. In this case, the housing association Arcades des Champs-Élysées failed to comply with the obligation imposed by the law of January 6, 1978 as amended.

The leniency of the sanction

The sanction as symbolic

The restricted committee limited the amount of the sanction to one euro. The sanction had no bearing on the state of the trustee's finances and budget. The symbolic nature of the sanction is explained by "the nature of the tasks to be accomplished and the will to ensure, by means of the processing, enhanced protection of goods and persons". Does this deliberately symbolic character of the sanction contradict the reasoning on the exceptional character of the constant surveillance of employees by video protection? The decision may give this impression, since it insists on the security of goods and persons, which is presented as a priority. And it is impossible not to notice this deliberate attenuation of the sanction. The security of people and property is an undisputed goal for those who support video protection, and the decision to restrict training highlights this. There is obviously some semblance of ambiguity.

The sanction as public

The restricted panel decided to make the sanctions public. Publicity allows commercial companies to realize that the risk factor is not high since it is limited to one euro. However, the legal reasoning is severe since this jurisprudence indicates that the acceptance by employees of video protection devices in no way justifies the constant surveillance of employees, except if the sole purpose is "the security of persons and property". According to the restricted committee, publication was motivated by the nature of "the evidence presented"[51], which is serious in nature.

The comments concerning the decision insist both on the sanction of one euro and on the useless character, from a legal point of view, of the acceptance by the employees of the video protection. The title of Cynthia Chassigneux's article[52] is "Pecuniary sanction against the surveillance of employees": it shows the legality of

---

51 Decision No. 2012-475 of January 3, 2013 of the CNIL "on the breaches observed and the publication of the decision".

52 Chassigc.blogspot.fr.

systems that have given rise to a pecuniary sanction. It is only by reading the article that the reader learns that the penalty is a symbolic one euro. And Chassigneux quotes one paragraph which mentions the following: "It is of little importance ... that new security agents accept the principle as long as the continuous nature of the surveillance resulting from the litigious treatment is not justified by an imperative of security of persons and goods but results from the will to control the activity of the employees."[53] The CNIL press release was also explicit: "The CNIL sanctions the constant surveillance of employees."

Generally speaking, observers emphasize the sanction relating to video protection with regard to employees, when this is not justified by the objective of the security of people and property. This is in line with the consultative practical sheet on the CNIL website "Video surveillance and video protection at the workplace" with five subtitles: "the purpose", "precautions to take while installing the device", "what to do when working with video surveillance", "who can view the images?" and "for how long should the images be kept?" "The purpose" reminds us that the only purposes that can justify the installation of video protection in a workplace are the security of goods and people, and the identification of the perpetrators of theft, damage or aggression. "Precautions to take while installing the device" indicates that cameras must not film employees at their workstations, except in special circumstances[54], and mentions that, in the workplace as elsewhere, employees have the right to privacy. "Who can view the images?" emphasizes that only authorized persons within the scope of their duties[55] are liable to view the images. "For how long should the images be kept?" cites the one-month period and specifies the following: "The maximum duration for storing the images should not be fixed solely according to technical capacity of storage of the recorder."

3.2.4.3. *Judgment of January 10, 2012 Mr. X. v. société technique française*

Since the LOPPSI 2, the Social Chamber of the Cour de Cassation has not had to rule on the legitimacy of video protection, but it has had to rule on the principle of loyalty and employee information. The case in question is the judgment of January 10, 2012, M. X. v. société technique française[56].

3.2.4.3.1. The facts

Mr. X. and other employees of the French technical cleaning company, TFN (*technique française du nettoyage*), were assigned to a client company, Guillet. They

---

53 CNIL, January 23, 2013.

54 In relation to safety requirement.

55 Selected illustration: the organization's security manager.

56 Cour de Cassation, chambre sociale, January 10, 2012, M.X. v. société technique française, 10-23.482.

applied to the labor court to obtain payment of, among other things, the time they spent getting changed. On September 3, 2008, their employer applied for and obtained an order appointing a bailiff to view the recordings of video surveillance cameras located at the entrance to the Guillet company for the period from April to August 2008: the purpose was to draw up a record of the arrival and departure times of the employees in order to make a comparison with the activity records drawn up by the team leader. The minutes drawn up on September 18, 2008 were produced by the employer as part of the industrial tribunal proceedings. The employees and the Maine-et-Loire CFDT services trade union requested in summary proceedings that the order be withdrawn on application and that the deeds be declared null and void.

3.2.4.3.2. The law

In order to deny the employees and the trade union their demands, the Court of Appeals' decision held that the purpose of the reinforcement of video surveillance by the Guillet company was not to monitor employees or the work of the service providers, but merely to monitor the access doors of the premises to strengthen security; the employer informed employees of the existence of this system on May 20, 2008; it thus fulfilled its obligation of loyalty by providing information which it was not obliged to provide[57], since the procedure had been set up by the company's client; in this context, the recordings arguably constituted a lawful means of proof.

The Cour de Cassation pointed out that while the employer had the right to monitor the activity of its employees during working hours, it was not entitled to authorize as a means of proof the use of the recordings of a video surveillance system placed on the site of a client company allowing the control of employees who had not been previously informed of the existence of the device. This obligation to provide information is mandatory. The letter of May 20, 2008 did not explain to the employees concerned that they were being filmed so that their arrival and departure times could be monitored. For these reasons, the employment division (chambre sociale) overturned the decision of the Court of Appeal.

Furthermore, the employment division reasoned on the law concerning the confirmation of the summary proceedings order issued by the Saumur district court, which rejected the request of Mr. X. and the eight other persons for the withdrawal of the order on a motion issued on September 3, 2008 by the president of this court and the annulment of subsequent acts. According to the Court of Appeal, it was no later than April 28, 2006 that Guillet's works council was notified of the installation of cameras "at each entrance". These cameras were installed at each staff entrance to the company solely to monitor intrusions and were not intended to monitor lateness. In addition, on May 20, 2008, the French technical cleaning company notified all of its employees working on the "Guillet site" by hand-delivered mail of the

57 Article L122-4 of the Labor Code.

installation of the video surveillance system thus installed. There was no need to ask the Court of Justice of the European Union for a preliminary ruling, which would not be relevant, according to the Court of Appeals.

According to the provisions of the French Labor Code[58], video recordings are strictly prohibited when they are made without the employees' knowledge, without the works council having been informed of the implementation of such a system. The Cour de Cassation[59] stipulated that the employer was not required to disclose the existence of procedures installed by customers of the company in which its employees worked[60], in particular when, as in the case of TFN and Guillet, the purpose of the cameras installed by Guillet was to control the access doors to its premises in order to enhance security after repeated thefts. Mr. X. and the other plaintiffs reported a connivance between the two companies, but this connivance, with the alleged objective of monitoring employees, was not obvious since Guillet did not have the power of subordination over the employees of TFN and would not have invested in monitoring the employees of its service provider. The Court of Appeal also argued that in May 2008, TFN employees were warned of plans to strengthen the client company's[61] video surveillance system. The increased vigilance of the Guillet company, marked by the installation of new cameras, was not intended to monitor TFN employees, but exclusively to control the access doors to the premises. Consequently, for the Court of Appeal, the video recordings constituted a lawful means of proof, since in labor law, a lawful means of proof is a means of proof that is not obtained without the employees' knowledge[62].

This reasoning did not convince the Cour de Cassation: on the basis of the principle of loyalty and Article L1222-4 of the Labor Code, the employer is not entitled to use a video surveillance system that would allow the monitoring and control of employees' activities without their prior notification. However, the Cour de Cassation indicated that "such a principle is applicable regardless of the workplace and the person in charge of the video surveillance", regardless of the notion of service provider or client company. The Cour de Cassation took the legal counterpart of the Court of Appeal: "by holding that a video recording made by a device installed by the client company constitutes a lawful mode of proof, since it was

---

58 Articles L122-4 and L2323-32.

59 Chambre sociale, April 19, 2005.

65 As of 2020, there will no longer be a works council, but ESCs (social and economic committees).

61 "TFN fulfilled its obligation of loyalty to its employees by providing this prior information, to which it was not bound", cited in Cour de Cassation, chambre sociale, January 10, 2012, M.X. v. société technique française.

62 Application of the provisions of articles 11 paragraph 2, 145 and 249 of the Code of Civil Procedure.

not intended to monitor the work of the employees of the company providing the service, but only to monitor the access doors to its premises, whereas the monitoring of access doors makes it possible to control the time of entry and exit of work and, consequently, the activity of employees." The Court of Appeal violated the principle of loyalty.

Finally, the Court of Appeal seemed to have forgotten the concept of good faith. Indeed, the letter sent to all employees, detailing the new supervision system installed by the company, would have, on the basis of a simple deduction, informed all the employees of the company providing the service that video surveillance had increased. This was not in line with reality. The letter mentioned by the Court of Appeal only relates to the establishment of a system of supervision regarding opening of emergency doors. The sole purpose of this letter was to order employees to "imperatively enter and exit through the main entrance". The Court of Appeal "distorted the mail" and violated the Civil Code[63]. There was no employee information, and the registration system had no legal basis.

Although the LOPPSI 2, the CNIL and the Cour de Cassation seem to be relatively concordant with regard to employees, whether in terms of information or proportionality, the CNIL is the main vector.

In many situations, employees "accept" more or less by adherence to a management system or more often by habit the intrusion of information technologies that have built an ideology of tacit proactivity to a diversified corpus of controls: the video protection devices. However, the process is not general and widespread. Some employees feel that the permanent, constant presence of cameras is an unbearable invasion of their privacy and have taken their case to the courts or the CNIL. Faced with this dichotomy, the doctrine remains divided. Human rights advocates want the use of cameras to monitor employees to be non-existent or very limited and justified by legal purposes. Other doctrines, more sensitive to economic freedoms, company and employer rights, consider that this antagonism must be overcome. They are following in the footsteps of Charles Hannoun[64]. Financing associates the liquidity of the firm with the liquidity of labor. "It reduces the firm to a numerical representation detached from concrete realities, whether it is a question of the production tool that is infinitely transferable … or of employees treated as a freely adjustable use value, independently of the constraints of its management and the other dimensions of the work community." Can we achieve a balance that satisfies human rights advocates, human resource management advocates and, why not, management controllers? The question remains up for debate.

---

63 Article 1114.

64 Hannoun, C. (2008). L'impact de la financiarisation de l'économie sur le droit du travail. *RDT*, 288.

3.2.5. *Video protection and terrorism*

Video protection has been frequently used to combat terrorism, notably in France in 2015. In 2016, after the arrest of Salah Abdeslam, the only surviving terrorist from the Bataclan attacks, indicted in Belgium, and currently imprisoned in France, the then Minister of Justice, Jean-Jacques Urvoas, initiated an order "on the creation of personal data processing relating to the video protection of detention cells". This text stipulated that monitoring should be applied to prison cells via video protection. Jean-Jacques Urvoas decided to place Salah Abdeslam under video surveillance 24 hours a day. Abdeslam's lawyer challenged this decision because, in his view, it was a "serious breach of the right to privacy" and an infringement of individual liberty. In July 2016[65], the Versailles TA and the Council of State rejected the appeal.

Nevertheless, in order to strengthen the legal basis for supervision, a law[66] took up the content of the decree. In March 2017, the Administrative Court of Versailles condemned the State for the period preceding the adoption of the text. The Administrative Court of Versailles ordered the State to pay 500 euros to Abdeslam for illegal surveillance.

Yet, video protection has become widespread, including in cases of terrorism, and video protection allows increased surveillance of citizens in most countries.

---

65 Order of July 15, 2016, Administrative Court of Versailles.
66 Law of July 21, 2016.

4

Biometrics or "the Second Circle"[1]

At the end of 2019, the Chinese government announced that to access the Internet or a cell phone number, facial recognition and scanning should be used (facial recognition is a very advanced technology in China). China and India use facial recognition to control and regulate. Facial recognition has evolved a lot internationally in the last decade. This is also the case for most other biometric processes. The rate of "false rejection, false acceptance" is gradually decreasing. The first biometric or anthropological fingerprints date back to the 19th century, along with digital fingerprints, which still play an essential role in travel documents today. But the concern for security and, to a lesser degree, the objective of good management have led to the increasingly frequent use, with an ever-wider spectrum, of biometric processes.

> If Marx were to return today, what phenomenon would he retain to characterize our society? It would no longer be capital and capitalism, but the development of technology, the phenomenon of technical growth[2].

Biometrics is an integral part of these technical developments. According to *Le Petit Robert*, biometrics is "the science that studies, with the aid of mathematics (statistics, probabilities), the biological variations within a given group". To the question "What is biometrics?" Actronix gave a pragmatic answer. He started from the observation that there are three ways to identify a person: possessions (card, badge, document), knowledge (password) and biometrics. This observation led to the following definition: "Biometrics allows the identification of a person on the basis of physiological or behavioral traits that are automatically recognizable and verifiable." Biometric technology has undergone spectacular expansion, first in

---

1 See Solzhenitsyn.

2 Ellul, J. (1982). Entretien avec Jean-Claude Gillebaud. *Le Nouvel Observateur*, July 17.

Western countries and then in the major Asian nation-states, notably China and Japan. Since the beginning of the 21st century, many researchers have been working on biometric techniques, with the aid of software, with significant returns on investment for the companies or states that funded them.

The industry classifies biometric systems into two categories: morphological or physiological biometrics and behavioral biometrics. Morphological biometrics identifies specific physical traits that are unique and permanent for each individual; it distinguishes between fingerprint recognition, hand shape, face shape, retina and iris of the eye, subsequently adding the contour of the ear lobe and lips, etc.

Behavioral biometrics identifies certain behaviors of a physical person such as the trace of his/her signature, his/her voice and speech[3], his/her gait and his/her way of typing on a keyboard.

The regulatory authorities in matters of personal data, since biometric fingerprints are personal data, such as the CAI[4] in Quebec and the CNIL in France, take up these distinctions. They have subsequently added the analysis of DNA, blood and odors – and the list is constantly growing.

4.1. Biometrics and international law

There is no specialized body comparable to the CAI in the field of tele-communications. Nevertheless, many parameters are transnational and are recognized as such.

The control of migratory flows is a concern for all states, especially since the terrorist threat has been introduced into the legal corpus of nation-states.

4.1.1. *The United States: a historical outline*

4.1.1.1. *The FAST device*

As early as 1993, US immigration authorities implemented a system called FAST at an airport in New York[5]. This system allowed the identification of

---

3 But voice recognition has progressed so far that the zek hero-scientist of Solzhenitsyn's *The Second Circle* would not recognize the fledgling science he was trying to examine.

4 *Commission d'accès à l'information.*

5 Future Automated Screening for Travelers.

passengers, following on from the INSPASS[6] project. The objective was to improve passenger processing. Volunteer travelers gave their identity and showed their palm at check-in. If it was not possible to use palm recognition, fingerprints were used. The vast majority of travelers in this program were American and Canadian.

4.1.1.2. *United States and migration flows*

The Immigration and Nationality Act applies the Alien Registration Act 1940[7] procedure to foreigners over the age of 14 who have been in the United States for more than 30 days. This has employed facial recognition.

4.1.1.2.1. Travel documents

The American continent and especially the United States have opted for security regulation via visas and passports.

4.1.1.3. *Visas*

Visas place limitations on the freedom of movement and settlement. They limit the length of stay. Some visas are tourist and business visas (allowing a stay of six months), student visas which allow foreigners to study in the United States, and work visas which are the only way to work legally in the United States. Fingerprint templates are mandatory for all visa applicants. According to section 414 of the Patriot Act, biometric identification mechanisms were implemented not only at airports, but also at all US ports of entry. Exemptions exist. For example, foreign nationals who are citizens of countries allied with the United States fall into the visa exemption category. The Visa Waiver Pilot Program allows allied nationals to apply for entry into the United States for a tourist or business visit of less than 90 days. The Enhanced Border Security and Visa Entry Act of 2002 makes the visa waiver conditional on the possession of a passport. As of October 26, 2006, citizens of allied countries[8] are exempt from visa requirements if they hold a machine-readable passport[9] or a passport which contains biometric data.

---

6 Immigration and Naturalization Service Passenger Accelerated Service System.

7 Which aimed to regulate the entry of foreigners into the United States.

8 Andorra, Australia, Austria, Belgium, Brunei, Denmark, Finland, France, Germany, Great Britain, Iceland, Ireland, Italy, Japan, Liechtenstein, Luxembourg, Monaco, Netherlands, New Zealand, Norway, Portugal, San Marino, Singapore, Slovenia, Spain, Sweden, Switzerland.

9 Delphine model.

Since September 30, 2004, visitors to the United States from foreign countries that benefit from the exemption program have been required to comply with the formalities set forth in the US-VISIT program, which regulates and, in some cases, limits freedom of movement in the United States. It was introduced on January 5, 2004 at 115 airports and 14 seaports. Under the US-VISIT program, foreign nationals are required to submit to the scanning of fingerprints from both index fingers and a fingerprint photograph. These provisions also apply to beneficiaries of visa exemption. According to the American authorities, freedom of movement has not been infringed upon.

4.1.1.4. *Passports*

The US Department of Homeland Security has chosen to insert a radio frequency chip in passports to strengthen border controls and combat false documents. It issued a call for tenders to four suppliers: Infineon Technologies of Germany, Bearing Point of the United States, Axalto of France and SuperCom of Israel. The passport includes a chip with an RFID radio identifier, and facial recognition for biometrics. The chip, which is very thin, is included in the cover of the passport. It stores the person's data, name, date and place of birth and a digital photo. When a person arrives at customs with the document, the data is transmitted to the control officer using a scanner located nearby. As of 2006, all passports are equipped with an RFID chip, which includes a digital signature and encryption technology.

In addition, the Ministry of Foreign Affairs and the Ministry of National Security decided to implement facial recognition systems at customs posts and airports. The State Department considered integrating other biometric data, fingerprints or iridial data, but no action was taken at that time as it involved taking the prints of the whole population, which seemed too expensive. Some security specialists wanted RFID technology to be abandoned in favor of a chip in direct contact with the scanner. According to these specialists, the RFID chip can be subject to dysfunctions and even criminal uses, such as clandestine access to information contained in passports.

Prior to the Patriot Act, citizens of the American continent were free to move freely within the United States. This is no longer the case. Since December 31, 2006, air travelers from Mexico, Canada and Bermuda have been required to present a passport or other acceptable document to US authorities. Since December 31, 2007, persons coming from the West Indies and traveling to the United States by plane, boat, road are subject to identical requirements. Finally, adults coming from Canada or Mexico with children to whom they are not related must prove that they have custody of the children and produce a letter from the parents or guardians authorizing the children to leave the country.

In 2020, at a time when the US has brought about a review of the old free trade agreement with Canada and Mexico, the new United States-Mexico-Canada Agreement (USMCA) demonstrates that the United States is the master of the game on the American continent, both in terms of trade and travel.

The ICAO[10], for its part, has long been in favor of the use of facial recognition.

4.1.2. *Standardization*

Compatibility and interface standards have been designed to facilitate the use of biometric techniques. As of February 13, 2002, HAAPI[11] and BAAPI[12] are the baseline generic standard. In 2002, the OASIS[13] established a working group with the aim of defining databases for data description and biometric functions based on the XML language (see the Common Biometric Exchange File Format).

Standardization first gained momentum in the United States, which allowed a research effort at a federal level. Because of the security issue, a collaboration was established between the Biometric Consortium and the NSA.

At the international level, it is the International Organization for Standardization (ISO) which tends to facilitate interoperability and exchange of data between applications and systems. These non-specific biometric standards include common file formats, application programming interfaces, biometric templates, template protection techniques, application and implementation profiles, and conformity assessment methodologies.

The International Electrotechnical Commission is also interested in biometrics. Much work is being done in the subcommittee of the ISO on identification of cards and persons and IEC joint technical committee on information technology. This is ISO/IEC JTC 1/SC 17. SC17 has worked on issues related to biometrics, including:

– the use of technologies that allow the identification of persons;

– the storage of biometric data in smart identification cards;

– the adoption of standards other than ISO and IEC;

---

10 International Civil Aviation Organization.

11 Human Authentication Application Programmer Interface.

12 Biometric Authentication Application Programmer Interface.

13 Organization for the Arrangement of Structured Information Standards.

– knowledge of the specific requirements of certain cards and card reading systems.

The SC17 working groups are developing standards to ensure uniform use of biometrics in all States. One such working group is the Identification Working Group.

In Canada, the Standards Council of Canada works with ISO and IEC. In Japan, a consortium includes three ministries – the Ministry of Economy and Industry, the Ministry of Land Infrastructure and Transport and the Gaimusho (Ministry of Foreign Affairs) – along with some 20 companies, including Hitachi, Mitsubishi and KDD. The objective is to unify the standards and technologies used in biometrics. In France, the AFNOR commission on CN37 biometrics was set up in January 2004. Two working groups have been created: WG1 on biometric techniques and WG2 on biometric profile uses.

The Cabal Report, which was tabled in the Assemblée nationale in mid-June 2003, emphasizes the value of standardization. The context is very fluid: biometric techniques are widely proprietary and dispersed. Standardization, which has legal aspects, reflects the industrial balance of power across borders. French manufacturers are not in a bad position[14]. Negotiations in the field of standardization highlight the winners of international standardization in the field of biometrics.

4.1.3. *The European Union and biometrics*

4.1.3.1. *The principle of freedom of movement*

Freedom of movement is a concept to which EU citizens are particularly attached. Biometric technologies are frequently used.

The first Schengen Agreement dates back to June 15, 1985[15]. The current one includes most of the nation-states in the EU. European citizens can move and reside freely. Nevertheless, security measures have been reinforced between the signatory states. A computer system called the Schengen Information System has been set up.

---

14 "We must participate in the standardization of biometric methods so that the selected processes correspond to the systems proposed by our companies", explains the then Cabal congressman, June 2003. news.zdnet.fr.

15 At that time, it included France, Germany, Belgium, Luxembourg and the Netherlands.

The SIS is a common database and a network of national files containing data that remain national. The persons on whom data is held include natural persons wanted for extradition, third country nationals not admissible on the national territory and missing persons, for example, minors on the run. The second-generation Schengen Information System was designed to take into account the increased flow of information, to control persons entering the Schengen zone and to integrate facial and iris recognition techniques into the central file.

4.1.3.2. *Visas and passports within the European Union*

Visas and passports are used in the European Union. On the occasion of the European Council of June 2003, the heads of state and government decided to introduce biometric data comprising fingerprints and irises in visas and passports by 2005.

The European Commission was already in charge of a study related to the development of a visa information system. It recommended the use of two biometric elements to identify individuals and to better secure residence permits and visas. The methods chosen were facial recognition – which must be digitized and stored on a smart card, inserted in identification documents – and fingerprints. The European Union adopts an approach closely aligned to the American guidelines.

In 2004, a regulation made fingerprinting mandatory. This text followed the meeting of the Council of European Ministers of the Interior and Justice, which introduced the addition of fingerprints as a second biometric identifier for travel documents issued by Member States for their citizens and residents. The majority of the European Parliament's group chairmen considered that this was not a significant enough change to bring about a review by the European Parliament's Committee on Citizens' Freedoms and Rights. If the group chairmen refused, the Council was prepared to initiate an emergency procedure. The document was adopted by 471 votes in favor, 118 against and 6 abstentions, with several amendments to the original text. MEPs said that only one biometric identifier was needed, while allowing individual member states to add fingerprints if they so wished and deemed it necessary. The Greens expressed their opposition for reasons related to the principle of freedom. In their amendments, MEPs argued that there should be no central databases of European passports as this would likely constitute a violation of the purpose and the principle of proportionality, where it could also increase the risk of this data being used for purposes other than those for which they were originally intended. Some MEPs also wanted biometric data to be used only to authenticate the document and identify the bearer, and for the Regulation to clearly designate the persons authorized to access such data.

The latter was adopted by the Board in December 2004[16]. Prior to this, the Article 29 Working Party had called for several guarantees to be implemented, including an assurance that biometric data would not be stored in a central database. The CNIL justified this position at the time: "The G29 considers that biometric data must be used exclusively to verify the identity of the document holder. A centralized database of photographs and digital fingerprints would necessarily open the door to other uses." In fact, this regulation responds, on the one hand, to the desire of member states to improve the security of travel documents by inserting biometric elements, and, on the other hand, to the American desire to require these travel documents from citizens of states that can enter the United States without a visa. Opponents of this text point out that the United States requires a single biometric identifier for travel documents: a facial image.

In addition, in 2004, the International Civil Aviation Organization recommended having a single identifier. The technology for machine-readable travel documents is called MRTD. Each type of MRTD contains, in a standard format, details about the identity of the holder, including a photograph or digital image. MRTDs include machine-readable passports, machine-readable visas and official machine-readable travel documents. MRTDS are developed by ICAO's Technical Advisory Group on Travel Documents, which establishes and adopts specifications, that is, detailed technical requirements. Indeed, ICAO recognized the importance of developing machine-readable passports and visas. It therefore recommended that States issue machine-readable passports and visas based on the model presented in Document 9303 and standardize the personal identification data included to be consistent with the details and format recommended in Document 9303. G29 recommendations regarding the confidentiality, integrity and authenticity of data have been taken into account. Indeed, the contactless chip that contains the photograph of the individual must have an electronic signature system that guarantees the authenticity of the data and its integrity; the data must be encrypted and not be read by anyone. This information is stored on the SIS II information system, which can be consulted by tens of thousands of officials throughout the Union. Tony Bunyan of Statewatch notes that this biometric data, collected for travel documents, can be misused[17].

---

16 Regulation 2252/2004 of December 13, 2004.

17 "No authority to collect personal data should be granted until national data protection authorities have been provided with adequate investigative resources and finances", 2006, Statewatch.

The European Commission considers that, with regard to visas, it is necessary to combat document fraud, which facilitates illegal immigration, human trafficking and terrorism. Visas must be biometric. The issuance of a biometric visa involves the passage of the passport holder at the counter. This is the application of the concept of personal appearance.

ICAO has recognized the importance of machine-readable visas. It has recommended that States issue machine-readable travel documents in the format set out in Document 9303. In March 2002, the ICAO Council adopted the Annex 9 standard requiring States to issue a separate passport to each person, regardless of age. The specifications of ICAO Document 9303 provide for the inclusion of biometric data confirming the identity of the holder or other data to verify the authenticity of the document. This results in a significant level of document security that allows border control authorities to have a high level of confidence in the validity of travel documents. Biometrics allows only the holder's information to be included in a machine-readable passport and complies with the guidelines for personal data.

The European Union as a whole is moving towards generalizing biometric passports. Since June 28, 2009, Member States have been issuing passports containing two fingerprints. Technically, this is sufficient to comply with the specifications adopted by the Commission. The Commission considers that the application is being implemented at a slower pace than desired. The desire to produce these new documents corresponds to a European will, as well as to the consideration of the geopolitical situation: the influence of the world's leading power, the United States, is not negligible in this context, since the American authorities are demanding the production of a new-generation document to enable the States of the European Union to continue to benefit from visa exemptions.

The cost, which is quite high, relates to malfunctions, and the risks relate to security. FIDIS[18] was able to demonstrate several years ago that RFID biometric passports are subject to loopholes in the protection of the private sphere of users and are likely to give rise to identity theft. Indeed, the data contained in biometric passports can be intercepted and read up to a distance of 10 meters from the bearer, without the person concerned being aware of it. Some passports are equipped with additional locks. For example, the US passport has a metal fiber mesh cover. Two researchers[19] have been able to prove that a simple half-inch opening is enough to intercept at a distance of 60 centimeters.

---

18 Future of Identity in the Information Society.
19 Mahaffey and Hering.

FIDIS also insists on the irrevocable nature of biometric data and the 10-year validity of passports. These specificities allow the fraudulent use of stolen information over a considerable period of time. Passports are exposed to interception, "brute force attacks", key theft, cloning of RFID tags and misuse of remote reading.

Based on its research, FIDIS drafted several recommendations, generally corrective, after the introduction of passports. In its view, they should not be used for authentication purposes in the private sector, but instead for informing citizens of the risks involved, for implementing procedures to be applied in the event of identity theft, and for establishing a policy to prevent the misuse of data contained in passports and, more generally, in travel documents.

In the longer term, FIDIS has advocated a new concept containing proven security measures for passports that are more reliable than those previously proposed and choices widely debated among security experts.

4.2. France

4.2.1. *Visa control*

4.2.1.1. *The November 2004 decree*

A decree of November 25, 2004 authorized the creation of a database – on an experimental basis and for a period of two years – containing, in particular, the fingerprints and digital photographs of persons applying for a visa at seven consular posts.

At the end of the experiment, the biometric data collection was generalized. A parliamentary commission of inquiry assessed the results of the biometric visa and the trial[20]. On this point, the financial issue was of paramount importance. All consulates were equipped to grant biometric visas in 2008.

4.2.1.2. *The law of November 26, 2003*

The law of November 26, 2003 relates to immigration. The law provided for the collection, storage and automated processing of a digital photograph and fingerprints of any extra-community national refused entry when crossing a border in the Schengen area. This group of people is in addition to the group already provided for by the Debré law, which includes applicants for residence permits, illegal residents or persons who have been expelled from French territory. Adopted under the Juppé

---

20 Biodev.

government, this measure had not been implemented for technical reasons. The law provided for an identical measure for visa applicants. Fingerprinting was provided for all those applying for a visa. However, not all visa applicants are criminals. Finally, the law did not make it necessary to obtain fingerprint and photograph data. The persons concerned are not those who had obtained a visa, but those who were applying for one. In order to authenticate the visa holder at border posts, an electronic component containing the scanned images of the visa holder's fingerprints and photograph could be combined with the visa sticker.

4.2.1.3. *The decree of December 19, 2006*

An order dated December 19, 2006 was issued pursuant to Article 7 of the Act of January 23, 2006. It created, on an experimental basis, an automated processing of personal data relating to passengers recorded in the air carrier departure control system[21].

The implementation of this automated processing of personal data was the responsibility of the Ministry of the Interior. A decision of the Minister of the Interior, communicated to the CNIL, specified the origins and destinations, located in States that do not belong to the European Union. This data includes the number and type of document used, nationality, surname and first name, date of birth, the gender, the crossing point used to enter or leave French territory, the Transport Code, that is, the flight number and the Air Carrier Code, the departure and arrival times of the transport, the boarding and disembarking point, and the inscription "known" or "unknown". Data specific to the fight against illegal immigration can only be consulted within hours of transmission. Automated processing is interconnected with the wanted persons file and the Schengen Information System.

4.2.2. *Passports*

For France, the issuance of the current generation of passports began in April 2006. This corresponds to a difficult path. In 2004–2005, the government initially considered applying to the National Printing Office. On July 15, 2005, an official from the Directorate of Public Liberties demanded that the Imprimerie Nationale provide a prototype, with a digitized photograph and optical reading zones protected by plastic film. The biometric chip was to be incorporated afterwards. On July 22, 2005, the then Interior Minister Nicolas Sarkozy requested the introduction of the integrated chip as of October 26, 2005[22]. As a result, the Ministry of the Interior

---

21 At the European Union level, the law obliges carriers to communicate passenger data.

22 "The project we found when we arrived at Place Beauveau was not up to the task. The Americans to whom we submitted it refused it outright. We had no other solution," said a member of the Interior Minister's office, July 2005.

issued an emergency call for tenders. Three main operators found themselves competing among one another: the Imprimerie Nationale, Thalès and the Swiss company Oberthur. The latter had good references and experience, in that it already produced Belgian biometric passports. Oberthur was granted the public contract, since it offered the most economically advantageous solution. The National Printing Office reacted quickly. It found itself in a difficult situation, having gone through a major economic layoff, and therefore wished to conceive a plan to safeguard jobs.

Located in Douai, the National Printing Office was also in an at-risk area in terms of employment. It was counting on obtaining this public contract and had received authorization from the European Commission to inject 197 million euros to support the restructuring plan. The trade unions brought the case before the administrative court, arguing that the company was "the only one authorized to produce the documents ... whose execution must be accompanied by special security measures, in particular identity papers, passports and visas". The National Printing Office got what it wanted, but the Ministry of the Interior appealed. In its view, this monopolistic position could not apply to the biometric passport[23]. The Council of State confirmed the ruling of the administrative court. In April 2006, the first passports were issued in the Hauts-de-Seine department. The process was then generalized. It has been issued throughout the country since June 2009. The chip stores the digitized photograph and two fingerprints of the passport holder. The passport is linked to the Delphine application – the first national biometric file used for administrative purposes.

By 2018, there would be seven different passport titles in France governed by ICAO standards. These are the ordinary passport, the frequent traveler passport, the temporary passport, the diplomatic passport, the urgent diplomatic passport, the mission passport and the service passport.

French passports are issued by prefectures (in France) and consulates (outside France). They are valid for 10 years for adults and 5 years for minors.

The biometric passport follows on from the e-passport. It does not rule in favor of Monique Chemillier-Gendreau, who declared in the 20th century[24]: "The 'national security' designated by the International Covenant on Civil Rights as one of the possible causes of this right ... shall not be interpreted in a manner inconsistent with the otherwise enthusiastic notion of 'general welfare in a democratic society' introduced in 1948 by the Universal Declaration of Human Rights." For

23 "How could we imagine that judges would integrate biometrics into their considerations?" declared Claude Guéant, then chief of staff to the Minister of the Interior.
24 Chemillier-Gendreau, M. (1998). La Déclaration universelle des droits de l'homme, entre célébration et méconnaissance. *Revue de la ligue des droits de l'homme*, November 1998.

Chemillier-Gendreau, free movement is "The idea of a common public good on an international scale. Visas and passports frame this public good."

4.2.3. *The TES database*

As new surveillance technologies become increasingly intrusive and as the surveillance of people through data develops, there is a growing concern that a culture of surveillance will become almost universal[25].

Since the beginning of the 21st century, security has been a concern for all those involved in economic and legal life. In 2016, in France, the debate began around the TES (Titres électroniques sécurisés; secure electronic identity documents) database, which illustrates these issues.

Identity cards, as travel documents, contribute to the control of migration flows. In European countries where the identity card exists and is considered a travel document, it is mandatory, except in Italy and France. In this country, holding an identity card was compulsory until 1955. Decree no. 55-1397 of October 22, as amended, founded the *fichier national de gestion* (national management database). Since then, usage has extended the use of the identity card as a travel document. It is recognized as proof of nationality within the European Union and the EEA[26], in accordance with the European Agreement on the Movement of Persons between Member States of the Council of Europe of December 13, 1957. The French decree of March 19, 1987 introduced a secure identity card, which has been widely issued since December 1995. The decree of June 5, 2003 specifies which documents must be included in the file. This system is valid for adults. A minor who is not accompanied by the holder of parental authority must produce, in addition to his/her card, a certificate of exit from the territory.

The TES database corresponds to the decree 2016-1460 of October 28, 2016, which brings together French files relating to the passport and national identity card, with a wealth of information, including biometric information from facial recognition and fingerprints. The "New Generation Prefectures" plan switched the database collected during the creation and renewal of identity cards to that created for passports.

---

25 Delmas-Marty, M. (2010). *Libertés et sûreté dans un monde dangereux*. Le Seuil, Paris, 69.
26 Austria, Belgium, Denmark, Finland, Germany, Great Britain, Greece, Iceland, Ireland, Italy, Liechtenstein, Luxembourg, Malta, Netherlands, Norway, Portugal, Spain, Sweden, Switzerland, Turkey.

The information already in the State's possession was gathered with a deadline of December 2018. Identity documents were gradually registered according to these rules. The town halls that did not have the necessary equipment were equipped with fingerprint collection devices. The experiment took place in the pilot department of Yvelines from November 8, 2016. The National Agency for Secure Documents[27], already in charge of passport files, is responsible for the connection and maintenance of the devices. As for the data, it is stored in the premises of the Ministry of the Interior.

4.2.3.1. *A generalized system in France*

The system is now generalized throughout France and even in the overseas territories.

4.2.3.1.1. The legal basis

The basis is not found in a law but in a regulatory act. A draft law on the protection of identity had previously been adopted[28], but had been referred to the Constitutional Council by parliamentarians of the opposition at the time[29]. The topic largely corresponds to the scope of article 34 of the French Constitution. Articles 32, 5, 7, 10, the 3rd paragraph of Article 6, and the 2nd phase of Article 8 were declared contrary to the Constitution, particularly with regard to identification. The law was largely emptied of its content. Was the decree the source of the desirable and appropriate law?

After the difficult path of the 2012 law, which took into account identification, not authentication, the government of Manuel Valls and his minister of the interior, Bernard Cazeneuve, decided to use the regulatory form. This is how the TES database appeared on the legal scene, replacing the 2005-1726 decree of 2005 and the FNG.

It is obvious that the themes addressed in the database are in connection with the scope of application of Article 34, in particular individual and collective freedoms. The CNIL expressed a preference for the legislative route: "As regards collective vigilance regarding this type of processing, the Commission notes[30] that, given the nature of this database, relating to identity documents, and, on the other hand, the debates on the protection of identity that took place on the occasion of the adoption of the aforementioned law of March 27, 2012, the Parliament should be seized as a priority of the envisaged project." The CNIL admitted that, from a legal point of

---

27 *Agence nationale des titres sécurisés* (ANTS).

28 Law 2012-410 of March 27, 2012.

29 On the basis of article 61, paragraph 2.

30 CNIL. Deliberation No. 2016-292 of September 29, 2016.

view, the decree cannot be questioned, but it "recommends that the government refer the project to Parliament". A debate without a vote was proposed by the Minister of the Interior, but this debate did not correspond to a legislative procedure, desired by the CNIL, the CCNUM, which would have allowed recourse to the impact study.

For its part, the *Conseil national du numérique* (National Digital Council) notes the lack of consultation. A dialogue with communities of experts could certainly have enabled the government to explore more resilient technical alternatives that respected citizens' rights, while achieving the same objectives. With one month to go before the Paris summit on the partnership for open government, chaired by France for one month, this opacity stood in stark contrast to the stated objectives of the public authorities in terms of transparency, not to mention the fact that it was part of the reverse of the consultation process initiated by Axelle Lemaire on the decrees implementing the law for a digital republic[31]. The opinion of the National Digital Council was published on December 12, 2016[32].

Although guarantees appeared in the text of the decree, fairly strong reservations were expressed by the CNIL, the National Digital Council, the ANSSI[33], the DINSIC[34], the INRIA[35] and the Human Rights League.

4.2.3.1.2. Purposes

In accordance with the law on personal data, the purposes, being legally invariable, are "legitimate"[36].

The system was part of the harmonization of procedures for processing and issuing national identity cards and passports. The general aims were to simplify administrative procedures and combat document fraud. The principle of territorialization was abolished: recourse was made to the digital archiving of documents and the recording of biometric data. A common processing system was to be set up to "establish, issue, renew and withdraw national identity cards and passports, and prevent and detect their falsification and counterfeiting".

---

31 *Conseil national du numérique* press release.

32 Self-selection as of November 7, 2016.

33 *Agence nationale de sécurité des systèmes d'information* (National Agency for the Security of Information Systems).

34 *Direction interministérielle du numérique* (Interministerial Digital Directorate).

35 *Institut national de recherche en sciences du numérique* (National Research Institute for Digital Sciences).

36 CNIL Deliberation No. 2016-292 of September 29, 2016.

Some contributors to the consultation related to the TES were hostile to a database containing so much personal information, including for authentication purposes. One contribution proposed to include the changing uses in the legal architecture that framed the prohibition of processing in order to limit and prevent the misuse of purposes. The widening of initial purposes occurred quite frequently, as has been demonstrated with the Eurodac system for asylum seekers, the visa applicants file or the STIC[37], in relation to which the CNIL has noted a certain number of errors.

The data in the TES is personal data. Among this personal data, a distinction must be made between traditional data and biometric or electronic data.

Traditional data, that is, data relating to the applicant or title holder, is:

– one's patronymic name, preferred name and first names;

– date and place of birth;

– gender;

– eye color;

– height;

– domicile, fixed address and possibly the address of the host organization;

– extraction: surnames, first names, dates and places of birth of the parents, information relating to their nationality;

– document attesting to the status of the legal representative when the ID holder is a minor or a protected adult under guardianship.

Biometric or electronic data is:

– scanned images of the face and fingerprints;

– email address, telephone number, when the applicant opts for an online pre-application for an identification document or wishes to use the secure postal service;

– in some cases, the connection code issued by the administration to the applicant in order to allow him/her to proceed to a declaration of receipt of the passport when the said passport has been transmitted by secure mail;

– the information relating to the identification document: document number and type, stamp duty rate, date, place, issuing authority, expiry date, notes and date of

---

37 *Le système de traitement des infractions constatées de la Police* (The Police's system for handling offences).

validation for the document, reason for invalidation, return of the document to the administration, its destruction, a note on the necessary supporting documents and information of a technical nature;

– information relating to the application for the identification document: application number, pre-application number if there was a pre-application, place the application was filed, date of receipt of the application, date on which the document was sent to the filing counter, reason for non-issuance;

– the date of delivery of the identification document, and, if necessary, the surname and first names identifying the honorary consul who is in charge of returning it; the address of the website for monitoring and identifying the carrier responsible for delivery when the document is transmitted electronically;

– information relating to the receipt of the passport by the applicant when the document is sent by a secure mail: date on which the passport is sent, secure mail tracking number, date of declaration of receipt, non-receipt or refusal of receipt, and notes on the supporting documents produced in support of the declaration;

– the data relating to the manufacturer of the identification document and the agents responsible for issuing the said document.

This personal data and information is kept for a period of 15 years if the identification document is a passport and for a period of 20 years if the identification document is a national identity card. The periods are reduced to 10 years and 15 years when the holder of the title is a minor.

Data and information concerning service passports and mission passports are kept for a period of 10 years.

Consultations, creations, modifications or deletions of data are subject to a record that includes the identification of the author, date, time and nature of the operation. The information is then kept for five years after registration. The TES database version of the national identity card includes a collection of several fingerprints, which was not the case for the previous national identity card.

4.2.3.1.3. Recipients

These are at once agents of the central services, agents of the local authorities and diplomatic agents tasked with issuing passports.

The central service agents are located in the Ministry of the Interior and the Ministry of Foreign Affairs. They are responsible for enforcing passport and national identity card regulations. They hold specific qualifications and, depending on the subject matter, are authorized by either the Minister of the Interior or the Minister of Foreign Affairs.

At the local authority level, it is the prefect who appoints, on the basis of individualization, and authorizes the agents of the prefectures and sub-prefectures who are responsible for issuing passports and national identity cards.

In the dependency of the Ministry of Foreign Affairs, the ambassador or consul designates and authorizes the diplomatic and consular agents in charge of issuing passports and national identity cards.

The Minister of the Interior may also designate and authorize officers who are responsible for issuing service passports.

These agents are able to access, by virtue of their duties, the data recorded in the processing mentioned in Article 1 and in the electronic component provided for in Article 2 of the Decree of December 30, 2005.

With regard to the data recorded in the electronic component provided for in Article 2 of the Decree of December 30, 2005 the agents that the mayor designates and authorizes in the municipalities are authorized to access it, within the framework of the collection of the application and the delivery of identification documents; for the mission passports, the Minister of Defense designates and authorizes the agents of the administrative divisions of the Ministry of Defense. The Ministry of Defense is authorized to delegate his/her powers in this specific area to the commanders of the administrative formations.

Recipients are linked to the conditions set by Article L222-1 of the Internal Security Code. Two categories of agents are concerned with regard to the exclusive needs of their missions and are authorized to access the data recorded in the processing provided for in Article 1, excluding the digitized image of fingerprints.

A director responsible for the defense of the fundamental interests of the nation[38] and the fight against terrorism appoints on an individual basis and empowers the officers of the national police services and the military of the national gendarmerie units.

The agents of the specialized intelligence services that appear in article R222-1 of the Code of Internal Security, for the same purposes, are very extensive.

Recipients who enter into collaboration with Interpol shall be authorized to access data recorded in the processing mentioned in Article 1 but not the digitized

---

38 Penal Code (Book IV, Title One), Law 92 686 of July 22, 1992. Concerns: treason and espionage, other attacks on national defense, consisting of attacks on the security of the armed forces and protected areas of interest to national defense and attacks on the secrecy of national defense.

images of fingerprints. These recipients who work with Interpol are agents of the Central Directorate of the Criminal Police. They develop exchanges with Interpol under the Common Position of January 24, 2005, the Interpol Rules on Data Processing[39]. They also establish relations with the competent authorities of the States that apply Decision 2007/533/JHA of the Council of June 12, 2007 on the installation, implementation and use of the second-generation Schengen system[40]. If an identification document is lost, stolen or invalidated, personal data may be transmitted to the competent authorities of the Interpol Member States or entered into the SIS II in order to invalidate or confirm the accuracy or relevance of the alert on the document. The information communicated to the Schengen Information System II shall be supplemented by the surnames, forenames, date of birth and date of issue of the document of the persons concerned.

To accomplish their mission successfully, the agents who are holders of the missions of research and control of the identity of natural persons, verification of the validity and authenticity of passports in the services of the national police, the national gendarmerie and customs can reach the data stored in the electronic component[41].

4.2.3.1.4. The prevalence of security concerns

Data aggregation

The aggregation of all the data collected, written and biometric, must serve to consolidate the perception of security as being necessary, in line with its original purposes. The objective, while respecting security, is to modernize the process of obtaining applications for passports and national identity cards; training platforms are common. The digitization of data provides good protection for data integrity, but fraud remains a problem. Common processing of passports and national identity cards enables the digitized image of fingerprints and photographs (facial recognition) of passport and national identity card applicants and holders to be combined and helps to combat document fraud and identity theft.

The CNIL wants the implementation of the secure electronic component previously provided for in the national identity card, which was not censored by Decision No. 2012-652 DC of March 22, 2012, but which has not been implemented. This limits the risk of misappropriation of purpose.

---

39 AG-2011, Res07, effective July 1, 2012.

40 SIS II, Articles 7, 38, 39.

41 Provided for in article 2 of the decree of December 30, 2005.

The legal reserves of the CNIL and the Conseil national du numérique (National Digital Council)

Reservations have been expressed by legal experts, in particular those of the CNIL and the National Digital Council

They essentially relate to the insufficient guarantees presented by a security text[42]. The CNIL and the National Digital Council would have liked Parliament to consider the various facets of the new database. On November 15, 2016, parliamentary debate would take place without a vote. Minister Bernard Cazeneuve explained the decree to parliamentarians and tried to show that mistrust is not justified. Not all parliamentarians were convinced.

Philippe Bas[43], president of the Sénat's law commission, intervened on November 16, 2016 during the debate. After mentioning the Sénat's investment as early as 2005 in the fight against identity fraud, he stated: "Yes to the fight against fraud, yes to protecting our fellow citizens against identity theft, but on the condition that the terms of this fight do not more seriously infringe on liberties, and on the condition that the database is effective."

Philippe Bas pointed out that despite the countless assurances given by the Minister of the Interior, uncertainties remain as to the technical possibility of fully guaranteeing the security of a centralized database against the risks of hacking and misuse of purposes; consequently, he asked for the implementation of the decree to be suspended pending the results of ongoing consultations, in particular the analysis of the National Agency for the Security of Information and Communication Systems. Claude Malhuret[44] agreed with Philippe Bas. He requested that the decree be suspended pending the final decision of the CNIL, the ANSSI and the *Direction des systèmes d'information et de communication* (Information and Communication Systems Directorate)[45]. Loïc Hervé[46] proposed a suspension followed by a trial.

---

42 "The Commission also considers that, given the nature of the data processed, the consequences of a misuse of the purposes of the file require subsistence guarantees and special vigilance", CNIL, deliberation no. 2016-292 of September 29, 2016.

43 LR, Senator of La Manche.

44 LR, Senator of the Allier.

45 DSIC.

46 UDI-UC, Senator of Haute-Savoie.

The Greens and the Communists were much more reserved. Esther Benbassa[47] demanded "the immediate suspension of the implementation of this decree, in order to stop any risk of diversion, and, to this end, to arrange the data and remove fingerprints". Eliane Assasi[48] demanded the withdrawal of the decree "which undermines democratic values and the rights of citizens".

The government announced that citizens/users of the TES would be able to opt out of fingerprinting. In fact, in a press release, it was stated that only the addition of fingerprints could be removed. The Ministry of the Interior wanted to ensure that police services were not deprived of the fingerprints of the millions of ID card holders. Before the Sénat, however, Minister Cazeneuve indicated that he would refer the matter to the relevant departments and take their recommendations into account. Bernard Cazeneuve's promises were not translated into a new decree.

4.2.3.1.5. The practice of requisitioning and biometric security

All the data contained in TES, including biometric data, may be subject to legal requisition, as may all data in administrative files. If legal bodies had intervened, and not simply the regulatory authority, an opportunity study would have been carried out in order to modulate the conditions for implementing these judicial requisitions, which would have been useful, according to the CNIL, "to take into account the unparalleled scope of this processing and the particularly sensitive nature of the data it will gather".

4.2.3.1.6. Particularly sensitive biometric data

The biometric database is made up of three distinct databases that correspond to a separation between photographs, fingerprints and the applicant's digitized signature. The biometric data on the database is subject to cryptology and the encryption keys are kept in HSMs[49]qualified by the *Agence nationale de sécurité des systèmes d'information* (National Agency for Information Systems Security). In addition, access to this data is secured by the implementation of a one-way link from the request for identification. The right of access and rectification is exercised as usual with the issuing authority. The right to object is excluded but the CNIL deems this justified in relation to the TES database.

The TES processing does not include a search feature that allows identification from the scanned image of the face or fingerprints. It is not possible to search for a person's identity based on their fingerprints or photograph. The effectiveness of this exclusion, according to the CNIL, must be imperative. It requires constant control of

---

47 Ecologist group, Senator of Val de Marne.

48 "Communist, Republican and Citizen" group, Senator of the Seine Saint-Denis.

49 Hardware security modules.

access to and use of the data. This requirement is an indispensable constraint. This control is essential and leads to precise information for citizens on the conditions of use of the biometric data collected. The CNIL requests that the use of biometric data be prohibited for identification purposes, whereas the use of facial recognition devices based on photographs for authentication purposes is desirable, subject to the exclusion of a facial recognition device for authentication purposes.

The CNIL also pointed out in its deliberation of September 29, 2016 that the storage of raw biometric data presents risks that could be circumscribed, or at least prevented, through the use of templates. It expresses reservations about raw biometric data and suggests[50] that raw biometric data be replaced by templates and by another technical device that would better guarantee the retention of biometric data.

4.2.3.1.7. User rights management

The management of user rights is entrusted to the hierarchical authority on which the agents depend. It is rather astute, with several functional profiles[51].

Consultations involve a registration that includes the identification of the consultant, as well as the date and time of consultation. The information is kept for five years.

The internal flows at TES are partitioned so that it is possible to verify their origin. The CNIL considers it necessary to adopt measures to protect the rights of the persons concerned in order to remedy the risks of false rejections and false acceptances. Security according to the CNIL is partly guaranteed, but the security requirement requires the updating of security measures taking into account the regular re-evaluation of risks; on this point, there is a shortfall that needs to be remedied. The problem is still ongoing. For their part, ANSSI/INRIA has criticized the risk of a loophole, which presents a misuse of purpose from a technical point of view.

4.2.3.1.8. The DOCVERIF

Cooperation with Interpol does not call for any particular remarks. No criticism seems justified with regard to the transmission of information to the national file for checking the validity[52] of improper use of such documents, against their falsification or counterfeiting.

---

50 This was not followed.

51 Collection, delivery, follow-up and instruction according to five levels.

52 Provided for by the decree of August 10, 2016.

The CNIL has suggested, for the sake of consistency with regard to the terms used in the decree of August 10, 2016, the use of the name DOCVERIF in the TES decree and that Article 7, which mentions the transmission of nominative data for "lost, stolen or invalidated" identification documents, should use only the term "invalidated", which includes identification documents declared lost or stolen.

4.2.3.2. *The centralized database and its possible misuses*

The TES system has a secure bubble and dedicated servers: the network on which the central application is operated has no links to the Internet. But this does not eliminate all risks.

4.2.3.2.1. A centralized database resistant to cyber threats

The database is effectively a target, with very high stakes, for cyber adversaries who are highly skilled in attacks against automated data processing and, in particular, against a centralized database. There is no impassable line of defense[53].

In April 2016, a security breach resulted in a massive data leak to 55 million Filipino voters. Almost at the same time, a database using the Turkish population census was put online, which included contact information. In Israel itself, a country that is highly effective in the various security sectors, a population register containing confidential information on nearly 9 million citizens appeared on the Internet due to the negligence of a subcontractor. During the public consultation on the TES database, some contributors emphasized the essential proportionality that is incumbent on the objective of fighting document fraud. Almost all contributors agreed that a system cannot be completely secure. Biometric signatures can, however, be used for secure access solutions to mobile or online payment services. Moreover, data centralization does not necessarily imply segmentation of data access. The centralization of sensitive or biometric data can lead to abuses by government services or hacking. Misuse by government agencies has already occurred.

4.2.3.2.2. Possible misuses

The choice made in favor of a centralized architecture for the storage of biometric data generates anxiety and concern. With the widespread use of digital technology, a centralized database, especially of biometric data and including encrypted and secure data, makes multiple abuses plausible.

---

53 Bill by Jean-Jacques Urvoas.

The initial purposes must be pursued; the misuse of purposes is prohibited by all sources of law regarding personal data. Technically, and with a multiform evolution of technologies, nothing can prevent the misappropriation or illegitimate extension of the initial purposes[54]. And the misappropriation can consist of a massive misappropriation of purposes. With misappropriation, it becomes possible to identify, and no longer to authenticate, systematically, members of the population with old passports and national identity cards, by using facial recognition for police or administrative purposes, which will easily replace the initial purposes. This widening of the initial purposes on a large scale has already taken place: it is worth mentioning, in a context that complies with the law, the Eurodac system for asylum seekers, the file of visa applicants or the STIC[55].

Nevertheless, it is quite possible that this enlargement may occur outside of the legal context. No technical guarantee seems sufficient for the time being. But the enlargement is developing more and more and is known by its terminology: privacy by design. The CNIL and the Constitutional Council advise keeping biometric data on an individual medium held by each person involved. Contributors to the consultation on the TES database consider that only a decentralized storage solution is likely to limit the risks; they want the file to be divided or duplicated in several interconnected database, and also want the use of hash functions. The CNIL (French Data Protection Authority) is requesting expertise in this area and an evaluation of the system. The National Digital Council cites[56] an electronic component that would be integrated into identity cards, as was done for passports, and in its opinion of December 12, 2016, it insisted on the sensitive aspect of centralizing information. It is skeptical about the need to store biometric data centrally in order to achieve the purposes. "Biometric authentication is only one indicator among others for the processing of applications for identity documents, and the expected gains in terms of efficiency, simplification and the fight against document fraud do not, for the most part, result from merging these two databases. On the contrary, considerable risks of misuse, theft or misappropriation of purpose may result directly from the creation of this file."[57] This use of individual media would be capable of combating document fraud while taking privacy into account. The retention of data in a centralized form should be compatible with the protection of individual and collective freedoms. It is therefore a serious alternative: "To sweep aside with a wave of the hand – whether we wanted to or not – is to ignore the state of available technologies and to hinder the

---

54 CNIL, "given the nature of the data processed, the consequences of a misuse of the purposes of the file require substantial guarantees and particular vigilance", deliberation No. 2016-292 of September 29, 2016.

55 System for processing recorded offences.

56 He adds, "This is not the only possibility", November 7, 2016 press release, Conseil national du numérique.

57 Notice of December 12, 2016 from the Conseil national du numérique.

progress of the rights and capacities of individuals in favor of a trusteeship of the population by its rulers." Independent audits could be put in place[58]. Encrypted automatic detection and access tracking systems should be systematically installed. The consent of citizens for the storage and use of their data would be required, which would be in conformity with the spirit of the regulation adopted by the European Parliament in May 2016, which was due to come into force in early 2018[59].

4.2.3.3. *Essential monitoring*

4.2.3.3.1. Independent monitoring of the use of the database

Monitoring the use of the database would fall to persons who would not be placed in a hierarchical relationship with the bodies that use the database. However, a question arises: does the protection of classified elements make it too difficult for intelligence services to effectively control the use of the file?

It is a true right for citizens to view a database that concerns them. Every citizen, at the European level, since directive 95/45, then the GDPR, must have the right to access his/her data and when, in view of the justifications, he/she considers the information inaccurate, unclear, insufficient or legitimate, he/she must be able to file a complaint. This right of access can be carried out either through a traditional right of access upon request by citizens, or through a system of notifying citizens when the file is consulted.

4.2.3.3.2. Strengthening or creating powers for independent administrative authorities

The CNIL

Some contributors suggested that a veto power could be given to it. This would undoubtedly be beneficial for individual and collective liberties, but for the TES database decree, the CNIL could only issue an opinion and it would be unthinkable that a right of veto would be acceptable. Moreover, since its creation on January 6, 1978, the CNIL is the first independent administrative authority.

It has seen its powers and competences in fields as varied as biometrics and video protection, etc., increase steadily. The CNIL does not have sufficient human and technical resources to cope with the increasingly diverse and important roles

---

58 Conseil national du numérique, Press Release, November 7, 2016.

59 Questions were asked by some contributors during the consultation, including: which services will be impossible to access if one refuses to provide one's fingerprints? Will there be a basis for "substitution" for those who have not given their consent?

that have been entrusted to it. As far as TES is concerned, the CNIL has announced that its agents will visit the services in order to determine whether the intelligence services have saved part of the database in their own secret databases.

The Conseil national du numérique

The *Conseil national du numérique* (National Digital Council)[60] is a purely consultative body. It played a significant role in the consultations that accompanied the adoption of the Digital Act, and although the body is advisory, the National Digital Council has steadily gained influence in the legal and digital sphere. Its remarks have often participated, directly or indirectly, in establishing doctrine in various fields related to innovation, protection of personal data, files and electronic communications.

The contributors proposed several solutions during the consultation for the TES:

– facilitation of security system audits by opening up the source code, promoting application expertise and detecting flaws, and even promoting traceability;

– introduction of technical constraints to the consultation of the file by authorized persons.

In its opinion of December 12, 2016, the National Digital Council called for a reform of the governance of technological choices within the State: the TES file highlighted certain shortcomings, including the lack of consultation with the scientific and technological communities that are best able, as actors or experts, to analyze the solutions presented, assess the risks and costs, and develop relevant architectures.

The consultation organized with the scientific and technological communities would go hand in hand with the start of a public debate between citizens, civil society stakeholders, the private sector and the public sector on the topics of administrative identity and online identity, as happened with the digital law. This would also enable certain issues already covered in the digital law to be extended: roles and links between FranceConnect and the CNIL, public and private digital identities, taking into account the widespread use of smartphones, the state of the art in terms of architectures[61], encouraging the development of public research, particularly for digital identity, biometrics and current security methods.

---

60 Or CNNum.

61 The December 12, 2016 opinion of the Conseil national du numérique cites web services, programming interfaces and cloud computing.

The National Digital Council asks the government, in its opinion, to:

– prepare a general framework consisting of standards and best practices among administrations and covering all digital projects that could have an impact on the various public concerned: "This framework could stipulate that any major technological choice be subject to a prior in-depth impact assessment explaining the choices made (along the lines of the data protection impact assessment required by the general data protection regulation)." This framework could be binding at the end of the process, but could also propose a first step that would define and attempt to implement the non-mandatory rules;

– open up the public decision-making process: the implementation of any technological project that could significantly affect a significant part of the population would involve a process of discussion, correction and amendment that would rely on institutional actors, as well as on experts and members of the academic world;

– improve the adaptation of the governance model for technological choices for the coming years.

In the conclusions of their report requested by the Minister of the Interior on November 17, 2017, ANSSI and DINSIC insist on the dangers of misappropriation for identification purposes, "despite the unidirectional nature of the computer link implemented to link alphanumeric identification data to biometric data"[62]. Presented at a hearing before the Parliament, these conclusions drew criticism, in particular, for the lack of legal protection of data when it is centralized, which can lead to misuse for different purposes. An approval committee gave its opinion the following February on "risk analysis and the conformity of risk management".

The TES file and its biometric information contribute to the desire of the actors, and in particular States, to safeguard national security, perhaps at the expense of certain freedoms, which corresponds to a trajectory that has been observed for several years. In the conclusions of their November 2017 report, ANSSI and DINSIC emphasize the dangers of misappropriation for identification purposes. Presented at a hearing before the Parliament, these conclusions drew criticism, particularly on the lack of legal protection of data when it is centralized, which can lead to misappropriation of purposes. An approval committee gave its opinion on the risk analysis the following February.

---

62 Report submitted by ANNSI and DINSIC to Minister Bruno Leroux on January 19, 2017.

4.2.3.4. *Installation*

4.2.3.4.1. The decree of February 9, 2017

A decree of February 9, 2017 established a list of necessary facilities. The first installation took place in Paris on February 21, 2017 and the other departments were included for implementation in February and March 2017.

On February 28, 2017, the Council of State was seized of a motion for the suspension of interim injunction. The appeals are those of the Quadrature du Net, the Ligue des droits de l'homme and the online platform of Jean-Marc Fedidia and Christophe Lèguevaques. The aim was to achieve the suspension of the decree and the order. These two lawyers were inspired by the audit report of the ANSSI and DINSIC, which stated that there was a risk of misappropriation of purpose with a switch to an identification system. In this situation, according to the lawyers, "there is a major risk of invasion of privacy without the expected gain for the stated purpose (document fraud) being achieved". In addition, Bernard Cazeneuve undertook to make the transfer of fingerprints for identity cards optional in the database. The measure did not come into force. Moreover, the choice of the centralized solution, as demonstrated in the INRIA report, does not guarantee privacy.

The suspension procedure, which would not be followed up, implied urgency. The petition that had been filed with the Council of State mentioned that the protection of privacy "in itself constitutes an emergency in view of the government's behavior, which turns a deaf ear to the alarms emanating from civil society, digital professionals and national representation". This suspension would be justified by "the right to resistance and oppression". Above all, the consent of the persons concerned by the secure documents should absolutely be gleaned prior to the collection of biometric data.

The TES file and its biometric information contribute to the desire of the persons involved, and in particular States, to safeguard national security, perhaps at the expense of certain freedoms, which corresponds to a trajectory that has been observed for several years.

4.2.3.4.2. Criticisms of AA

To accomplish their missions successfully, the agents who are holders of the missions of research and control of the identity of natural persons, verification of the validity and authenticity of passports in the services of the national police, the national gendarmerie and customs can get to the data stored in the electronic component[63].

The recipients are duly listed, and this helps to protect the privacy of passport and national identity card holders.

4.2.3.4.3. An overriding concern for security

The grouping of all the data collected, written and biometric, must serve to consolidate a security necessity, in line with its initial purposes. The objective, while respecting security, is to modernize the process of obtaining applications for passports and national identity cards: training platforms are common. The digitization of data enables the integrity of the data to be properly protected.

The common processing of passports and national identity cards enables the digitized image of fingerprints and photographs (facial recognition) of passport and national identity card applicants and holders to be combined and helps to combat document fraud and identity theft. A comparison is made between each applicant's fingerprints and previously registered fingerprints. This facilitates the authentication of applicants, reduces administrative procedures and avoids misappropriation for identification purposes.

The CNIL wants the implementation of the secure electronic component previously provided for in the national identity card, which was not censored by Decision no. 2012-652 DC of March 22, 2012, but which has not been implemented.

4.2.4. Setting up Alicem

Decree no. 2019-452 of May 13, 2019 authorized the creation of Alicem. Passed through the GDPR sieve, the text authorized Alicem's processing to read the data recorded in the electronic component of passports and securities.

As prescribed by the Ministry of Interior, Alicem allows the civil service access to facial recognition. It consists of scanning the biometric passport photo and implementing a video of the face by moving the head to prove one's identity. Facial biometrics is already used not for security purposes, but for practical management purposes[64]. This device complies with the European directive on payment services, designed to limit fraud. Facial biometrics is also used to secure access to sensitive areas and high-profile sporting events, as well as when starting a car-sharing scheme.

---

63 Provided for in article 2 of the decree of December 30, 2005.
64 Such as unlocking a cell phone or computer.

Companies working on facial recognition, such as Thales, Cisco and Idemia[65], are arranging with the public authorities. "We are still along the lines of experimentation and learning," explains Guillaume de Saint-Marc, director of innovation at Cisco.

The CNIL is considering whether to deploy metal detectors at the entrances to the Ampère high school in Marseille and Les Eucalyptus high school in Nice. Several associations consider this project disproportionate. It should be recalled that a few years ago, palm recognition was introduced, regarded as preferable to fingerprinting, to monitor the management of school canteens, and that this was considered disproportionate by activists opposed to social control over minors, even with a "playful" biometric such as it appeared at the time with palm recognition.

An impact analysis has been conducted on facial recognition in some of its uses: "test duration, information on the learning algorithm, data exploitation mode" lists William Eldin, founder of the start-up XXII, which specializes in real-time analysis of video streams.

Facial recognition can be used as an identity document and boarding pass for the traveler. The biometric boarding card was tested in 2018[66]; ADP and Air France launched the experiment in 2020. The purpose is the fluidity of ever-increasing passenger travel, and therefore increased profitability for airlines.

Facial recognition is also used in banks. Société Générale authorizes the opening of an account using facial biometrics and video. It is expected that the recording of a facial image in its banking app will enable it to validate Internet purchases and financial transactions. In the European Union, the use of facial recognition is governed by the GDPR, which requires free and informed consent from persons being filmed. On the other hand, the identification of persons in a public space by automatic analysis without prior consent is prohibited, except in the case of a flagrant violation or if a judge authorizes the cross-referencing of videos from surveillance cameras with a police file to track down a criminal[67]. An experiment was carried out in this field in February 2019 in Nice, in part of the carnival grounds. The Republican mayor of Nice[68] was pleased with the results, which all seemed positive. He insisted on the general public's acceptance of the technology

---

65 Merger of Morpho and Oberthur.

66 Thus, the traveler did not have to present his/her passport.

67 In France, the police and the gendarmerie interrogate a database of 8 million photos with the so-called criminal record processing file. An experiment was carried out in this field in February 2019 in Nice, in a part of the carnival grounds.

68 Christian Estrosi.

and on its technological reliability[69] – in spite of the situations tested out by the software, the existence of monozygotic twins, the fact that some people had aged, etc. – and the biometric data was then erased. However, the CNIL was less enthusiastic. According to the CNIL, the work was carried out too hastily in that "the circumstances were not such as to favor in-depth work on the planned device".

4.3. Facial recognition at the heart of globalization

In France, the idea that the technology could be hijacked and lead to mass surveillance is a cause for concern. Those who are strongly opposed emphasize the unreliability of the algorithms and the risk of bias. According to an NIST[70] study, algorithms are more effective with males than with females. They recognize white skin more easily than other skin colors. On this subject, in the United States, it has been shown that, for the moment, the error rate is infinitely higher with African American people than with white people. On the other hand, in China, the error rate is lower, but the ethnic homogeneity is greater. American labs promise to correct these aberrations. "The artificial intelligence that is at the heart of program learning has made considerable progress. Every year, the error rate is halved," says Vincent Bouatou, Director of Innovation at Idemia.

Beyond that, the reticence concerns the fundamental liberties of the citizen. La Quadrature du Net, which attacked the decree creating Alicem before the Council of State, demands the "pure and simple prohibition" of facial recognition.

All the stakeholders who accept facial recognition, including potential industrial users and regulatory authorities, want to open a debate on this technology, which plays a key role in usage.

There is unanimity on the imperfections of the regulatory framework, as noted by Sébastien Louradour, who is studying these issues for the World Economic Forum[71].

In Europe, in Denmark, in July 2019, the Brondby stadium used CCTV cameras linked to a database of those banned from the stadium during several soccer matches. "Everything was done in compliance with the GDPR, but the Danish regulation is more flexible than in France," said Panasonic, who supplied the equipment.

---

69 No error rate.

70 National Institute of Standards and Technology.

71 Organizer of the Davos forum.

China, for its part, has instituted a rating system for its citizens based on facial recognition. The Chinese government has played a major role in the introduction of facial recognition software. The country's "social credit system" has been implemented in recent years to prevent exceptions to the rule. Facial recognition cameras can now be spotted at pedestrian crossings to ensure that no one crosses the road at places other than crossings.

In the United States, views are divided. Facial recognition software exists just about everywhere, but its reliability is far from perfect, and some states have stepped in for that reason. This is the case in Oregon, New Hampshire and California.

In California, law AB1215 prohibiting the use of "all biometric surveillance" in police body cameras was signed on October 8, 2019 by Governor Gavin Newson. The law also allows citizens to prosecute officers who violate the new regulations.

Last year, Brian Brackeen, the CEO of Kairos, a company specializing in artificial intelligence technology, said that when we talk about body cameras with artificial intelligence, we are talking about superhuman capabilities.

According to Chronicle, the California Peace Officers Association has confirmed that facial recognition technology is not currently used by any California law enforcement agency. The new law expires in 2023.

India is creating the world's largest facial recognition system. Like China, India relies on artificial intelligence to enhance its security.

For the world's most populous countries, ensuring the safety of their citizens is an important issue. India has an insufficient number of police officers. In order to compensate for this deficit in terms of manpower, India is turning to artificial intelligence. The Indian government has launched a call for tenders to encourage private companies to help develop a comprehensive central repository of surveillance data. The selected companies will be responsible for developing a system that will link facial recognition data with information such as citizens' passport numbers and fingerprints.

One drawback is the issue of Indian cybersecurity. In the past, the Aadhar national identification system has been subject to numerous data leaks and it is unlikely that this new facial recognition system will be well-armed against abuses. Moreover, the privacy of Indians is likely to be compromised by this new system.

Thus, biometrics plays a pivotal role in security and all observers are aware of this. The typology of biometric fingerprints has evolved considerably and, along with artificial intelligence, in a globalized economy, biometrics is part of the Big Brother society.

5

Personal Data in the United States and Europe

Personal data is ingrained in all the technologies that contribute to security, as we have seen.

Personal data is concerned with security; it was first established in the 1970s primarily by public bodies, and the Safari affair, which is well known in France, was interesting in this respect. Nowadays, personal data is circulating in a globalized market.

In geopolitical terms, a clear distinction is made between the GDPR and the less protective US regime[1], but new thinking is emerging in the United States. Furthermore, personal data has been around for a very long time. The US Privacy Act was passed in 1974. Laws were passed in the 1970s in Sweden, Germany and France. Convention 108 of the Council of Europe Convention was designed to make freedom of movement and the protection of privacy compatible. Resolution 45/95 of the General Assembly of the United Nations emphasizes the principles of lawfulness, fairness, accuracy and purpose.

The preamble to Council of Europe Convention 108 of January 28, 1981 recognizes the need to reconcile the fundamental values of respect for private life and freedom of movement between peoples.

Personal data is defined in Convention 108[2] as any information concerning an identified or identifiable natural person.

---

1 The Safe Harbor Principles agreement was invalidated by the European Court of Justice.
2 Article 2.

Article 7 on data security states: "Appropriate security measures shall be taken for the protection of personal data stored in automated files against accidental or unauthorized destruction or accidental loss, as well as against unauthorized access, alteration or dissemination."

5.1. The United States and the protection of personal data in the European Union: Directive 95/46

Personal data has been virtually unprotected in the United States for decades. Minimum protection was based on self-regulation by industry, but since January 2020, California has had a more protective regime.

The European Union is very protective of personal data. The first national laws were already protective. But a dichotomy showed between the United Kingdom (then a member of the European Union), which was attached to general principles, and the majority of the other States of the European Union, which wanted precise and detailed protection.

Directive 95/46 of October 24, 1995 concerns the protection of individuals with regard to the processing of personal data and the free movement of such data.

This directive served as the basis in Europe for the protection of personal data until the GDPR came into force in 2018.

The definition of personal data initially employed the definition contained in the Council of Europe Convention 108 but introduced greater detail: a person is deemed identifiable if they can be identified, directly or indirectly, in particular by reference to an identification number or to one or more elements specific to his or her physical, physiological, mental, economic, cultural or social identity (Article 2a) of Directive 95/46.

Personal data shall be processed fairly, for explicit and legitimate purposes, for a specified period of time. Misuse of the purpose is prohibited.

5.1.1. Sensitive data

"Sensitive data" may not be processed if it provides information on social or ethnic origin, political opinions, religious or philosophical beliefs, trade union membership, health or sex life. Sensitive data would be stored in the following circumstances:

– if the person concerned has given his or her consent;

– the processing is necessary for the protection of the vital interests of the data subject or of another person who is physically or legally incapable of giving consent;

– the treatment pursues a managerial purpose, carried out by persons engaged in legal activities, having a political, philosophical, religious, or trade union character. The files are constituted to gather information on their members; they cannot be transferred, neither in return for payment nor free of charge;

– in health matters, exceptions are made in the interest of the patient or in the field of preventive medicine, medical diagnostics or administration of care. The data processing is carried out by a professional who is bound by an obligation of discretion or by professional secrecy. Sensitive data also relates to journalism and literary or artistic creation.

5.1.2. *The right of access*

The person concerned has a right to access his or her data. They may have any incomplete or inaccurate data corrected, erased or blocked. They also have the right to object, for legitimate reasons relating to their particular situation.

The automated processing of data must not harm the interests of the natural person: a decision cannot be based solely on the consideration of data, in particular in the evaluation of personality, professional performance, credit, reliability or behavior.

5.1.3. *Security*

Emphasis is placed on security. All actors recognize that security is a condition for freedom. The data controller shall implement technical measures and adequate organization to prevent any accidental destruction or loss, alteration, dissemination or unauthorized access. The level of security is assessed with regard to the risks incurred by the processing. If a subcontractor is chosen by the data controller, he shall provide sufficient guarantees: like any other subcontractor, he will only act on the instructions of the data controller.

With transborder data flows, a principle of reciprocity is pursued with regard to the protection of nominative or personal data: "Member States shall provide that the temporary or permanent transfer to a third country of personal data undergoing processing may only take place if the third country in question ensures an adequate level of protection." The criterion of adequacy refers to the nature of the data, the purpose, the duration of the proposed processing, and the laws or regulations in force in the third country. Negotiations are envisaged in delicate situations. Indeed, the freedom of exchanges and the protection of automated personal data are essential concepts in the European and international legal corpus.

5.1.4. The directive of December 15, 1997[3], followed by the directive of July 12, 2002[4] and supplemented by the directive of November 25, 2009[5]

The directive of December 15, 1997 integrates digital technologies. Member States shall ensure, through the use of national regulations, the confidentiality of communications by means of a public network. It is prohibited for any person other than the users, without the consent of the users concerned, to intercept or store communications. This prohibition does not apply to legally authorized interception of communications.

Personal data appearing in directories, whether printed or electronic, is limited to the identification of a particular subscriber, unless the subscriber gives their consent to the publication of additional information. A subscriber who prefers not to be listed in the directory obtains permission not to appear and, if he or she so wishes, to mention data that cannot be used for canvassing purposes.

The identification of calling lines can be problematic in terms of individual freedom. The calling user must be able to eliminate the calling line indication. If calling line identification is offered, the called subscriber has the right to refuse incoming calls when the calling user has removed the calling line identification. The protective regime is lifted when a subscriber is subject to malicious calls. In this case, the data identifying the caller is retained, communicated by the provider. The protection also does not apply to emergency calls, which are recognized as such[6].

Unsolicited calls for the purpose of direct marketing are not permitted without the consent of the account holders.

In terms of security, the provider of an electronic communications service must take all technical and organizational measures to ensure the security of the services.

---

3 Directive 97/66/EC of the European Parliament and of the Council of December, 15 1997 concerning the processing of personal data and the protection of privacy in the telecommunications sector.

4 Directive 2002/58/EC of the European Parliament and the Council concerning the protection of privacy in the electronic communications sector.

5 Directive 2009/136/EC of the European Parliament and the Council dated November 25, 2009, supplements Directive 2002/58.

6 Firefighters, police services, gendarmerie.

When a particular risk of a network security breach is detected, the provider should inform account holders of the risk, the means of dealing with it and the cost of those means.

The Internet is overturning traditional business structures by providing a common global structure for the provision of a range of electronic communications services.

Repeated and unwanted commercial requests, known as "spam", are prohibited. Canvassing is possible if a person has already made a transaction with the merchant service provider, but the person concerned may terminate this canvassing if he or she no longer deems it appropriate.

5.1.5. *Geolocalization*

When location data, other than traffic data, relating to users or subscribers of public communications networks is collected, it will be processed only after being made anonymous or with the consent of the users, to the extent and for the duration necessary for the provision of a value-added service. The service provider is obliged to inform users, before obtaining their consent, of the type of location data other than traffic data that will be processed, along with the purposes and duration of such processing. Users may withdraw their consent to the processing of location data other than traffic data at any time.

5.1.6. *Cookies*

Cookies changed between 2002 and 2009.

5.1.6.1. *2002*

In 2002, cookies[7] could be a legitimate and useful tool, for example, to assess the effectiveness of a site's design and advertising, and to monitor the identity of users conducting online transactions. Where cookies were intended for legitimate purposes, such as facilitating the provision of Information Society services, their use was permitted provided that users were given clear information as required by Directive 95/46.

However, users had a right to object to cookies; they could refuse to allow a cookie or similar device to be installed on their terminal equipment. This was

---

7 Recital 25 of the 2002 Directive.

particularly important in cases where users other than the original user had access to the terminal equipment and the sensitive private data stored on it.

Information regarding the use of multiple devices to be installed on the user's terminal equipment, as well as the right to refuse such devices, could be offered at one time during the same connection and could cover future use that may be made of such devices during other connections. The 2002 Directive insisted on the user-friendliness that would accompany the communication of information, the offer of the right to refuse.

5.1.6.2. *2009*

An essential change came with the directive of November 25, 2009. Cookies could only remain with the user's consent. There was therefore a shift from the right of refusal to prior consent.

However, is consent in 2009 really free and informed? No. Users can only access cookie-carrying sites if they give their consent while they are in a hurry to access the information on the cookie-carrying site. Can this consent be considered partially biased? The question was put to a legal expert.

At the level of the European Union, the G29, a grouping of regulatory entities referred to in Article 29 of Directive 95/46, were not required to take decisions but to conduct studies that lead to decisions. Research on spam, prospecting, profiling and cookies brought together a great deal of expertise, which contributed to the development of a doctrine.

The national regulatory authorities, for their part, ensured that practices comply with the transposition of the directives into national law, at that time, in France, the law of January 6, 1978, amended by the law of August 6, 2004.

Penalties were set by these national regulatory authorities, but they were not very dissuasive.

The regimes that applied in each country are quite different, with authorization, then declaration in France, and, currently, data protection delegation.

5.2. The GDPR

The GDPR (General Data Protection Regulation) has worked to make data protection legislation more protective.

5.2.1. *Consent*

Emphasis is placed on prior consent, the right to oblivion and profiling supervision. The powers of regulatory authorities are strengthened. When a rule is not complied with, financial penalties of up to 4% of worldwide revenues may be applied to a company that violates the rule. Indeed, personal data is a treasure trove for companies, and file transfers are a constant and integral part of marketing development.

The GDPR was adopted in 2016 but came into force on March 25, 2018. In France, a new law that takes into account the evolution marked by the GDPR came into force on June 20, 2018.

5.2.1.1. *Profiling*

5.2.1.1.1. Definition

Profiling is primarily based on behavioral analysis and allows us to determine a person's profile. Before being used for commercial purposes, profiling was used in the field of criminal matters (i.e. criminal profiling), which made it possible to determine the psychological profile of a criminal. Now, profiling plays a different role since it allows companies to collect personal data that they will use. Profiling is therefore able to classify individuals into different categories through the automated processing of personal data collected about them. Profiling appears in the GDPR[8].

5.2.1.1.2. Profiling and Big Data

Profiling results in decisions being made that are tailored to individuals by predicting their future behaviors in various domains. This tool is used by both private and public structures. For private companies, profiling conditions promotional activity. With public structures, profiling contributes to ensuring the public security of a State thanks to the information collected. In both cases, the emergence of Big Data has played a major role. Big Data is the set of massive data that is created every day and that no conventional management tool can process. With Big Data, everyone has access to a great deal of information in giant databases.

The profiling technique obtains its generated information with the aid of loyalty cards or cookies. The issue is essential for private companies and it is potentially dangerous for individuals, as their data is collected.

---

9 Article 4 of the GDPR: "Any form of automated processing of personal data consisting of the use of personal data to evaluate certain personal aspects relating to a natural person, in particular to analyse or predict aspects concerning that natural person's performance at work, economic situation, health, personal preferences, interests, reliability, behavior, location or movements."

5.2.1.1.3. Control of profiling

For this reason, the GDPR establishes limits for profiling. Profiling involves the automated processing of data: these are decisions/predictions made by a computer, without human intervention, in an automatic way, which have significant effects on the person concerned. An example of this is a credit card application with an online bank that is rejected, or a response to a job offer that is also rejected, but without any human intervention in the evaluation. How can we prove that no human has acted as a complement to the machine? The process is legal and authorized when:

1) the user has given his explicit consent;

2) the decision is necessary for the performance or execution of a contract;

3) it complies with the law of the European Union limited by specific provisions.

Exemptions are provided for in special cases as stipulated in Article 9.2. For example, consent to the use of data may be given where "necessary in the public interest".

Profiling also concerns connected devices. Can we talk about consent when it comes to the processing of this data? We still don't have a clear answer.

Sensitive data is more numerous: biometric and genetic data are now part of sensitive data, along with religious, political and trade union opinions, ethnic origin, health and sexual tendencies.

5.2.1.2. Cookies in the GDPR

5.2.1.2.1. Duty of information and prior consent

The GDPR established prior consent for cookies, meaning that operators must obtain the informed consent of Internet users after giving them clear and precise information before they can install cookies on their computers.

Two exceptions remain: prior consent for the installation of cookies is not required when:

– cookies are intended solely to enable or facilitate electronic communication;

– cookies "that are strictly necessary for the provision of a service expressly requested by the Internet user", such as cookies that allow the creation of shopping carts on e-commerce sites.

The modalities of prior consent of the Internet user

The main problem is that of the fluidity of navigation, which would be very limited if consent were to be strictly required. The inconveniences are not negligible for both Internet users and operators. In France, debates on this have emphasized the indispensable nature of increased transparency: in-depth information on the purposes, nature of the data collected and the recipients, with a specific heading at all times, in clear and understandable language.

French law follows a proposal set out in point 66 of the preamble[9] by stating that the consent of the Internet user may come from appropriate parameters of his or her connection device or any other device under his or her control.

There are no further details on how to obtain consent. Differences of interpretation are evident within the European Union, even if the G29[10] opted for the "opt-in".

5.2.1.2.2. Privacy regulation: cookies in the new "privacy and electronic communications" regulation

As stated in the pre-project impact assessment, "the end user is being asked to accept tracking cookies without knowing what they are and, in some cases, is even being asked to accept cookies without consent. This rule is both too inclusive, as it also covers practices that do not infringe on privacy, and too exclusive, as it does not expressly cover certain tracking techniques (digital fingerprinting) that do not necessarily involve accessing or storing data in the device. Finally, its application can be costly for companies."

The proposed regulation implies a strengthening of the duty to inform and of the requirement of consent. The burden of proof for the collection of consent lies with the data controller, withdrawal of consent should be as easy as giving consent, and the absence of consent can only prevent access to the service if the data processing concerned is necessary for the operation of the service. Above all, the request for consent must be presented to the person concerned in a distinct, easily accessible form, not lending itself to problems of comprehension nor to imprecisions that are difficult to reconcile with the philosophy of law; simple and clear terms will be used subject to unenforceability. For this reason, sibylline, incomplete consent applications may be declared unenforceable by the judges. As things currently stand, legal experts have not decided on the possibility of imposing a sanction with respect to unenforceability.

The proposed Privacy Policy states that where technically feasible, the user's consent will be expressed through a positive action on their part: using technical means, such as configuring the web browser, can be user-friendly.

---

9 Article 32II of the French ordinance 2011-1012.

10 Succeeded by the European Data Protection Committee.

The purpose of consent expressed through technical means is to reduce the "spillover" effect of consent requests to users that is implied by the current widespread use of cookies, trackers and various other tracking techniques.

Software that enables electronic communications[11] is now set up in such a way that user tracking and storage of information on the terminal is prohibited.

During set-up or initial use

When installing or using the software for the first time, the user is informed of the privacy settings that are provided by default up to that point and the possibility of changing these settings, that is, the possibility of changing or confirming the privacy settings provided by default by confirming the setting.

While using the browser

While using the browser, the parameters that are offered to the user must be easily accessible so that the user is able to modify them at any time and be able to express specific consent, even after installation. The parameters must also be presented in such a way as to enable the user to make an informed decision. The information provided must not have the effect of dissuading the user from selecting higher privacy settings than those provided by default by the browser or software. In particular, the user will be informed of the risks involved in tracing information from terminals.

Not only should there be default settings, but also providers of software enabling electronic communications will be required to provide the user with sufficiently detailed options for the various categories of purposes for which tracker cookies may be deposited on a terminal.

The various options offered to the user must include at least the following purposes: tracking for commercial or non-commercial direct marketing purposes[12], tracking for the purpose of personalizing the content offered, tracking for analysis purposes, tracking of location data and transfer of personal data to third parties.

According to the European Parliament, the implementation of such technical means that allow the user to give his or her consent using transparent and user-friendly parameters should allow the prohibition of cookie walls on electronic communications services.

---

11 See web browsers or communication applications.
12 Behavioral advertising.

The user must accept the cookies deposited on his or her terminal in order to continue his or her use of an online communications service, whether or not he or she has paid to access this service. Indeed, the European Parliament considers that such a practice does not allow the user to control his or her personal information and privacy, nor to be properly informed about his or her rights since he or she has no real choice if he or she wants to continue the consultation. Moreover, consent shall be re-requested every 6 months "for as long as the processing continues".

It is possible for each user to prohibit cookies, and therefore third-party cookies, *a priori*, from his or her browser settings.

Moreover, "device fingerprinting" is also envisaged, just as Recital 20 of the future regulation mentions "digital screenshots". Just like pixels, spyware will have to be prohibited without the user's consent.

The requirement for default settings, which stems from the "Privacy by design" principle in the GDPR, was not part of the original proposal. The original proposal only provided for a "do not track" option, whereby the user could, once the software, browser or application was installed on their terminal, select the types of cookies that they would allow or not allow for all future browsing based on the source of the cookie.

While the European Commission proposed a parameter setting option, the European Parliament created a default setting obligation. Where the Commission differentiated between them in terms of the origin of the cookie, the Parliament differentiated between them in terms of the purpose of the cookie.

The "do not track" principle does not contradict the "Privacy by design" principle, which has not given the user the power to decide what happens to their data; it is merely a question of ensuring that digital tools structurally respect their choices. Furthermore, the "do not track" principle corresponds to the requirement of strict necessity of collecting identifying data.

In order to remedy the malfunctions, the European Commission has therefore proposed to centralize users' consent by using the privacy settings of their Internet browser. According to the Commission, this measure, which would be mandatory, would avoid a compliance cost that would be too costly for website publishers. As far as the user is concerned, the use of privacy settings from his or her browser is a significant gain in time and control. Browser settings should offer a choice between different levels of privacy, similar to what Internet Explorer offers.

Nevertheless, the concentration of browser roles that define the parameters of confidentiality, and also of the issuer of cookies, of advertising management within a single legal entity such as Google, is at the origin of debates, the virulence of which is growing insofar as this issue is far from neutral.

It is obvious that the problems of online tracking and advertising are at the heart of discussions between economists and lawyers. The current version of Apple's Safari browser includes an anti-tracking system. This tracking blocker is based on a *deep learning*[13] system that analyzes the Internet user's browsing habits and determines which cookies should be blocked and which should not. Concerns have been raised about the potential abuse of this dominant position, as large online advertisers such as Google and Facebook go from strength to strength.

By continuing to browse the site, the Internet user accepts the use of cookies for audience measurement and advertising targeting purposes. This is a more demanding process than validation via a cookie banner, which appears as soon as you visit a website's homepage. Thus, the Internet user can set his or her browser to prohibit by default certain categories of cookies by sorting between cookies perceived as intrusive or tolerable.

This is coupled with a novelty factor, which obliges publishers of commercially available software that enables electronic communications, including the retrieval and presentation of information on the Internet, to offer users the ability to prevent third parties from storing information on their terminal equipment or processing information already stored on the terminal. This primarily concerns browsers that are required to provide the user with a choice at the time of installation of the software such as "block all trackers", "accept all trackers" or "choose on a case-by-case basis".

The Commission is of the view that the choice to block all trackers at a browser level "does not deprive website operators of the possibility of obtaining consent by sending individual requests to end-users and thus maintaining their current business model".

5.2.1.3. *The position of publishers*

This development is causing concern among online newspaper publishers who have a great need for reader-generated data to improve their editorial offerings and

---

13 Also called in-depth learning.

services. In October 2017, they wrote an open letter, which was signed by the vast majority of press unions in France.

Categories of professionals in the field of publishing and online advertising have expressed reservations: "We remain mobilized at the French and European level to defend our industry," said the French branch of the IAB[14] in its October 2017 contribution.

Online publishers have emphasized the significant economic potential that could harm players in the event that users get a massive choice of privacy settings on their browsers. As a result, advertisements will no longer be targetable, and advertisers' revenues will likely be reduced.

In a press release signed by some 30 press publishers, including well-known general-interest magazines such as *Der Spiegel*, *The Financial Times*, *Le Monde* and *Libération*, a change in the project was called for. Indeed, according to the communiqué, "the number of readers is higher than ever" and this favorable outcome is explained by the financing of journalists through advertising. They are worried about the multinationals or American companies that control the browser market. There is a globalized economic struggle, since Facebook and Google monopolized the vast majority of global advertising spending in 2017. This may contribute to a distortion of competition.

The dominant position of the major data players may be strengthened. If an Internet user decides to accept, once and for all, or refuse cookies, the Internet user who refuses would make himself or herself invisible from the sites, and the latter would be deprived, in the case of start-ups, or even SMEs, of the personal information valued thanks to targeted advertising. Browsers or interfaces owned by large multinationals or the most influential technological players would be likely to continue to impose their conditions of use on Internet users, since their position is then unavoidable.

The main professional organizations of the French press[15] insist on the risks that the removal of cookies would constitute for the written press, but also, contrary to appearances, for consumers/Internet users.

---

14 Interactive Advertising Bureau.
15 SPQN, UPREG, SEPM, FNPS, SPHR.

5.2.1.3.1. The position of Pierre Chappaz

"By making cookies disappear, we would inexorably reduce the advertising market to only those players on the Web who collect data without using cookies," insisted Pierre Chappaz, executive chairman of Teads in a comment published by *Les Échos*. However, it is hardly possible to view Pierre Chappaz as a defender of the pluralism of freedom of information. Indeed, Pierre Chappaz, with Teads, has become a leading figure in online video advertising. In 2017, Teads was bought by Patrick Drahi's Altice. This agreement between two French entrepreneurs based in Geneva corresponded to a vision that would present, for Pierre Chappaz, an international alternative to online advertising, compared to Facebook or YouTube. Of course, Altice has a large amount of data, but it is not obvious that it is an alternative to Facebook or YouTube.

5.2.1.3.2. Professional organizations

The professional organizations of the European press, such as the European Publishers' Council and the European Magazine Media Association, are joined by other digital players, such as the operator Orange, Criteo, the German online sales group Zalando and professional organizations of start-ups, such as France Digitale and the German company Deutsche Startups.

Jean-David Chamboredon, co-president of France Digitale, states: "We risk leaving the complete monopoly to a few players, who will in any case manage to capture the data"; "there will be the small ones who will have very little data and the right to do nothing"[16]; "and the big ones who will have all the data, will be able to do everything". This last sentence refers to Facebook and Google[17]. As these two companies are American, this would mean that almost all targeted advertising would be the prerogative of American commercial companies.

Conversely, consumer associations such as BEUC[18] support the position of the European Parliament.

5.2.2. *Metadata and the "Privacy" bill*

5.2.2.1. *Anonymization of data*

Without the Internet user's authorization, metadata of a very private nature will have to be anonymized or deleted by the entity that possesses it, except in certain specific cases, such as invoicing.

---

16 In the area of targeted advertising.

17 Source: *Observatoire français de l'e-pub*.

18 The European Consumer Organisation.

This corresponds to the progressive awareness of the importance of metadata in economic life. However, companies want their competitiveness to be taken into account.

In a compromise of April 2018, the Bulgarian presidency proposed that companies could process metadata without consent "for network optimization and management" or "for statistical counting at the request of an authority". The text was to be considered by the Council's Telecom Working Group on April 19, 2018.

In the European Parliament, the S&D group wanted the text to provide greater protection for communications. The field mainly concerns hosting companies, electronic communications operators, Internet service providers, and also professionals who offer, including as an accessory and free of charge, public access to a communications network, who must themselves comply with the obligatory nature of the collection[19].

Note that the term metadata is rarely used in legal texts: "technical data", "connection data", "traffic data" and "location data" are preferred. Nevertheless, it is easy to distinguish between metadata and correspondence when it comes to electronic correspondence. Correspondence is the content of the correspondence, or the messages. Metadata corresponds to the signs present that are not part of the content of the correspondence.

5.2.2.2. *Metadata collection*

The metadata of all connected devices and terminals is collected and stored by Internet and telecommunications professionals for a wide variety of purposes:

– the invoicing of the services that professionals render to their clients;

– the security of the information systems of these same professionals;

– information essential for the investigation, establishment or prosecution of criminal offences. In addition, the prosecution of offences relating to illegal downloading, pursuant to the Hadopi law[20].

Within the bill, "privacy" covers "the processing of electronic communications data carried out in connection with the provision and use of electronic communications services in the Union and information related to end-users' terminal equipment".

---

19 Example: Wi-Fi network of hotels.

20 Law No. 2009-669 of June 12, 2009 promoting the dissemination and protection of creation on the Internet, supplemented by Law No. 2009-1311 relating to the criminal protection of literary and artistic property on the Internet.

This wording has been changed by the Council of the European Union. Electronic communications data means content exchanged by means of electronic communications, in particular in the form of text, voice, video documents and sound. The actors are also the OTT[21] operators, which allow communication via the Internet without the intervention of a traditional network operator. This includes Messenger and WhatsApp.

5.2.2.3. *Electronic communications services*

They apply not only to Internet access services and services consisting wholly and partly of the transmission of signals, but also to interpersonal communications services, whether or not based on numbering, such as voice over IP, online messaging services and Web-based email services[22].

5.2.2.4. *Machine to machine*

Devices are increasingly communicating with electronic communications networks. The implementation of machine-to-machine communications is also an electronic communications service. Machine-to-machine communication combines information and communication technologies with so-called intelligent objects, with the aim of providing the means to interact without human intervention with the information system. The machine to machine allows the miniaturization of hardware, chips, sensors, the enrichment of communication capabilities (proximity or remote, self-organized networks), the improvement of energy autonomy, the storage capacity of information, and the provision for industrialists of software infrastructure that allow devices from different suppliers to receive the same software or service[23].

The machine to machine is used in particular in the automotive[24], waste treatment and food industries.

The French positions are rather favorable with regard to the "Privacy" bill.

Isabelle Falque-Pierrotin, who has had a prestigious career when it comes to the Internet[25], declared on May 28, 2017 that the "Privacy" bill "corresponded to the end of the blank check on data". She believed that this regulation was capable of

---

21 Over the top.

22 Considering 173 of the GDPR.

23 Examples: Oracle, MicroEJ, STMicroelectronics, with Java technologies in electronic devices and gateways.

24 Detectors for parking spaces, autonomous cars.

25 She chaired the Conseil d'Etat's study "Internet and digital networks" (July 2, 1998), then chaired the Internet rights forum, the CNIL and the G29.

harmonizing the fundamental rights of citizens in their private lives with certain aspirations of the major Internet companies. She saw, not a relationship of power, but a balance. The Department of Justice also wanted to strengthen the protection of privacy. On the contrary, the Minister of Culture at the time, Françoise Nyssen, without doubt quite sensitive to criticism from online advertisers, believed that publishers may no longer be able to collect data on the habits and tastes of Internet readers and that this may weaken their business model.

The association for the defense of online freedoms, La Quadrature du Net[26], was a fastidious and cautious observer. It regretted "the disappearance of class actions, the exemption of metadata generated outside of communications and the possibility of refusing access to a site if an advertising blocker is detected"[27].

In Germany, the publishers' campaign was just as virulent as in France. The regulatory authorities were convinced that an agreement was not possible before the summer of 2018 and were betting on a two-year implementation period.

The European Parliament's rapporteur at the time, Birgit Sippel, did not allow herself to be influenced by the "reluctance to change" on the part of German publishers. She pointed out that "following users without their consent is prohibited" according to the European legislation in force at the time.

She also believed that a relative balance had been struck between GAFA and citizens. The "Privacy" bill was not adopted under the Bulgarian presidency.

A new version of "Privacy" was published online. The Romanian Presidency of the Council reviewed the text after the final meetings of the telecom working group in February 2019. The definition of data processing had been extended to non-personal data[28]. States could impose the retention of data for the general interest for a limited period of time[29]. The text entrusts the control of processing to the data protection authorities[30] and their European Committee[31]. Finally, operating systems are encouraged, alongside web browsers, to facilitate the management of cookies[32]. This version was discussed on February 26, 2019 in a telecom group.

At the request of the Belgian data protection authority, the grouping of European authorities examined the prerogatives of the latter regarding processing in the field

---

26 Founded in 2008.
27 January 13, 2017.
28 Article 4-2.
29 Article 11.
30 Article 18.
31 Article 19.
32 Recital 20 a.

of the GDPR and "Privacy" and the possibility that the same processing falls under both the *lex generalis* and the *lex specialis*. The EDPB specifies when the GDPR and "Privacy" do not apply and where both apply. In a situation where both texts are concerned, the data protection authority may be competent if the Member State has given it this power in the transposition text. The "Privacy" bill was on the agenda of the Telecom Council of June 8, 2019, where ministers were invited to express their views on the proposals of the Bulgarian presidency. The lobbies Etno, GSMA and Cable Europe wrote to them to ask for support for "an innovative use of metadata". In particular, they wanted subsequent processing of metadata to be possible without the consent of the user, when the purpose of the processing is compatible with that of the initial collection. Parliament, for its part, refused. In fact, the economic, political and legal dimensions make it difficult to reach a point of balance.

5.3. Cloud computing

5.3.1. *Definition*

Cloud computing involves the use of remote computer servers[33] over a network, most often the Internet, to store or use data. Cloud computing is very flexible: it is possible to manage one's own server or to use remote applications.

5.3.1.1. *The main services*

The main services are:

– SaaS (Software as a Service);

– PaaS (Platform as a Service);

– IaaS (Infrastructure as a Service).

Operating systems, infrastructure software and application software either fall under the responsibility of the supplier or under the responsibility of the customer. Cloud computing takes advantage of increased server power and lower storage costs.

Amazon, Citrix, Google, HP, IBM, Intel, Microsoft, SalesForce and Sidetrade are among the largest companies in the industry.

5.3.1.2. *Contractual aspects*

The contractual aspects have given rise to many legal studies: companies contract the cloud computing services they purchase. The clauses focus in particular

---

33 They are becoming increasingly frequent.

on data confidentiality, traceability of operations and quality of services. From a regulatory point of view, it is the client company that is legally responsible and the supplier is treated as a subcontractor.

5.3.1.3. *Practical advice from the CNIL*

In France, the CNIL publishes practical advice and model contractual clauses that are often inserted in cloud computing service contracts.

The development of cloud computing is driving the growth of data centers or data processing centers. Savings are made, as the cost is based on the length of time the service is used and requires no prior investment.

The disadvantages are primarily environmental, as cloud computing contributes to global warming. They are also related to security, since the Cloud exposes users to risks of cyber-attacks and breaches of confidentiality. Finally, they raise the question of location. The laws in force apply, but for which server, which data center and, above all, which country[34]?

For Richard Stallman, the founder of the GNU Project, cloud computing "is a trap" because users lose control of their applications. It is mostly a fad, as Larry Ellison, founder of Oracle, points out. As for Steve Wozniak, co-founder of Apple, he insists on data outsourcing and its risks.

File sales, every thousandth of a second, are both a source of profit and tracking. The circulation and transfer of files generally respect, as far as the countries of the European Union are concerned, the rules of mutualized respect. However, this proved impossible with the United States.

5.3.2. *The Safe Harbor Principles agreement*

The Safe Harbor Principles agreement was a compromise between the American philosophy of data protection and the philosophy of Directive 95/46. Regulation in the United States was the responsibility of the Federal Trade Commission and criticism was growing in Europe. The agreement was invalidated by the European Court of Justice on October 6, 2015[35].

---

34 Rogier, C. (2010). Enjeux juridiques du *Cloud Computing* [Online]. *OCTO*, September. Available at: http://blog.octo.com/cloud-computing-risques-juridiques.

43 The Schrems decision, which concluded that the Safe Harbor Principles do not provide adequate data protection.

5.3.3. *Privacy Shields*

The Privacy Shields or data protection shield between the United States and the European Union is the successor to the Safe Harbor Principles. It is based on self-certification. It came into force on July 12, 2016 and has been adopted by the states of the European Union[36].

This text takes the form of provisions in the United States and a commitment at the European Union level. Reservations have been expressed in France because organizations that defend individual and collective freedoms consider that the text is not sufficiently protective. The National Digital Council has partly associated itself with these criticisms.

5.3.4. *Two models*

5.3.4.1. *The EU model*

For a long time, the European Union seemed to embody a certain conception of personal data protection, while the United States seemed to embody the markets and be hardly concerned about the protection of personal data. The ACLU has often expressed concern about this.

5.3.4.2. *The California CCPA*

However, there has been an evolution in some states, in particular California, where the California Consumer Privacy Act came into effect on January 1, 2020, giving Californians some control over their personal data.

Companies that possess personal data on more than 50,000 individuals or have revenues in excess of $25 million and derive more than 50% of their annual revenues from the sale of personal information of California residents must inform users about the personal data they collect about them and how it is used.

This only concerns the most important companies. SMEs and VSEs in California are not concerned.

5.3.4.2.1. The definition of sales in the CCPA

Selling is defined by the CCPA as "selling, renting, leasing, publishing, disclosing, disseminating, making available, transferring, or otherwise communicating orally, in writing, electronically or otherwise, personal information

---

36 With the exception of Austria, Croatia, Slovenia and Bulgaria.

of a consumer by the business to another business or third party for monetary consideration or other benefit"[37].

When a company shares a common brand[38] with another company that must comply with the CCPA, the other company has the same obligations as the CCPA.

Under the CCPA, California residents[39] are entitled to exercise the right to opt out of the sale of their data to third parties, the right to request disclosure of data already collected, and the right to request deletion of data collected.

California residents have a right to information and the right to equal services and prices. Under no circumstances shall they be discriminated against in the exercise of their rights.

5.3.4.2.2. Violation of CCPA rules

Failure to comply with the CCPA may result in fines of $7,500 per violation and $750 per affected user for damages.

The authority to enforce the CCPA rests with the California Attorney General's Office, which is expected to specify the terms of enforcement in July 2020. However, the interim period between January and July 2020 is not a closed period: companies have been exposed to civil lawsuits regarding the collection and sale of data since January 1, 2020.

If a company corresponds to one of the three thresholds mentioned above, and has an Internet domain, certain changes shall be made to the website.

The duty to inform

The website informs its users before or at the time of data collection of the categories of personal information it collects and for what purposes and interests. In addition, the website is required to include a "do not sell my personal information" link that users can use to remove their sales data from third parties.

Minors

When a website has minors under the age of 16 years[40] among its users, their prior or positive consent[41] must be obtained before it is possible to sell or disclose

---

37 1798.140.t1.

38 Common name, service mark, trademark.

39 Or consumers.

40 The age of the driver's license in the United States.

41 Opt-in.

their personal data to third parties. If the minor is under 13 years of age, consent is required from the parent or legal guardian.

Confidentiality

A company shall update the privacy policy on its website to include a description of the rights of the resident-consumer and how to exercise those rights. The privacy policy also requires the company to update an annual list of the categories of personal information that the company collects, sells and discloses.

If the company receives a request from a resident-consumer requesting the communication of personal information collected within the last 12 months[42], the company is prohibited from discriminating on the grounds of the consumer's choice to exercise his or her right to withdraw, request communication or delete the data.

The CCPA definition of personal data

Personal information is defined by the CCPA as "information that identifies, relates to, describes, can reasonably be associated with, or could reasonably be expected to relate directly or indirectly to a consumer or household"[43].

Personal information, according to the CCPA, includes direct identifiers[44], unique identifiers, such as cookies, IP addresses and account names, biometric data, such as face or voice recordings[45], geolocation data (such as location history), Internet activity (such as browsing history, search history, data about interaction on a web page or application), and sensitive information: health data, personal characteristics, behavior, religious or political beliefs, sexual preferences, employment or education data, financial and medical information.

Personal information also includes data that, by inference, can lead to the identification of an individual or household. As in Europe, the notion of identification is at the heart of the definition, and sensitive information is almost identical to sensitive data.

Aggregated and anonymous data are not covered by the CCPA unless they have the possibility of being re-identified. This means that data that is not in itself personal information is likely to become personal information under the CCPA if it can be used by inference or in combination with other data to identify an individual or household.

---

42 With the sources, the commercial objectives.

43 1798.140.o1.

44 Name, pseudonym, mailing address, social security numbers.

45 In biometrics, the CCPA focuses on voice recognition and facial recognition.

Cookies in the CCPA

Cookies or other tracking technologies on websites are classified as unique identifiers that are personal information according to the CCPA. This is especially important because cookies are one of the most widely used technologies used by websites worldwide to collect personal information about individual users.

Proprietary cookies are set by the website itself. They often collect anonymous data for its essential functions which are deleted as soon as the user closes the browser.

Third-party cookies are set by technology companies and social networking platforms and often collect a great deal of personal, sometimes sensitive, information about consumers that can be kept for up to 100 years.

Data collected on a website through cookies that may not constitute personal information *per se*[46], but by inference or combination with other data for the purpose of identifying and connecting devices, creating profiles and delivering personalized advertisements may ultimately be considered information under the CCPA.

If a company meets one of the CCPA's three compliance thresholds, the company is responsible for all forms of personal information that is collected about California residents through website cookies. Consumers may request disclosure of their relevant personal information on the website within the last 12 months and request that their data be deleted.

With the CCPA, it is possible to find out what data the website collects, how it is collected and for what purposes, as well as the third parties with whom the site shares this data.

Cookiebot[47] is a world-class consent management platform that ensures compliance with the European GDPR and the CCPA. It is a technology that conducts extensive scans of websites for all cookies and trackers and automatically controls them, so that end-users can be sure they know what personal information is being collected and which third parties have access to it.

It also allows companies to be CCPA compliant by putting in place the "do not sell my personal information" link with the cookie statement.

The CCPA was voted on in June 2018, shortly after the GDPR came into effect. The question arises as to whether the CCPA can serve as a legal reference for other

---

46 Such as analysis data made anonymous.
47 www.cookiebot.com/fr.

US states. Personal data security is a growing concern with cyber-attacks and the development of artificial intelligence.

On the contrary, in spite of the duty to inform and prior consent, users that are Internet users continue to be tracked, including by cookies.

This ambivalence will increase with the rise of connected devices, which will play an eminent role in the years to come. These machines, according to Jacques Ellul's definition, are at the heart of economic and legal life.

6

Cybersecurity and Privacy

The term cybersecurity is a neologism that refers to the role of laws, policies, tools, devices, concepts, security mechanisms, risk management, training, best practices and technologies that are used to protect people and the tangible and intangible IT assets – directly or indirectly connected to a network – of States and organizations. Its objectives are availability, integrity and authenticity.

The risks brought about by the omnipresence of information and communication technologies, and their interconnection and data exchange capacities, have led to cybersecurity being considered a discipline.

Cybersecurity, which concerns the digital security and sovereignty of nation-states, includes economic, strategic and political issues that go far beyond the security of information systems. It applies to business computing, industrial computing, embedded computing and smart objects. It takes into account economic, social, legal, technical, diplomatic and military aspects and is concerned with long-term visions.

The International Telecommunication Union has developed a global cybersecurity index[1]. The GCI assesses countries' commitment to cybersecurity by domain.

Reaction and decision cycles are short. ISACA encourages the use of a simple process, developed by NIST[2], to identify threats, detect attacks, be able to respond to them and then return to normal operations. It is mandatory to report attacks. ISACA places this process within the framework of a methodology based on risk analysis to

---

1 Global Cybersecurity Index (GCI); www.itu.int/en/ITU-D/Cybersecurity/pages/GCI.aspx.

2 *Framework for Improvising Critical Infrastructure Cybersecurity.* www.nist.gov/cyber.

identify information assets, define security objectives and the most effective fight against risks. The aim is to manage cyber-attacks in real time, react and give orders for swift action.

An ISOC[3] is a component of the implementation of cybersecurity policies in public and private organizations. To be reliable, an ISOC manages the components of an information system and is able to detect the characteristics of a cyber-attack and then adapt the best reactivity of the components of the information system.

Currently, cybersecurity is benefiting from research in the areas of Big Data and artificial intelligence. It concerns not only cybersecurity itself and cryptology but also mobility, PNR and smart cities.

6.1. Cybersecurity itself

Faced with the increasing dangers, regulation is international, with each country having a State responsible for cyber defense and guarantor of cybersecurity.

6.1.1. *Cybersecurity in the United States*

For the United States, the 2013 and 2015 guidelines and the creation of a cybersecurity agency, the CTIIC, are noteworthy. The US Department of Defense is updating its cyber strategy, which in 2019 included the provision of artificial intelligence and the development of cybersecurity skills. The United States has identified five priorities:

– protect US infrastructure;

– improve the ability of the United States to identify cyber-attacks;

– develop international partnerships to promote freedom on the Internet;

– secure the networks of the different states by defining clear and measurable objectives, and hold federal agencies accountable for achieving the objectives;

– educate with a view to having an expert workforce aware of cybersecurity issues.

The CISA Directive, which specifically creates a legal framework to encourage the exchange of information between private companies and the federal government regarding cyber threats and defense mechanisms, was signed into law by Barack Obama on December 18, 2015. It is effective until September 30, 2025:

---

3 Information Security Operations Center.

– in early 2016, Barack Obama strengthened these initial initiatives with a national cybersecurity action plan. This plan, known as the CNAP, aims to better protect privacy and public safety, improve economic security in the digital environment and increase the awareness and protection of stakeholders. CNAP had a budget of US$19 billion in 2017;

– in February 2016, the US Department of Homeland Security published a benchmark for assessing the maturity of cyber surveillance organizations[4]. Cybersecurity was a priority for Donald Trump. On November 2, 2017, a Shield Act strengthened security in New York State. In June 2019, Trump launched a cyber-attack against Iranian missile launch systems and an Iranian spy ring.

The cybersecurity repository developed by NIST in 2013 could be extended to the Internet of Things.

6.1.2. *Cybersecurity in China*

In China, on November 7, 2016, the Chinese National People's Congress passed its first cybersecurity law. This law came into force on June 1, 2017. It implements the concept of national sovereignty in cyberspace.

The Cybersecurity Act is designed to maintain IT security. It is a matter of managing cyber-attacks in real time, reacting and issuing orders so that rapid computer measures can be taken to safeguard national security and public interests, protect citizens' rights and personal data and promote the healthy development of information technologies.

This law on cybersecurity provides a legal framework for defining the levels of security offered by computer networks and their components. For the geolocation of data in China, the focus is on operators of vital importance. Lastly, it insists on the definition of IT security standards that are more rigorous than the previously recognized standards.

6.1.3. *Cybersecurity in Japan*

Japan took an early interest in cybersecurity. As early as 2010, Japan wanted to give more responsibility to its National Information Security Center[5] so that this

---

4 EU coordinated risk assessment of 5G network security [Online]. Available at: Eeas.europa.eu/delegations/united-states-america/68637/eu-coordinated-risk-assesment-5g-network-security_me.
5 NISC.

entity would be able to coordinate all operational cybersecurity actions of national interest, which became effective with the second version of the "Cybersecurity Strategic Plan" published in September 2015[6]. For this reason, the NISC was renamed the National Cybersecurity Strategy and Incident Preparedness Center. This version of the "Cybersecurity Strategic Plan" anticipated, among other things, the problem of the massive use of the Internet of Things in the run-up to the 2020 Olympic Games. The Japanese government wants to expand its cooperation in the field of cybersecurity within the Asia-Pacific region, with North America in the context of Japan–US agreements and with most Western states.

6.1.4. *Cybersecurity and the European Union*

Within the framework of the European Union, a draft directive on the security of networks and information systems of the European Parliament and the European Council was the subject of a consultation in 2013[7]. These measures were intended to ensure a common high level of network and information security in the Union, which would impose a common minimum level of security for digital technologies, networks and services in all Member States. The text also proposed to oblige certain companies and organizations to report major computer security incidents which they fall victim to. The European Union's cybersecurity strategy thus defines the approach adopted by the European Union to best prevent and respond to computer attacks and disruptions. It looks at actions to increase the cyber-resilience of computer systems, to reduce cybercrime and to strengthen the European Union's cybersecurity and cyber defense policy at an international level.

The International Cybersecurity Forum is part of a process of reflection and exchange aimed at promoting a European vision of cybersecurity and strengthening the fight against cybercrime, a priority of the European Union, in the Stockholm Programme for 2010–2015.

The European Cybersecurity Organization (ECSO)[8] was created in June 2016 with the aim of providing assistance to projects that would develop and promote cybersecurity initiatives in Europe.

In July 2016, the European Parliament and the Council of the European Union adopted the Directive on the Security of Networks and Information Systems, known as the NIS Directive. This directive provides for the strengthening of national cybersecurity capabilities; the establishment of a framework for voluntary

---

6 Cybersecurity Strategy Plan (September 4, 2015).

7 Reference SWD 2013-31 and 32.

8 European Cybersecurity Organisation.

cooperation between States; the strengthening by each State of the cybersecurity of so-called essential service operators (ESOs) and the establishment of common European rules on cybersecurity for digital service providers in the areas of cloud computing, search engines and online marketplaces. May 2018 was the transposition deadline for the NIS Directive. The NIS implementing regulation was published in the Official Journal of the European Union on January 30, 2018.

The legal component of cybersecurity has been strengthened by the GDPR: on October 5, 2019, the members of the European Union, with the support of the European Commission and the European Union Agency for Cybersecurity, were due to publish a first report on the assessment of the risks linked to the arrival of fifth-generation mobile networks (5G).

6.1.5. *Cybersecurity in the United Kingdom*

On November 1, 2016, the United Kingdom published its 2016–2021 strategic plan on cybersecurity. The plan is based on three objectives:

– defend the United Kingdom against threats and be able to respond effectively by ensuring that private companies and the public sector have an appropriate level of knowledge and the ability to protect themselves;

– deter potential attackers, from cyber-attack detection to criminal prosecution;

– develop a business sector around cybersecurity with special efforts dedicated to research and development.

These objectives are complemented by strengthened international cooperation. This strategic plan is the subject of an announced investment to the tune of £1.9 billion. Its implementation is mainly based on a government agency, the National Cyber Security Centre, created in October 2016.

The assessment of government measures published in December 2016 in the United Kingdom confirmed that the GDPR would serve to improve the management of cybersecurity risks.

6.1.6. *Cybersecurity in France*

In France, Jean-Marc Ayrault, then head of government, declared on February 21, 2014: cybersecurity "is a matter of national interest that concerns all citizens, all French people, and that is why it is important that the government is fully committed". On July 6, 2015, Axelle Lemaire, then Secretary of State for Digital Technology, stated: "The government will present a comprehensive national strategy on cybersecurity at the beginning of the new school year." As planned, Manuel Valls, successor of Jean-Marc Ayrault at the head of the government, presented this national strategy for digital security on October 16, 2015[9], which was to be based on training and international cooperation (proposal to draw up a roadmap for Europe's digital strategic autonomy; strengthened participation of France in multilateral negotiations on cybersecurity within the UN and the OSCE)[10].

This strategy, drawn up in conjunction with all the ministries, sets out the objectives to be achieved and the resulting directions to be taken in order to strengthen the security and defense of critical infrastructures and support the digital transition by defining the human, technical and operational factors that are essential to boost innovation, economic development and the confidence of the French people in digital technology.

Finally, the implementation of a system likely to assist victims of cyber malevolence throughout the country, announced in 2015, was confirmed in early 2017 by the ANSSI.

This device provides, via a digital platform called ACYMA (Actions against Cyber Surveillance), a help desk for filing a complaint and referral to local actors who can provide technical assistance best suited to the victim's situation[11].

Also in France, Article 15 of the Military Programming Act for 2014–2019 details the obligations that the Prime Minister may impose on operators of vital importance (OVIs) in terms of securing their network, qualifying their detection systems, providing information on attacks they may suffer and submitting to controls.

It also provides for the criminal penalties applicable in the event of non-compliance with these obligations. The fact that these obligations are dealt with in the Military Programming Law simply shows that national defense and security must be dealt with comprehensively and consistently.

---

9 www.ssi.gouv.fr/actualite:la-strategie-nationale-pour-la-securite-du-numerique-une-reponse-aux-nouveaux-enjeux-des-usages-numeriques/-digital-security-a-response-to-new-digital-use-issues/.

10 Organization for Security and Cooperation in Europe.

11 ANSSI (2017). Le dispositif national d'assistance aux victimes ACYMA se dévoile au FIC. Press release.

Article 22 of this law requires OVIs to set up computer attack detection equipment and to operate it by ANSSI-qualified service providers or by other State services designated by the Prime Minister.

Actually, cybersecurity is one of the 12 areas of the Vigipirate plan, which concerns ANSSI, OVIs, their subcontractors and administrations. Local authorities and non-OVI operators are encouraged to implement the Vigipirate plan, consistent with overall security. Permanent security objectives common to all are also considered conditions for the successful implementation of the Vigipirate plan[12].

Among the many associations active in France in the field of cybersecurity, it is worth mentioning the Alliance pour la Confiance Numérique[13], Tech in France (software company) and Hexatrust[14], an association that brings together small and medium-sized IT publishing and integration companies. These three associations are members of the FIEEC, which ensures that their respective work is linked together.

A "France Cybersécurity" label has been created to raise user awareness, attest to the quality and functionalities of the labeled products and services, promote French cybersecurity solutions in France and internationally and increase their visibility and use to improve the level of protection for users.

In January 2018, the General Council for the Economy, Industry, Energy and Technology published a report on cyber-resilience to strengthen inter-ministerial governance and measure the level of maturity of organizations in this complementary and essential sector for cybersecurity.

6.1.7. *The dangers of cyber-attacks*

Cybersecurity specialists in every country fear cyber-attacks. A cyber-attack is an act based on malevolence against a computer device via a cyber network. A cyber-attack can come from a single individual[15], a group of hackers, or large organizations with geopolitical objectives.

Definitions are numerous; they vary according to countries, NGOs and international organizations.

---

12 Source Vigipirate, public part of the government plan, 2013.

13 ACN.

14 www.hexatrust.com.

15 Kevin Mitnick is very well known.

For A. Coustillère, Vice-Admiral in charge of French cyber defense, a cyber-attack is defined as "a deliberate, offensive or malicious action, carried out through cyberspace and intended to cause damage to information and the systems that process it, which may harm the activities for which it is used"[16].

The ANSSI defines a cyber-attack as "an attempt to attack information systems with malicious intent. Its objective may be to steal data (military, diplomatic or industrial secrets, personal banking data, etc.) or to destroy, damage or alter the normal functioning of information systems (including industrial systems)".

Danino prefers the term "cybernetic vandalism". Leman-Langlois, for his part, speaks of virtual vandalism.

Intentional and planned, cyber-attacks result "from the use of cyber capabilities to achieve objectives in or through cyberspace ... using networked computers to disrupt, disable, degrade, manipulate or destroy information in the target information system". It is, in fact, one of the methods used to weaken, paralyze, corrupt or destroy a target that is totally or partially dependent on the cybersphere.

According to N. Ténèze, the term cyber-attack can be confusing. Indeed, online attacks reduce the scope of reflection. Cybernetics is a portmanteau integrating cyber (governance according to the Greek root), cyber (encrypted in English), electronics and automatism.

According to N. Ténèze, attacks in the cybersphere are distributed as follows:

– DSAs (Denial of Service Attacks to neutralize an information system and make it inoperable);

– cyber espionage;

– cyberbullying;

– cyber fraud (e.g. falsification of official documents);

– cyber whistleblowing;

– cyber-counterfeiting and the black market (online purchase of illegal goods);

– criminal cyberfinance;

– cyber propaganda;

– cyber identity theft;

---

16 France, Défense nationale. Glossaire interarmées de terminologie opérationnelle. PIA-7.2.6.3_GIAT-0(2012), No. 001/DEF/CICDE/NP.

– cyber burglary (data theft);

– web defacement (changing the appearance of a site, blog, etc.).

In 1982, the US Secret Service allegedly voluntarily introduced a bug in the Canadian software used to manage a Trans-Siberian gas pipeline, causing an explosion in an uninhabited area.

In 2007, the first recorded cyber-attack targeting a state structure for several weeks, with sufficient means to saturate the targeted sites and cause a prolonged denial of service, came from Russian sites against Estonian government sites, as well as those of Estonian banks and newspapers. The majority of Estonian institutions had adopted a paperless, computerized and Internet-linked bureaucracy. This was a simple and effective attack, which consisted of connecting devices to a network and thus triggering saturation. This method was then often used for its discretion (traceability level) because it is directed by a single person controlling several computers infected by it.

Although NATO case law does not yet take such attacks into account, Estonian officials considered the organization and duration of the cyber-attack to be an act of war because the targeted structures were rendered inoperable.

In 2008, it was Georgia's turn[17]. Russia launched a classic military invasion, but just before doing so, cyber-attacks partially destroyed the infrastructure of the Georgian state.

In February 2016, the Central Bank of Bangladesh fell victim to hacking.

In 2017, on May 12 and 13, a cyber-attack paralyzed the computers of multinationals and public services in a hundred countries. This cyber-attack spread through emails with an Internet link that, once clicked, allowed the virus to be downloaded to the computer without the user's consent. The virus also spread through the SMB protocol, and then exploited the obsolete Windows XP system and all versions prior to Windows 10 that had not been updated, to release a payload of malware, which encrypted the data contained in the computer before demanding ransom from the user in exchange for the decoding keys. It is estimated that more than 230,000 computers in 150 states were infected with the virus.

At the same time, another cyber-attack[18] claimed hundreds of thousands of victims. It uses the resources of infected computers to create a virtual currency, Monero.

---

17 www.pagasa.net/georgie-recit-dune-cyber-attaque.
18 Named Adylkuzz and quieter than WannaCry.

On November 2, 2018, HSBC Bank revealed a security incident affecting an unspecified number of customers: "HSBC learned that unauthorized users accessed online accounts between October 4 and October 14, 2018."[19]

On January 4, 2019, the revelation of a major cyber-attack in Germany involved the online publication of confidential documents belonging to politicians.

At the end of January 2019, Airbus was the victim of an intrusion into the information system of its commercial aircraft branch. And the aircraft manufacturer is an expert in computer security!

In March 2019, Kapersky researchers reported that hundreds of thousands of Asus computers had fallen victim to malware[20].

In June 2019, the United States launched cyber-attacks against Iran.

Also in June 2019, the *New York Times* reported that the US government had stepped up cyber-attacks against the Russian power grid. According to the weekly newspaper: "The Trump administration, in the broader context of a digital cold war between Washington and Moscow, is using new powers to deploy IT tools more aggressively." Following this article, Donald Trump attacked the newspaper on social media, calling the article a "virtual act of treason".

6.1.8. *Two interesting cases*

6.1.8.1. *Case one: TV5 Monde (cyber-attack against an international French-language television channel)*

As a result of a cyber-attack against TV5 Monde, broadcasting of programs on an international French-language television channel TV5 Monde ceased, and messages of support for the Islamic State were published on its social networks.

TV5 Monde is an international French-language general-interest television channel created on January 2, 1984. It is owned by French, Belgian, Swiss, Canadian and Quebec public audiovisual companies. It is one of the three largest television networks in the world. It broadcasts 10 distinct regionalized signals, two thematic channels and two web TV channels.

---

19 Lecher, C. (2016). Denial-of-service attacks are shutting down major websites across the internet. *The Verge*, October 21.

20 Des centaines de milliers d'ordinateurs Asus victimes d'un piratage sophistiqué. *Le Monde,* March 26, 2019.

At the end of March 2015, the ANSSI informed TV5 Monde of a fraudulent use of one of its unprotected servers. The agency retrieved the server in question and the international channel started looking for a service provider for a security audit.

On April 8, 2015, TV5 Monde launched its thematic channel on the "French art of living", TV5 Monde Style HD, in the presence of the then Minister of Foreign Affairs, Laurent Fabius. The channel intended to broadcast programs on fashion, luxury goods, hotels, jewelry, gastronomy, oenology, design, garden design, architecture and cultural and historical heritage in the Middle East and Asia[21].

On April 8, at 8:50 p.m. CET, TV5 Monde's broadcasting infrastructure, fell prey to a cyber-attack. Both the main and backup infrastructure were neutralized in one fell swoop; however, the channel's CIO and his team believe it must be a technical failure. Minutes later, the email server is destroyed, confirming the existence of a cyber-attack. For the CIO, it was "a blistering attack that was probably very well prepared".

By way of damage control, the technical teams shut down the entire computer network around 10:00 pm, which interrupted the channel's television broadcasts around the world[22].

At the same time, TV5 Monde's Twitter and Facebook accounts were also hacked. Messages of support for the Islamic state in English, Arabic and French were published. A message questioned President of the Republic François Hollande for having committed "an unforgivable mistake" by having waged "a war that serves no purpose", compensated by the "January gifts to *Charlie Hebdo* and the Hyper Cacher"[23].

> Soldiers of France, stay away from the Islamic State! You have the chance to save your families, make the most of it.... In the name of Allah, the All-Merciful, the Most Forgiving, the CyberCaliphate continues to conduct its cyberjihad against the enemies of the Islamic State.[24]

---

21 Dupont-Calbo, J., Debes, F. (2015). TV5 Monde: Comment les pirates ont débranché la chaîne [Online]. Available at: https://www.lesechos.fr/2015/04/comment-les-pirates-ont-debranche-la-chaine-242308.

22 Alonso, P., Mathieu, L., Guiton, A. (2015). TV5 Monde débranchée par des pirates. *Libération*, April 9.

23 Attacks in January 2015 in the Parisian capital.

24 Excerpt from the message published on TV5 Monde's Facebook account on April 8, 2015.

Shortly before midnight, the technical teams managed to regain control of the social networks and send explanations to Internet users. The CEO of TV5 Monde, Yves Bigot, spoke of "an extremely powerful cyber-attack"[25].

On April 9, starting at 5:00 a.m. CET, the computer system and television signals were gradually relaunched with the participation of computer security engineers from ANSSI, which had been sent on site. Around midnight, the network's channels were restored but could only broadcast pre-recorded programs rather than its own productions.

6.1.8.1.1. The inquiry

On April 9, 2015, the Paris Public Prosecutor's Office referred the matter to the *Direction générale de la sécurité intérieure* (General Directorate of Internal Security) (DGSI), the *Sous-direction anti-terroriste* (Anti-Terrorism Sub-Directorate) (SDAT) and the *cyberpoliciers de la direction centrale de la Police judiciaire* (cyber-police officers of the Central Directorate of the Judicial Police) (DCPJ). The prosecutor retained "access, the fraudulent maintenance and obstruction of an automatic data processing system" and the "association of criminals in connection with a terrorist attack". ANSSI experts were in charge of analyzing the modus operandi of the cyber-attack.

On April 10, 2015, the Ministry of Defense announced that no confidential documents relating to the French army nor the identity of military personnel and their families had been broadcast during the TV5 Monde cyber-attack. On the other hand, 01net spoke of a "gigantic hodgepodge where one finds a jumble of CVs, screen shots, invitations to CHSCT[26] training sessions, invoices from town halls and photos".

On April 13, the authorities indicated that the attack could not have been carried out by a single individual but by a group of dozens of highly skilled hackers who may have been hired as mercenaries. For the ANSSI, the attack had been meticulously prepared over a long period of time. In its view, the hackers had been infiltrating TV5 Monde's networks for weeks. The investigation specified that the hackers used the technique of phishing by sending an email at the end of January to all the channel's journalists. Three of them replied, allowing the hackers to penetrate the network via a Trojan horse. Three weeks before the attack, a computer virus spread to several computers, taking advantage of a computer architecture that mixed the "business" part, which is the heart of the channel, with the office automation part, which is open to the outside world. The hackers would have created accounts

---

25 Ce que l'on sait de la cyberattaque sans précédent de TV5 Monde. *L'Obs*, April 9, 2015.

26 Committee for Hygiene, Safety and Working Conditions (*Comité d'Hygiène, de Sécurité et des Conditions de Travail*).

with administrator rights giving them the possibility to circulate wherever they wanted.

In June 2015, the media claimed that the investigation was moving away from the jihadist track, and towards a group of Russian hackers.

6.1.8.1.2. The consequences

The then Minister of the Interior Bernard Cazeneuve, the Minister of Culture Fleur Pellerin and the Minister of Foreign Affairs Laurent Fabius visited the headquarters of TV5 Monde on April 9 to lend their support to the editorial staff. Bernard Cazeneuve announced that an investigation had been opened and that the resources allocated to cybersecurity would be reinforced, with the creation of 500 additional jobs. Fleur Pellerin announced that she would bring together "all the managers of the major audiovisual media and perhaps even the print media" to ensure "the points of vulnerability or risk that may exist and how best to deal with them"[27]. Prime Minister Manuel Valls condemned "an unacceptable attack on the freedom of information and expression".

In July 2015, the channel's journalists were still not able to access the entire computer network: they could not use Wi-Fi, Skype or document scanners because the Internet had still not been reconnected. The cost of the attack was estimated at nearly 5 million euros for 2015. In October, the internal messaging system was still regularly inaccessible. TV5 Monde decided to invest in cybersecurity.

6.1.8.2. *Case two: the cyber-attack of 2016 against Dyn*

The 2016 cyber-attack took place on October 21 and involved a massive denial of service (DDoS) attack of more than one terabyte per second, targeting the Dyn Managed DNS service. Many sites that use this service[28] other than DyndNS, such as Twitter, Ebay, Netflix, GitHub and PayPal, were inaccessible for about 10 hours. The attackers used hacked smart objects (such as surveillance cameras) infected with malware called Mirai to relay the massive packet flow[29].

---

27 Trois ministres au chevet de TV5 Monde, victime de piratage. *Le Monde*, April 9, 2015; TV5 Monde victime d'un piratage sans précédent. *France Inter*, April 9, 2015.

28 Dyn Status Updates Delivered. *Dynstatus*. October 21, 2016.

29 "Nearly 100,000 smart objects used in the giant cyberattack/piracy", *La Presse,* October 26, 2016. Friday's global cyber-attack by the Mirai malware that attacks smart objects: www.futura-sciences.com/tech/actualites/informatique-cyberattaque-mondiale-vendredi-due-malware-mirai-prend-objets-connectes-64922.

The US Department of Homeland Security launched an investigation. The activist group New World Hackers claimed responsibility for the attacks on Twitter on October 22, 2016. According to the computer security company FlashPoint, this attack could have been the work of amateur hackers.

6.2. Cybersecurity and cryptology

While cybersecurity applies to all technologies, it has a special relationship with cryptology.

Cryptology has a dual use: civil/commercial and military. In the United States, the freedom to use cryptography as a means of expression was an instrument of freedom of speech guaranteed by the First Amendment to the Constitution. This was not the case with exports and imports, and it was at the end of the 20th century, under the double lobby of cryptography providers and supporters of Internet commerce, that cryptology could be exchanged with countries that were not enemies of the United States.

In France, cryptology was assimilated as a weapon of war and could neither be used, nor exported, nor imported. The liberalization of telecommunications[30], then the Internet lobby, with the law to support confidence in the digital economy[31], led to total freedom of use. It is not the same with exports and imports, since the sole purpose is not authentication nor integrity control. The digital law of October 2016 deepened this liberal trend.

In the digital age, with the use of electronic messaging, e-commerce platforms, online practices and smart cards, cryptography is used systematically, with encryption being the most important security measure.

Cryptology, the science of secrecy, owes its longevity to all those who, over the centuries, have been able to detect new applications and exploit their potential.

6.2.1. *Cryptology: the science of secrecy*

Initially reserved for military[32] and diplomatic use, cryptology has been an integral part of our daily lives since the rise of the Internet.

---

30 Article 28 of the LRT of December 29, 1999.

31 Law of June 21, 2004.

32 Even in the United States, despite the guarantee of freedom of expression, cryptography was first assimilated to ammunition.

Today, as an unavoidable science, cryptology offers countless possibilities. This technology is in fact deployed in many public applications such as WhatsApp or Telegram. "Of course, these applications are encrypted, but these tools are not suitable for professional use, and even less so for the exchange of sensitive data. The whole issue of Shadow IT is at stake here, i.e., the use of consumer solutions that are often free of charge for professional purposes," says Raphaël Basset[33]; he adds: "by using this type of solution, the entire address book is swallowed up by the servers".

The ANSSI points out that "the integration of cryptographic applications in a professional environment concerns a very large number of business sectors and requires specific know-how, and even the intervention of experts specialized in the implementation of these solutions and support for these uses". But these experts alone cannot guarantee the cybersecurity of institutions, businesses and individuals without a collective awareness of the challenges posed by digital technologies and the assimilation of best practices; an effort to raise awareness, combined with the maintenance of relationships of trust with the people and entities concerned by these issues, as designers or end-users of these solutions. Making each link in the information systems chain accountable is a priority.

Commercial companies have only recently become aware of the risks involved and of the urgent need to implement encryption solutions for their security. It is not generalized, but it is increasingly used, stresses Raphaël Basset, acculturated by awareness campaigns and the work carried out by ANSSI in particular, as well as by the increasingly frequent publications on corporate security breaches.

In order to democratize the use of encryption both in companies and institutions, the battle of data must be won, "and that means", says Basset, "by the emergence of European champions, supported by Europe and a truly proactive security policy". The first encrypted telephone on a presidential airplane dates back to 2002, when 200 ERCOM terminals were deployed at the French Ministry of the Interior. Overall, the national government market is no less than tens of thousands of units. "Today, we need to scale up and have more orders to lower our costs and be able to offer this end-to-end encryption solution to as many people as possible" (Raphaël Basset). "Only on a European scale", Basset adds, "will we be able to achieve this objective, which is also a necessity for the future of our industry".

This move to scale also relies on partnerships with major integrators[34] with whom ERCOM collaborates on the design of secure communications and terminal solutions.

---

33 VP Marketing & Business Development at ERCOM.
34 See Samsung and IDEMIA.

> We have significantly evolved our CryptoMart solution to simplify the deployment process for users. We have also created a WhatsApp type application, but dedicated to the professional world, departments or companies, which can be adapted to any type of terminal.

Partnerships allow technologies to acquire a real maturity and to make good export proposals.

This allows not only large companies but also SMEs to tackle international markets. "We need these manufacturers to carry our solutions, to develop new ones, but also to conquer markets abroad. For the economic equation to work, we need to go beyond the French sector," says Guillaume Poupard[35].

2018 marked a turning point in the exploration of these solutions within the Ministries of Defense, Interior and Foreign Affairs.

Within the Ministry of the Interior, directives issued by the then Prime Minister's Office required the deployment of encryption solutions qualified by the ANSSI for mobile telephony. After an experiment conducted at the end of 2016, the Ministry integrated the solutions developed in particular by ERCOM in May 2017. "Today, within 24 hours, an ERCOM terminal shall be deployed for any request issued and we are working to drastically reduce these delays," notes Thierry Markwitz[36]. By the end of 2018, nearly 2,000 terminals were operational. "This corresponds to the extension the Ministry wants to make to equip not only ministerial offices, but also the prefectural corps and general directors." Being simple and transparent for the user, despite end-to-end encryption that includes voice, the technology is also deployed in times of crisis; this was the case, for example, when the Ministry's forces were sent to the territories ravaged by hurricane Irma. "Thanks to this technology, we were able to use different media and guarantee our operational capacity when no network was available in the area. Deployments are also set up as part of the border control missions carried out by the Ministry."

6.2.1.1. *Waiting for 2022*

Within the Ministry of the Interior, the National Police is set to expand the Trustway program[37], which has already been tried and tested and is now being deployed within the gendarmerie. More significant investments are planned than for the gendarmerie. This concerns in particular videoconferencing and web conferencing.

---

35 Director General of the ANSSI.

36 Deputy Director of Infrastructure at the Ministry of the Interior.

37 From Bull.

In addition to the equipment, the encryption layers for the data stored on the workstations will be provided by the Cryhod solution[38], an encryption software that enables full encryption of the hard drives of the institution's portable workstations.

Access to the data is only possible for authorized and duly authenticated users[39]. Data exchanges between users will be encrypted by Zed containers[40], comparable to a "diplomatic suitcase" with sensitive files that only the identified recipients are authorized to read.

As part of the Public Action 2022 program, global digitization will be accompanied by digital security adapted to the new challenges of nomadism and proximity, as well as volume: the Ministry of the Interior has just under 200,000 workstations. This workstation will be homogeneous throughout the country, autonomous with OS applications[41].

An upgrade is planned in real-time detection for an in-depth defense of the information system.

The quantum computer poses a problem. The technological breakthrough of the quantum computer raises the question of cryptographic power and encryption keys. These will be strengthened. Renaud Lifchitz[42] insisted more than 2 years ago on the fragility of asymmetric cryptography: "It will quickly be necessary to double all symmetric key sizes to remain out of reach of quantum attacks.... It is asymmetric cryptography, using RSA type algorithms, which risks being quickly outdated."

This has detrimental consequences for many security protocols: PKI, SSL, SSH, HTTPS, smart cards, etc. Scientists are unanimous in their view that within 25 years, all these protocols will be breakable. It is necessary to set new standards within the next 5 years.

6.2.2. Risks

The progress made in the field of quantum computers and their computing power also implies risks for the encryption of smart objects, which is in full development.

---

38 From Prim'X.

39 At the preboot.

40 Prim'X.

41 Smartphone, Linux or Windows workstation.

42 Econocom Digital Security expert.

The rise of smart objects is leading to undeniable progress, but they are also a privileged target for those who want to capture data[43]. The cameras, microphones, network access and other applications that connected objects are equipped with are all gateways that will allow or facilitate an attack.

These objects with heterogeneous systems evolve within constrained environments, are not sufficiently armed against the threats that await them and do not have resources dedicated to security. However, scientists have pointed out that by integrating the end-to-end security component, based on the fruits of research in light cryptography, smart objects will be able to convert to cybersecurity. Nevertheless, the question remains as to whether the hardware and processor of the IoT will be able to support encryption.

6.2.2.1. Homomorphic encryption

The French Ministry of the Armed Forces, which has at its disposal multiple pieces of equipment with these technologies, places the issue of encryption among the strategic stakes. At the DGA Innovation Forum held at École Polytechnique[44], the DGA presented homomorphic encryption as a breakthrough technology, along with IoT, artificial intelligence and quantum computers. Cryptography is therefore, not surprisingly, one of the major directions of the French Ministry of the Armed Forces.

Homomorphic encryption allows a user[45] to entrust previously encrypted data to cloud computing without the server having to decrypt the data. The Cloud thus has an outsourced storage and computing capacity.

Homomorphic encryption can also be used in the case of electronic voting. The latter has often been criticized for possible instances of fraud that could distort the results.

Each vote can be encrypted separately; the sum of the votes is calculated homomorphously on the encrypted votes and the trusted authorities that share the private key meet once to decrypt the sum obtained.

Of course, other checks are used to prove the validity of votes, and homomorphic encryption is only part of the electronic voting protocol.

Lastly, homomorphic encryption can be used in the fight against terrorism or organized crime.

---

43 Health elements, bank details, strategic information.
44 In 2017.
45 Whether it is an individual or a company.

6.2.2.1.1. The CNIL and public authorities' access to encrypted data

The CNIL was not consulted as part of the bill to strengthen internal security and the fight against terrorism. However, it was consulted on the access of public authorities to encryption. For the CNIL[46], "encryption is an essential element of the resilience of our digital societies and information heritage". For the digital law, the consultation was broad and the CNIL was a stakeholder.

For the CNIL, encryption must not be weakened under any circumstances. Indeed, encryption solutions not only help to preserve the confidentiality of data transmitted over the Internet but also to ensure its integrity against cybercrime, which tends to access confidential or sensitive information as much as to modify, copy or delete it.

According to the CNIL, encryption is part of cybersecurity, which is a vector and factor of confidence for users, both professional and non-professional, and contributes to innovation for manufacturers.

The objectives of protecting the privacy[47] and security of the information assets of public and private actors will have to be reconciled with the need for public authorities to have access to the information they need.

Access by judicial authorities or intelligence services to computer data that can be encrypted is thus subject to numerous specific legal provisions.

The set of tools that can be mobilized to access encrypted data or bypass encryption devices forms a fairly robust arsenal.

The CNIL was not satisfied with these provisions. "It intends to reaffirm, as the ANSSI has done, that the implementation of backdoors in encryption systems and 'master keys', or the ban on the general public using data encryption techniques in the hands of users, would endanger the very principle of operation of current encryption technologies, which are based precisely on the prohibition of access by third parties to the data thus protected."

Indeed, this would create a collective risk of lowering the level of security of individuals and institutions, and increase their exposure to serious economic, political or public safety harm.

Homomorphic encryption, which is moving towards controlling the sovereignty of a company or a State, can really prove to be a major asset reconciling the

---

46 *SD Magazine*, January 24, 2018.
47 Pursuant to the GDPR.

protection of privacy and personal data and the fight against crime. Cryptology is therefore a major component of cybersecurity.

This cybersecurity applies to PNR and smart cities.

6.3. PNR data

Cybersecurity is also par for the course. PNR (Passenger Name Record) data therefore plays an active role in cybersecurity.

PNR data must be transmitted to the authorities to ensure flight safety. Passenger data is of great interest to hackers, and this has been demonstrated with the theft of passport and bank data of 9.4 million Cathay Pacific customers and the information from 429,000 payment cards stolen from British Airways.

The International Civil Aviation Organization[48] has long been concerned about the Passenger Name Record.

Airlines collect information from passengers as part of their reservation services. This information is stored in the databases of the reservation systems, then exchanged between the companies involved from the time of the reservation until the services requested by the passengers are provided.

The data in these databases are internationally standardized information records known as PNRs.

The PNR contains, according to the services offered by the companies and requested by the customer, precise pieces of information: the name and surname of the customer, information on the travel agency where the reservation is made, the itinerary of the trip, the flight details: number of successive flights, date, times, class, the group of people for whom the same reservation is made, the passenger's contact on land; telephone and electronic contact details, accepted fares, the status of the payment made and payment method via bank card, hotel or car reservations on arrival, services requested on board: seat number assigned in advance, meals, specific health requirements. It is rare that all fields are filled in.

6.3.1. *Element of definition*

PNR data is not to be confused with APIS[49] data, which is collected by airlines during the passenger check-in phase of a flight.

---

48 ICAO.

49 Advance Passenger Information System.

They include the number and type of travel document used, nationality, full name, date of birth, border crossing point used to enter the territory of the Member States, Transport Code, departure and arrival times of the transport, total number of persons transported and the original boarding point.

There is less APIS data available than PNR data. Nevertheless, APIS data is interesting as it is verified by carrier personnel during check-in for a flight. PNR data is provided by travelers at the commercial booking stage, which can change before boarding.

Prior to 2001, PNR data stored for commercial purposes by operators could be required by judicial authorities to meet the needs of an investigation or inquiry.

After the attacks of September 2001, and the extensive media and political exploitation of these events, security laws were passed in the United States and then in other countries allied with the United States, notably Australia and Canada. The United States, Australia and Canada subsequently set up "PNR systems", which then gave rise to agreements with the European Union.

The American system is the oldest and most successful. On November 19, 2001, the United States passed the Aviation and Transportation Security Act; on May 5, 2003, a fairly strict law on the conditions of entry into the United States[50] came into force.

The Aviation and Transportation Security Act of November 19, 2001 requires this data. The 2002 law stipulates that as of March 5, 2003, airlines must provide US customs and security services with personal information about their passengers, failing which they will be subject to tighter controls, fines and even suspension of landing rights.

These provisions apply not only to individual travelers but also to legal entities such as airlines and US security services[51]. The purpose of the IAO was to ensure technological, automatic and permanent monitoring of all possible forms of information that would make it possible to report the signs of a terrorist act. This project, called Terrorism Information Awareness[52], aimed to establish links between police and judicial data and behaviors such as visa applications and credit card use. The TIA had several other components such as the monitoring of medical databases or the automatic transcription of communications in foreign languages. This project,

---

50 Enhanced Border Security and Visa Entry Reform Act.
51 In January 2002 the Information Awareness Office (IAO) was created.
52 TIA.

which was hotly debated by individual freedom advocates, was abolished in September 2003 and replaced by CAPPS[53] and CAPPS2, the latter of which applies only to air transport users.

6.3.2. *PNR data and nation-states*

The United Kingdom is the only state to have a comprehensive PNR system under the e-borders program. It came into force in March 2008 and combines both APIS and PNR data collection. The UK system does not *a priori* distinguish between flights from a member state of the European Union (which the United Kingdom used to be) or from a third state.

In Belgium, the police services are able to ask airlines for access to their PNR data if they obtain legal authorization.

In France, article 7 of the law of January 23, 2006[54] authorizes the collection and use of PNR and APIS data. In fact, this concerns APIS data, PNR data, data collected from the optical scanning strip[55] of travel documents, national identity cards and visas of air, sea and rail passengers; using this technique, it is possible to record the data contained in the optical bank, even when border officials are faced with the arrival of several flights. However, the 2006 law prohibits the use of so-called sensitive data for the purpose of Directive 95/46 and for the purpose of Article 8 of the law of January 6, 1978 as amended by the law of August 6, 2004. Thus, data concerning the types of meals on board[56] or the state of health of the passenger are not likely to be transmitted.

The implementation of the law of January 23, 2006 led to the creation of the air passenger file by an order dated December 19, 2006.

This experiment was not conclusive due to the lack of rigor in the transmission of data by certain companies and the multiplicity of errors due to homonyms or inaccurate name transcriptions. However, France is not inexperienced, since it applies Article 65 of the Customs Code, which allows customs to request PNR data for certain flights on an ad hoc and urgent basis.

---

53 Computer Assisted Passenger Prescreening System.
54 Law No. 2006-64 of January 23, 2006 on the fight against terrorism.
55 Known as "MRZ".
56 Which may be indicative of religious beliefs.

Australia and Canada have implemented PNR systems. Despite the differences in personal data protection between EU law and the laws of Australia and Canada, technical problems have been resolved in the management of travel data by operators, who nevertheless want harmonization to reduce the cost of transmissions.

This harmonization has not ceased to pose legal problems as part of agreements between the European Union and Australia, the European Union and Canada, and the European Union and the United States. The PNR has long stalled at the EU level.

6.3.2.1. *The European Union and PNR*

6.3.2.1.1. Council Directive 2004/82/EC of April 29, 2004

Directive 2004/82/EC obliges carriers to communicate passenger data, based on the Schengen Agreement, and regulates the exchange of PNR data for the official purpose of fighting terrorism and illegal immigration. According to Article 12, it authorizes "the use of such data as evidence in proceedings for the enforcement of laws and regulations on entry and immigration, including provisions relating to the protection of public policy and national security".

6.3.2.1.2. The May 2004 United States/European Union agreement

The United States approached the European Union in 2004 to obtain full access to the PNRs of trans-European companies. In May 2004, the United States and the European Union signed the 2004 Passenger Name Record Data Transfer Agreement, which gives the CBP access to 34 pieces of information contained in the PNR. At that time, the European Union was satisfied with the level of data protection guaranteed by the US authorities, insofar as they used the data within the intended framework, namely "preventing and combating terrorist attacks and international organized crime". However, these US requirements ran contrary to European rules on the protection of personal data. This agreement was invalidated by the European Court of Justice[57].

6.3.2.1.3. The 2006–2007 Agreement

The agreement was necessary to ensure that the airlines would know how to regulate the flow of information. The agreement was concluded on October 19, 2006 and came into force on August 1, 2007.

---

57 ECJ, Grand Chamber, May 30, 2006, European Parliament, Council of the European Union, Joined Cases C-317/04 and C6318/04 (Decision 2004/235 is excluded from the scope of Directive 95/46.

The agreement, materialized by the Council decision of July 23, 2007 falls within the framework of the third European pillar, devoted to police and justice issues. It lasted for 7 years and was applicable as of July 23, 2007. After 7 years, the data should be stored in an inactive database for a period of 8 years, during which access to the Department of Homeland Security is only possible in exceptional situations or when lives are at stake. The number of pieces of information is reduced to 0-19. Nevertheless, the DHS may transfer PNR data to other government authorities and it is allowed, albeit in limited cases, to access sensitive data, that is, data that may reveal ethnic origin, religious or political beliefs, or a health problem; the purposes of the system are broad and evolving. There is no guarantee that the data concerned will be destroyed after 15 years, that is, after the initial 7 years and the additional 8 years.

This is why this agreement was often criticized within the European Union, among some MEPs, at the institutional level, at the level of personal data regulatory bodies, including the G29, and at the level of associations for the defense of human rights and individual freedoms.

As early as December 2007, the G29 published a report questioning the basic principles of the agreement: "As currently drafted, the proposal for a framework decision provides for the collection of a large amount of personal data relating to air passengers or passengers leaving the European Union, regardless of whether they are suspected or innocent. This data will then be stored ... for possible future use, thus enabling the profiling of passengers. This proposal is in addition to the fingerprinting of all travelers applying for passports and the retention of all telecommunications traffic data within the European Union.... A European PNR regime cannot lead to the generalized surveillance of all passengers."[58]

The United States, on the other hand, considered it a good agreement for EU law. It was felt that this agreement would protect both the data collected and the privacy of individuals. No cases of misappropriation of PNR data by the US government have been detected since the start of the transfers. It should be noted that the 2007 agreement is an interim agreement.

Following numerous criticisms from some MEPs, the latter announced in May 2010 that they wanted to strengthen the protection of air passengers' personal data in the PNR database. On May 5, 2010, the European Parliament adopted a resolution calling for a renegotiation of the agreement. On December 2, 2010, the Council authorized the Commission to negotiate a new agreement on the transfer of PNR data.

---

58 G29, Opinion 2/2007 on passenger information regarding the transfer of shared file data to the US authorities, adopted on February 15, 2007.

The objectives are clearly determined: fostering cooperation between the United States and the European Union in a spirit of transatlantic partnership, fighting terrorism while respecting fundamental rights and recognizing the importance of privacy, taking into account traveler security and border protection. The United States entered into negotiations because it was concerned that the 2007 agreement, which was provisional, would not be renewed in 2014. The precedent of the SWIFT affair led the United States to take the European Parliament seriously.

6.3.2.2. *Controls within the European Union*

6.3.2.2.1. The European Court of Justice

The May 28, 2004 agreement was terminated by the European Union following the May 30, 2006 ruling of the European Court of Justice because it did not have an appropriate legal basis.

Indeed, the agreement of May 28, 2004 was based on the first pillar. The fields of competence of the European Union are divided into three pillars: the first pillar covers matters relating to the internal market and free movement; the second pillar is concerned with defense and foreign policy issues; the third pillar is concerned with police and justice issues.

In 2004, the rules for adopting European texts differed according to the pillars: the first pillar corresponded to qualified majority, that is, co-decision with the European Parliament and control by the Court of Justice; the third pillar corresponded to unanimity, that is, simple opinion of the European Parliament and no control by the Court of Justice. The latter considered that the 2004 agreement was not appropriate since it was adopted within the framework of the first pillar. Indeed, the purpose of the processing linked to the transfer of PNR data to the US authorities was public security; an agreement had to be concluded under the third pillar.

6.3.2.2.2. The G29

The G29 did not make decisions but made its opinion known on the agreements and in particular on the 2007 agreement. It was useful in the fight against terrorism and crime.

The G29 pointed out that the United States "has never conclusively proven that the considerable amount of passenger data collected is actually necessary to combat terrorism and serious crime... The only substantiated information available for this purpose indicates that API data is more widely used than PNR data".

Moreover, the G29 pointed out that the European Union already has the Schengen Information System[59].

6.3.2.2.3. Reciprocity and democracy

The G29 was concerned about the possible consequences of the agreement and, in particular, the consequences of automatic reciprocity with third countries that use a PNR system: "It must be realized that the existence of a European PNR regime could encourage undemocratic or corrupt regimes to demand the communication of PNR on the basis of the principle of reciprocity. It is therefore necessary to ask whether the consequences of this reciprocity have been sufficiently studied." In particular, the G29 mentioned the possession of credit card information by officials of a member state unable to suppress corruption.

On the other hand, the fight against terrorism can be understood in different ways to that which prevails in the European Union: "Reciprocity could thus allow a dictatorship to establish an assessment of the risks presented by dissidents, based on PNR data."

6.3.2.3. *The European Data Protection[60] and Profiling Supervisor*

The EDPS criticized the profiling technique that develops risk hypotheses from personal data that do not correspond to an offence. The shaping of movements and behavior leads to decisions being taken against individuals who would subsequently have great difficulty defending themselves against these decisions. Above all, according to the European Data Protection Supervisor, the principles of purpose and proportionality would not be observed. Data protection law is unclear or non-existent, while the retention period seems excessive.

6.3.2.3.1. The European Parliament

Parliament initially expressed reservations. The Washington agreement of May 28, 2004 between the United States and the European Union was criticized by the European Parliament. This Washington agreement allows the United States to retrieve additional personal information from reservation systems that may be of interest to it.

The agreement establishes a list of PNR data to which CBP has access: "CBP will extract information from airlines' reservation systems until such time as the airlines are able to export this data to CBP." The Washington Agreement may be in substantial conflict with European data protection legislation. The European Union has aligned itself with US air transport legislation.

---

59 SIS.

60 Notice of May 1, 2008.

Article 4 of the 2004 PNR Records Agreement states that "CBP shall process PNR data received, and the persons concerned by such processing in accordance with U.S. law and constitutional requirements".

Therefore, on the basis of Article 230 EC, the European Parliament sought to quash the Council's decision to approve the agreement with the United States on the one hand, and the Commission's decision finding of adequacy in this agreement on the other hand. Among the elements relied upon by the European Parliament to challenge the Council's decision, the following points should be highlighted:

– violation of the right to personal data protection from the point of view of the framework directive 95/46/EC. Infringement of the principle of proportionality, which implies that the actions taken, and the means used by the European Union are not disproportionate and do not overstep the objectives of the Union Treaties;

– violation of the principle of loyal cooperation;

– the spurious choice to use Article 95 EC as the legal basis for the Council decision. Indeed, Article 95 EC refers to the adoption by the Council "of measures for the approximation of the laws, regulations and administrative provisions of the Member States which aim to establish and operate the internal market". It cannot therefore serve as a basis for the approximation of legislation between the European Union and third countries such as the United States.

In the case concerning the Commission's decision on the adequacy of PNR agreements, the European Parliament raised, among other things, the following points to challenge it:

– abuse of power, violation of fundamental rights and violation of the principle of proportionality;

– violation of Article 300 of the Framework Directive 95/46/EC on the protection of personal data. An amendment to this directive implies that the transfer of such data to a third country is only possible if the third country has an adequate level of protection. If the Commission decides that this presupposition is fulfilled by the United States[61], what will happen if the United States decides to transfer this data to a foreign partner?;

– violation of the essential principles of Directive 95/46 and in particular Article 25, which stipulates that "persons whose data are processed have the right to be informed about the processing, to have access to the data, to request its rectification and even to object to the processing in certain circumstances".

---

61 Safe Harbor Principles, then in force and since invalidated by the European Court of Justice.

Finally, European legislation provides a very clear framework for the collection of personal data. This collection can indeed be done in the context of public security and for law enforcement purposes. However, in this case, the data contained in PNR files are collected as part of a service provided by airlines. Consequently, it can be considered that the collection of PNR data as part of economic activity has no legal basis in European law. And the Parliament did not vote for the 2004 agreement.

6.3.2.3.2. The 2007 PNR agreement

The negative opinion on the agreement was not taken into account. The Parliament adopted a resolution dated November 20, 2008[62]. It shared the European Data Protection Supervisor's judgment on the imprecision of the text but was more nuanced on the usefulness of PNR data for the services in charge of the fight against terrorism and serious crime. The European Parliament considered that this data could be useful as evidence in an investigation. On the other hand, it had doubts about the relevance of possible preventive profiling. Controls therefore largely highlighted the shortcomings of the 2004 and 2007 agreements.

The text adopted by Parliament in 2012 emphasized security and some criticisms remained. The new text further reflected a concern for security and sought to strike a balance.

On November 11, 2011, the European Union and the United States initialed a new agreement on the transfer of air passenger data on flights from the European Union to the United States.

6.3.2.3.3. Sharing with the European Union

US authorities are required to share PNR and analytical information derived from such data with law enforcement and judicial authorities in the European Union to prevent, detect and prosecute transnational crime or terrorist offences.

6.3.2.3.4. Use and data retention

The US authorities use PNR data for the prevention and detection of terrorism and transnational crimes punishable by a prison sentence of at least 3 years. Minor offences are excluded: it concerns serious offences such as drug trafficking, human trafficking and terrorism. PNR data is depersonalized 6 months after it is received by the US authorities. After 5 years, the depersonalized data is transferred to a non-active database, to which US officials have conditional access. The total period of data retention is limited to 10 years in general, but the data will be accessible for 15 years for terrorism cases. It is recalled that PNR data is transferred to the US

---

62 Resolution No. 2008/0561.

authorities from airline databases[63] and not from reservation systems[64], except in certain limited circumstances[65], such as when airlines are technically unable to transmit the data.

6.3.2.3.5. Protection of personal data

The protection of personal data is the subject that has given rise to the greatest number of legal controversies.

Cecilia Malmström[66] emphasized this aspect: "The protection of personal data has been my priority since the start of the negotiations in December 2010 and I am satisfied with the result achieved, as it represents a clear improvement compared to the current 2017 agreement. This new agreement contains strong guarantees for the respect of the privacy of European citizens without undermining the effectiveness of the agreement with regard to the security of the European Union and the United States."[67]

Congress has required the appointment of a privacy officer in the Department of Homeland Security who must report to Congress annually on the status of privacy issues and whose findings are binding on the department. The privacy officer has agreed to receive and urgently process the actions of data protection authorities in the European Union on behalf of citizens who consider that the Department of Homeland Security has not satisfactorily resolved their complaints.

Passengers can obtain access to, correct and delete their PNR data. They also have the right to seek administrative and judicial remedies as provided under US law. Air carriers must also accurately inform passengers about the use of PNR and how to exercise their rights. The agreement prohibits US authorities from taking decisions that could harm someone solely on the basis of automated data processing; this is consistent with concerns about profiling. The agreement also sets conditions limiting the use of sensitive data that could reveal, for example, the religion or sexual orientation of passengers. To this end, mechanisms are put in place to filter and mask sensitive data.

Appropriate technical measures and organizational arrangements must be put in place to protect the personal data contained in the PNRs from accident, destruction,

---

63 According to the "push" transfer method.

64 According to the "pull" method.

65 For example, when air carriers are technically unable to transmit the data.

66 Formerly the commissioner in charge of internal affairs.

67 European Commission press release by Cecilia Malmström on the agreement of PNR data, November 18, 2011.

loss, alteration, access, use or unlawful processing. Data protection, confidentiality and integrity with encryption, authorization and documentation procedures must be ensured. Disciplinary action is taken against any person responsible for an incident involving private data, including seizing of or refusal of access to the system and suspensions.

Even if a concern for balance appears and if the United States is taken into account, at least partially, in the European Union law on the protection of personal data, the agreement reflects the primacy of the security requirement. The crimes and offenses for which the United States may use PNR data to investigate and prosecute are numerous: they include, on the one hand, terrorist attacks and certain other crimes, and on the other hand, serious international crimes.

Crimes that are included under the heading of "terrorist attacks" are those that pose a threat to human life, property or infrastructure, or are allegedly intended to intimidate or influence a civilian population through intimidation or government policy, or affect the conduct of a government by means of mass destruction, assassination, kidnapping, hostage taking, fundraising carried out with the intention, directly or indirectly, of carrying out any of the above acts, or attempt, complicity, or threat to carry out any of the above acts. Serious international crimes are defined in Article 4 of the Extradition Agreement between the United States and the European Union.

Criticism remained, particularly at the level of the European Parliament. In May 2010, the European Parliament postponed its vote on a PNR agreement with the United States, which had been provisionally applied since 2007, mainly due to concerns about the protection of personal data. MEPs then urged the European Commission to negotiate a new agreement, which it did in 2011. The agreement took effect after it was adopted on April 19, 2012 by 409 votes to 226, with 33 abstentions, due to strong support for the text from the main parliamentary groups. The president of the social-democratic group indicated that he supported the agreement despite its shortcomings, but that he would respect the voting freedom of the members of his group.

Nevertheless, the vast majority of Social Democratic MEPs voted in favor of the agreement. Since the conservative groups[68] supported the agreement, the result was a foregone conclusion.

A minority of MEPs voted against the agreement. This significant minority rejected the agreement as these parliamentarians were not convinced by the guarantees

---

68 Notably the EPP.

taken in the field of personal data protection. Rapporteur Sophie In 't Veld withdrew her name from the report because she had many reservations.

The liberal group stated that it was against the text, and its president, Guy Verhostadt made this known. The Liberals were joined by the Greens. For these parties, a blow had been dealt to European law and, in particular, to European law on personal data: "Today's decision by the conservatives and social democrats to vote in favor of the agreement is a step towards a police state"[69] and "for the first time in ten years, the Parliament had the opportunity to stop profiling ... but a majority chose to let it pass them by". In 't Veld explained: "Some things are non-negotiable, such as fundamental rights and respect for European Union law[70]. Apparently, the Parliament believes that transatlantic relations are more important." She also wondered why the Parliament "which rejected the agreements in 2007, then in May 2010 and even went to court, ended up accepting an even worse agreement[71]? Why would the Parliament accept PNR and reject ACTA[72]?" Note that the shift in opinion to oppose ACTA had been partially taken into account, as a petition against ACTA was signed by more than 2 million people.

The European Data Supervisor, Peter Hustinx, expressed his reservations. He did so vigorously and tried to make himself heard by MEPs, but to no avail. He clarified the EDPS' line: "Personal data of air passengers could certainly be needed for law enforcement purposes in specific cases, when a serious threat supported by concrete indicators arises. It is their use in a systematic and indiscriminate way for all passengers that raises particular concerns."[73] The EDPS acknowledges that improvements in data protection compared to the 2007 agreement are notable, in particular as regards the restriction of the scope and conditions for processing PNR data.

Nevertheless, the new agreement does not comply with European legislation. The very fact that it requires air carriers to provide EU member states with Passenger Name Record data for flights to or from the territory of the European Union in order to combat terrorism and serious crime is questionable.

---

69 Statement by Jan Philip Albrecht.

70 Recommendation of the rapporteur contrary to the report, D66, The Netherlands, April 19, 2012.

71 Since the Treaty of Lisbon, the Parliament has had to decide whether it is for or against.

72 The agreement on counterfeiting concluded between Western and formerly industrialized countries, criticized by emerging countries that are not involved.

73 Opinion of the European Data Protection Supervisor, Peter Hustinx, April 19, 2012.

Such a system would not be necessary, and the text provides no evidence to the contrary. Indeed, the need to collect or store large amounts of personal data must be based on a demonstration of the relationship between use and result[74].

The EDPS therefore regretted that the scope of the data collected remains too wide. Furthermore, no data should be kept beyond 30 days in an identifiable form.

The G29, for its part, criticized the lack of provisions to ensure the security of personal data with respect to privacy: "As currently drafted [it] provides for the collection of a large amount of personal data[75] relating to air passengers entering or leaving the European Union, regardless of whether they are suspected or innocent. This data is then stored … for possible future use, allowing for the profiling of passengers. This is in addition to the fingerprinting of all citizens applying for a passport and the retention of all data related to telecommunications traffic within the European Union. A PNR regime cannot lead to the widespread surveillance of all passengers."

6.3.2.3.6. Criticism from legal experts

Some legal scholars focus on certain points – which they feel are controversial – in the agreement.

PNR and extradition

The reference to extraditable crimes has no place in an agreement on PNR, since this notion only refers to suspects or guilty parties and not to persons who are *a priori* innocent. This clause would be likely to extend the use of PNR data to any purpose, provided it is ordered by a court. PNR data would also be likely to be used, in some cases, to ensure border security, when its use is intended to prevent terrorism and serious crime, not to track illegal migrants or to combat customs offences.

Moreover, these processes are not always effective, particularly in the area of terrorism, given that it is the fight against terrorism that has justified the PNR and PNR agreements. The United States has reported that thanks to PNR, two "dangerous terrorists" have been arrested[76]. Two terrorists in 10 years is not a very convincing record. The Indian authorities were outraged by the ease with which one

---

74 Principle of necessity.

75 G29 Notice, March 29, 2012.

76 They were Faisal Shahzad and David Headley.

of the "terrorists"[77] managed to fly so often between Pakistan, India and the United States.

Duration of use

The duration of use goes far beyond the draft agreement with Australia[78]. The latter agreement is considered balanced and more favorable to the European Union. The data retention period is not 15 years, but indefinite. It is true that access to the data by the US Department of Homeland Security will be progressively restricted. Nevertheless, the data will not be erased. It is even possible to speak of a step backwards compared to the 2004 agreement if we consider the storage period. Finally, criticism has been leveled at the reversibility of depersonalization. The agreement foresees that PNR data can be concealed after 6 months, but it can be re-personalized by persons with special access rights.

Sensitive data

The agreement does not provide for the immediate deletion of so-called "sensitive" data, contrary to the 2004 agreement. For example, a food preference may be indicative of a religious affiliation. A hotel reservation or a choice of itinerary may give indications of sexual orientation. A request for medical assistance may indicate a state of health. Now, this sensitive data will not always be erased after 30 days if it is part of a specific investigation. There is therefore a potential risk of it being diverted for other uses.

Data security and errors

Several countries, including Germany, Austria and Belgium, are concerned about the risk of data leaks when transmitting data to third countries, particularly with regard to the transfer of PNR data. In addition, errors can and have already occurred in the processing of air passenger data[79].

The right of recourse

The proponents of the 2012 agreement insist on the right of recourse, which would protect passengers against possible violations of their rights. Passengers have the right to "administrative and judicial recourse in cases where data protection rules have been violated, as well as the right to compensation. But it is not clear how

---

77 David Headley, perpetrator of the 2008 Mumbai bombing.

78 Agreement of October 27, 2011.

79 The media took up the case of Maher Arar, the Syrian-Canadian who was arrested at New York's JFK Airport and then imprisoned, before he was released, and it was legally acknowledged that no evidence of any crime could be held against him.

individuals would know whether or not there has been a violation". Thus, the possibility of recourse appears limited.

The 2012 agreement on certain points seems to reflect some progress, but this is not true in all areas. These include the questioning of the principle of proportionality and the issues induced by territoriality.

The principle of proportionality is at the center of personal data law. The retention period of PNR data in the agreement approved by the EU Parliament is a real problem. It is too long, and it seems disproportionate to advocate the right to be forgotten and to keep PNR data for such a long period of time, even though certain guarantees have been negotiated and granted, especially since the Parliament has real power and no longer merely gives an opinion; and the 19 PNR data metrics are likely to give rise to profiling, which also hardly corresponds to the principle of proportionality. The 2012 US/EU PNR agreement also raises questions of territoriality. The provisions apply to all citizens of the various European Union states, with the exception of Denmark, the United Kingdom and Ireland. They are more often inspired by common law[80] than by Romano-Germanic law. The PNR legal system as a whole is distinctly inspired by common law. Because of the territorial dimension, effective access to justice in the event of interpretative disputes remains pending and the possible legal costs generated by interpretation or possible litigation are not mentioned.

Last but not least, there is the issue of passenger consent. This consent is presumed. From the moment a person is registered for a trip, he or she is supposed to accept the basis and clauses of the PNR agreement. In reality, most passengers are unaware of some of the clauses of the PNR agreements even though carriers have an obligation to provide information.

With reference to French law, the motion for resolution No. 252(2008–2009) presented by Simon Sutour on behalf of the Committee on European Affairs on the proposal for a framework decision on the use of passenger data for law enforcement purposes[81] was examined on May 13, 2009 by the Law Committee. The motion for a resolution was approved for the most part, but criticisms were made about the right to privacy and the protection of personal data did not seem to present sufficient guarantees.

---

80 Which applies, with notable differences, to the United States, the United Kingdom and Ireland in particular.

81 E3697.

The PNR agreement approved by the Parliament of the European Union does not have the same degree of legal certainty as the agreements with Canada, where common law is partly counterbalanced by the civil law tradition.

Moreover, the United States has never conclusively proven that the considerable amount of passenger data collected is necessary to fight terrorism and serious crime. The G29 had also indicated that the existence of a European PNR regime could lead undemocratic regimes to demand the disclosure of PNR on the basis of the principle of reciprocity. In 2012, the question was whether the consequences of such reciprocity had been sufficiently studied.

Despite the positive vote of the Parliament, the European PNR project was abandoned in 2014. The wave of terrorism in 2015 would revive the process. On December 4, 2015, the Council approved the compromise text agreed with the European Parliament on the proposal for a directive on the use of Air Passenger Name Records.

The Parliament, as far as its minority is concerned[82], had the same criticisms as in 2012. But the directive has now been in force for several years. Data is kept for 6 months, then concealed and kept for an additional period of 4 and a half years. The PNR system works just about everywhere, with a deliberate focus on security.

6.4. Smart cities

Cybersecurity in smart cities, especially those dedicated to Big Data, refers to all the laws, devices and best practices for managing risks in the digital and IT sectors.

From the beginning of the 21st century, the "machine to machine" has been introduced. It is subject to testing and is then traced. This is what appears in the *Le profilage des populations*[83]. The "machine to machine" concerns movement in particular, for example autonomous cars, and the health sector.

Initially, the public authorities played a decisive role, but nowadays, public/private partnerships are common and companies, large and medium-sized, not to mention start-ups, play a key role. Cybersecurity is at the heart of the system. This cybersecurity is increasingly being challenged, with increasingly frequent instances of hacking.

---

82 32 votes for, 26 against.
83 Mattelart, A., Vitalis, A. (2014). *Le profilage des populations*. La Découverte.

Cybersecurity has not been an immediate priority[84]. The white paper led mainly by César Cerrudo in April 2015 insisted on the overly reserved assessment of smart cities by providers of cybersecurity. Initially, relatively isolated attacks drew attention to security flaws even though, at first, the perpetrators did not dare to target cities. In 2008, a Polish teenager hacked into the city of Lodz's streetcar management system. The Ukrainian power grid was attacked for the first time in December 2015, causing power cuts during the winter. The ANSSI considered that security efforts should focus on smart objects that have physical interactions with the city, such as water and electricity management.

According to Thierry Bonhomme (ANSSI), the fragmentation of smart city projects is dangerous because it is not comprehensive enough: "Different projects with different companies are starting up in the same city: one will take care of air control, another of street lighting, a third of traffic…." Security is almost guaranteed when several aspects of the smart city are brought together in a single project, as in Doha, where Orange is managing the "end-to-end" installation of 500,000 sensors to connect a downtown neighborhood. Yves Verhoeven does not share Thierry Bonhomme's point of view. Globalization, according to this head of Orange Business Services, would have serious drawbacks. "If we move towards complete integration, there will be a better homogeneity of systems. But the service provider may become too powerful. Relevant e-governance is not indifferent." Cybersecurity has to be considered from the very outset of the project. Encryption of the smart city's communications is essential. Partitioning is necessary. Systems only communicate with each other if they have to. A contingency plan to initiate a response in the event of an attack is desirable. The resilience of strategic information infrastructures corrects weak points and conceives of solutions.

For example, Singapore, one of the most developed smart cities, has implemented some of these measures. In 2016, Singapore announced the deployment of a protection program. This includes, for both public services and businesses, estimates of recurring risks and vulnerabilities, plans to enable restoration and continuity of services that would eventually be subject to attacks and regular cybersecurity exercises. In addition, Singapore has a cybersecurity research center. The Anil Das company has launched the Clean Tech Park, a complex that brings together companies that respect the environment and have green buildings. However, Singapore is a special case as it is both a city and a state[85].

In Barcelona, Spain, the city has focused on a public data system; the Mobile ID application allows direct access on cell phones with a secure authentication system.

---

84 Adam, L. (2015). Smart cities: la cybersécurité trop souvent négligée? *zdnetfr*, April 20.
85 Analysis by Hervé Debar.

In France, in Issy-les-Moulineaux, residents can consult the availability of parking spaces in real time.

In the United States, 21 cities adopted guidelines in September 2016 to ensure infrastructure security. These principles were established by New York City Hall, drawing on timely practices observed in some 50 cities. However, the risk remains and the San Francisco subway, one of the signatory cities, was hacked a month after the guidelines were adopted.

6.4.1. *The development of standardization and certification*

The standard that plays the key role for legal entities under public and private law with regard to cybersecurity is ISO/IEC 27032.

The latter tends to study the various securities in cyberspace, with regard to information security, network security and the protection of key infrastructures. It provides a realistic solution in the protection of private data, as well as in the fight against phishing, hacking and cyber threats.

European certification was adopted by the European Parliament in December 2007, and the EQF level[86] was introduced in all certifications in 2012, but certifications are costly for companies.

The NIS Directive[87] of July 6, 2016[88] relates to measures to ensure a common high level of network and information system security in companies in the European Union's smart cities.

Malicious intentional actions are on the rise. Security incidents are a serious nuisance for companies. They lead to large financial losses for large and medium-sized commercial companies and can undermine the confidence of customers and users. A cooperation group bringing together representatives of the Member States, and the Commission and the European Union Agency for Security and Information[89] has been established, with the objectives of supporting strategic cooperation and facilitating security policy.

---

86 European Qualifications Framework.

87 See Quémener, M. (2016). La directive NIS, un texte majeur en matière de cybersécurité. *Sécurité et Stratégie*, 3.

88 Directive 2016/11148 of the European Parliament and of the Council.

89 ENISA.

Within the banking union, the application and monitoring of the requirements is reflected in a single supervisory mechanism. It is relevant for the supervisory authorities to work on exchanges of experience on security-related issues. The same reasoning applies to members of the European System of Central Banks that are not part of the euro area.

CSIRTs[90] participating in the CSIRT network are invited to provide information for publication on the Internet, without involving confidential or sensitive information.

In many cases, personal data is compromised as a result of incidents. In these circumstances, data protection authorities exchange information on various aspects of the fight against personal data breaches following incidents.

Member States shall identify the operators of essential services that have an establishment on their territory. These essential service operators shall provide a service necessary to maintain critical societal or economic activities; an incident would cause a disruptive effect on the provision of the service. The disruptive effect is based on the number of users in relation to the service provided, the dependence of other sectors, the consequences brought about by the incidents and the entity's market share.

6.4.2. Strategies and CSIRTs

Each Member State has a national strategy for network and information system security.

It designates a single point of contact for network and information system security. This single point of contact collaborates with the CSIRT network. Each CSIRT has sufficient resources to accomplish its missions. The CSIRTs have obligations and tasks.

With respect to bonds, CSIRTs avoid single points of default and have several means of being contacted and contacting others.

As far as the tasks of the CSIRTs are concerned, they include monitoring incidents, activating the early warning mechanism, announcing and disseminating information on risks and accidents to interested parties and conducting a dynamic analysis of risks and incidents. When they are separate, the competent authority, the single point of contact and the CSIRT of a State collaborate effectively. The CSIRTs

---

90 Computer Security Incident Response Team.

receive incident notifications. The single point of contact ensures coordination with the outside world. A network of national CSIRTs is created.

Standardization or the use of European or internationally recognized specifications for network and information system security are encouraged. Entities that are not considered essential service operators and are not digital service providers may report incidents that impact the continuity of the services they provide. On May 9, 2019, the Commission presented a report to the European Parliament and the Council assessing the consistency of the approach taken by Member States to identify essential service operators. The Commission periodically reviews the operation of the Directive and reports to the European Parliament and the Council. The first chapter of the NIS Directive provides for a regulatory framework to enhance the cybersecurity of operators of services that are necessary to ensure the proper functioning of the economy and society.

The text of the law adopted by the French Parliament was published in the JORF on February 27, 2018 and sets the general context for establishing regulation in the area of information systems security. Implementation measures are taken by decree in the Council of State, published on May 25, 2018 and by orders of the Prime Minister in the second half of 2018. The head of government establishes the implementation of the system and inter-ministerial coordination with the support of the ANSSI, which works to identify essential services.

France has established a list of essential services based on the NIS Directive (Appendix II of the Directive) as well as feedback from its national experience, in particular the protection of vitally important operators brought about by the 2013 military programming law. The list corresponds to the work carried out by ANSSI with French private and public companies and European partners[91].

The list of essential services introduces the list of essential service operators. These are large companies, SMEs and public service operators[92]. Member States are required to notify a list of essential service operators, which are subsequently updated, to the Commission.

The essential service operator must designate a representative to the ANSSI, identify its essential information system(s), implement the security rules within the given deadlines, declare to the ANSSI all security incidents likely to have an impact on the continuity of the services provided and submit to security controls carried out at the request of the Prime Minister, by the ANSSI or qualified service providers.

---

91 See cooperation group.

92 Public institutions that must protect themselves against possible attacks.

6.4.2.1. *Safety rules and the decree*

ANSSI has taken an active part in the French risk management method. This concerns:

– network security policy development and network and information system security certification, in the field of network and information system security governance;

– architecture security and network administration, in the field of network and information systems protection;

– the detection and treatment of security incidents that are able to affect networks and information systems, in the sphere of network and information systems defense;

– crisis management when security incidents occur that have a major impact on essential services, in the area of resilience of the various activities of smart city companies.

6.4.2.2. *Sanctions and controls*

Penalties are provided for in the event of non-compliance with the regulations. The controls conducted by the ANSSI correspond to a cost that has been the subject of wide and careful discussion and is specified in a decree: law and economy can only be inseparable in the various layers of cybersecurity of smart city companies.

Cybersecurity is now ubiquitous in all smart cities. However, according to Sami Ben Jabeur and Vanessa Serret, the increase in cyber-attacks around the world increased by 140% between 2013 and 2016. Cyber-attacks represent an average annual cost of US$13 million in 2018, which penalizes shareholders. The phenomenon is well perceived by all players since the Wannacry attack of May 12, 2017, which affected 300,000 computers in 150 countries, and the global Nopetya attack of June 2017.

Smart cities are therefore constantly confronted with advances in cybersecurity and attacks that contribute to ever-changing financial and geostrategic games.

7

Security Instruments in Texts Relating to Terrorism

Even before the end of World War II, the writer and essayist Georges Bernanos denounced the advent of a society where men would be subjected to machines and robots, in *La France contre les robots*. Fritz Lang's *Metropolis* had previously materialized this vision in the form of a cinematic poem. For Bernanos, technical progress is the means of questioning human freedom. In the 21st century, robots and men are supposed to be reconciled with artificial intelligence. The most intelligent robots are better chess players than human world champions. However, artificial intelligence is on track to relieve humanity of the most repetitive of tasks.

Devices play a major role in the fight for security, with millimeter wave scanners, body cameras and drones. They are indirectly covered by anti-terrorism texts, and they triumph with artificial intelligence.

7.1. Security instruments

7.1.1. *The millimeter wave scanner*

Over the last 20 years or so, techniques have invaded the perspectives of purpose, and this is true of biometrics. On the face of it, the body scanner seems to relate to a means of doing something, but the question of its relationship with the ends remains[1]. It forms part of the security measures that have been around since the 21st century, when the media coverage of attacks made it possible to get the

---

1 Latour, B. (2000). La fin des moyens. *Réseaux Communication-Technologie-Société*, 10(100), 39.

majority of the population to accept measures that, in a different context, would have been perceived as destroying freedoms.

There are two forms of body scanners: the millimeter wave body scanner and the body scanner that uses the X-ray backscatter technique. The millimeter wave scanner is most widely used in the United States, United Kingdom, the Netherlands, Germany, Italy, France and Canada.

Body scan detectors work with the aid of microwaves. Household appliances that use millimeter waves play a prominent role in most Western countries, such as microwave ovens, cell phones and Wi-Fi networks. In contrast to ultraviolet, X- or gamma-rays (known as ionizing rays), microwaves interact with the superficial layer of the skin and are not energetic enough to penetrate skin tissue. Only an insignificant portion of the radiofrequency energy emitted by the scanner is absorbed on the body's surface, while most of the radiation is reflected and then captured to produce a three-dimensional image.

The millimeter wave solution was chosen by Aéroports de Paris[2]. In particular, it is able to detect weapons and traces of explosive powder that body searches and metal detectors are not able to detect. Millimeter waves are reflected by water and stop at the surface of the skin.

A schematic image represents the human body in the form of a computer avatar; a holographic image represents the human body in 3D.

Two checks are carried out: a computer analysis by the computer and a visual check by an operator of the same gender as the passenger.

7.1.1.1. *The United States*

Body scanners have been installed in large numbers in the United States. Half of them are millimeter wave devices[3]. The others have been questioned because they emit strong radiation. The rays emitted by the Rapiscan Systems can cause dangerous changes to cells.

It was the United States that launched the introduction of full-body scanners in most Western countries, in the context of airports, with the aim of making air travel safer. Some states have resisted American pressure, but most are following their lead.

---

2 ADP.

3 They were manufactured by L-3 Communications.

Yet even within the United States, body scanners are causing controversy for medical and legal reasons.

In the medical field, studies have been conducted. They have not come to any definitive conclusions, but there are fears about cancer. Even the scanners manufactured by L-3 Communications, which emit only low levels of radiation, alarm many people. The federal government is insistent on the safety of all body scanners installed in airport terminals, but faces the mistrust of the people concerned, both aircrew and passengers, who are not convinced by the U.S. FDA's repeated assurances. The scientist Peter Rez[4] claims that "the most worrying thing is what could happen if the equipment stops working and emits too much radiation". The risk is much higher than with a medical scanner because airport scanners work more often than medical scanners and are used by TSA[5] employees who have no medical training. In addition, the Health Physics Society, an association of scientists working on radiation safety, reports that someone working as a pilot has a higher risk of cancer than the average population. Many citizens would like to see the precautionary principle applied in this area.

Many Americans also consider body scanners to be an invasion of privacy. Studies on this were carried out as early as 2002 in Florida. A quarter of potential passengers refused to comply with the full-body scanner and opted instead for the metal detector and body search.

The body scanner reveals, if only to TSA agents, the intimate parts of the people being checked, and many citizens fear that their naked photograph will end up on the Internet. This fear has been exploited by companies, one of which has developed a new line of underwear that is supposed to block radiation and enforce privacy. US citizens can refuse the use of the full-body scanner, but they must then submit to a thorough physical search, which does not respect privacy either.

A boycott of the body scanner was launched the day before Thanksgiving Day 2010. Thanksgiving was chosen because it is a day when Americans travel a lot and use airports. The slogan of the protesters was "travel with dignity". All it takes is one or two passengers refusing the use of body scanners to seriously delay travel. The right to privacy and intimacy posed by the body scanner has been relayed by multiple human rights associations. The EPIC[6] subsequently filed a complaint to suspend the deployment of body scanners in American airports on the grounds that

---

4 University of Arizona Physics.

5 Transportation Security Administration.

6 Electronic Privacy Information Center.

they would be "illegal, invasive, and ineffective"[7]. In spite of these oppositions, the body scanner is mandatory in the United States.

7.1.1.2. *Within the European Union*

On May 24, 2011, the Committee on Transport and Tourism in the European Parliament approved the report prepared by the Spanish conservative Luis de Grandes Pascual with a very large majority[8]. This report is devoted to air security and, in particular, the use of body scanners in airports.

The use of full-body scanners enhances aviation security in theory. This machine is notably used in the United Kingdom, the Netherlands, Finland and France. In Italy, full-body scanners were deployed in four airports in the country, but after a few months, the scanners were withdrawn because they were considered incompatible with privacy[9]. Since 2008, when the European Parliament stated its opposition to the introduction of body scanners, the situation has changed significantly: "Four years later, we consider that these devices can offer added value in terms of security without risk to the health of passengers or doubt about the respect of their fundamental rights." The report calls on Member States "to use technology that is the least harmful possible[10] to people's health" and bans scanners that use ionizing radiation, that is, scanners that use X-rays, in order to cater to vulnerable people who may be frail. People considered vulnerable are pregnant women, the elderly, children and the sick.

Privacy must be respected. Refusal to be subjected to a body scanner results in an obligation, in case of refusal, to submit to an alternative method of inspection that is just as effective. The refusal "must not cast any suspicion on the passenger".

However, Luis de Grandes Pascual acknowledged that the alternative – the use of manual body searches, as has already become evident in the United States – could complicate and delay the boarding of passengers who refuse to have body scanners used on them.

When people agree to be screened by the millimeter wave body scanner, random selection is applied and passengers must not be selected on the basis of discriminatory criteria: "Any form of profiling based on gender, race, colour, ethnic or national origin, genetic characteristics, language, religion or belief is unacceptable." This is in full compliance with the law on personal data.

---

7 http://epic.org/privacy/airtravel/backscatter.

8 37 votes for, 2 against, 3 abstentions.

9 Statement by Vito Riggio, President of ENAC, the Ente nazionale per l'aviazionale civile.

10 The report does not claim to guarantee absolute safety.

The image should not be an absolute identifier. Human dignity and intimacy must be taken into account. Only stick figure silhouettes should be used. No image of the human body should be stored or recorded. The images, according to MEPs, should be destroyed immediately after the security check.

Above all, "the technology used must not be capable of storing or backing up data". MEP Sylvie Guillaume points out on her blog that significant progress has been made since 2008, and that the criticisms made at the time with regard to health and privacy have not been ignored. Nevertheless, she remains skeptical about the usefulness of millimeter wave body scanners. Other monitoring techniques which are less intrusive in theory are able to carry out identical checks in airports. Body scanners have not shown themselves to be completely effective. No comprehensive study has proven that they add value in the fight against terrorism, even though this was the main justification for installing them. The German conservative Markus Ferber is more reserved than Sylvie Guillaume, believing that "body scanners infringe on privacy, without any obvious gain in terms of security".

Sylvie Guillaume has noted the link between technology and industry: several companies offer body scanners on the market that are expensive[11] but are the source of significant returns on investment for manufacturers. The latter effectively constitute a lobby for airport control and know how to make their voice heard. They are able to upgrade their equipment and products so that they meet the legal requirements for privacy and data protection.

MEPs have called for EU-wide collaboration on aviation security. This implies mutual recognition of the measures envisaged and a single security check for passengers, baggage and cargo at EU airports. In fact, the States of the European Union coordinate.

Discussions have continued between the United States, which was the first to introduce the body scanner, and the European Union, which is probably more committed than the United States to health and privacy requirements.

On July 6, 2011 the European Parliament adopted a resolution to regulate the use of body scanners as a result of the Pascual report.

The resolution preceded the commission's decision to authorize full-body scanners at airports. The parliament was able to overturn the decision within three months.

---

11 Between 100,000 and 200,000 euros each.

MEPs wanted European governments to have the appropriate technology in place before the end of April 2013, when the ban on transporting liquids by air was lifted. For this reason, the Commission announced the establishment of a working group comprising state representatives and industry and aviation officials, which were due to meet after summer 2011.

The question of discrimination arose, however. The Commission stated in its communication[12] that passengers would not be selected "solely" on the basis of sex, race, color, social or ethnic origin, religion or belief. By using the word "solely", the Commission was suggesting that these criteria would be used in the selection of passengers. However, since these data are sensitive, one can only be astonished by the prospect of such discrimination. The risk of profiling, racial or otherwise, is high.

7.1.1.3. *The body scanner in France and LOPPSI 2*

A trial based on the use of the millimeter wave technique was carried out at Paris Airport. The trial attempted at Nice Airport was abandoned following protests from a number of passengers and human rights organizations. The LOPPSI 2 has legislated in France on body scanners.

The body scanner used in France is the millimeter wave scanner, for health reasons. Indeed, serious reservations are likely to be expressed as to the absence of dangers of the waves emitted during the controls. No in-depth impact study has been conducted on the safety of devices that use X-rays in a non-medical context. Only the millimeter wave scanner, in this context, is acceptable, although it is also not certain that this body scanner is harmless.

The recommendations of the CNIL have been followed. The visualization of the images produced by the body scanner can be intrusive and detrimental to people's privacy. In order to limit this invasion of privacy, the French legislator heeded to the advice of the G29 and the CNIL.

The viewing of images is restricted to competent and authorized personnel in premises that are not open to the public. The persons carrying out the control are of the same gender as the passenger. These provisions had previously been introduced for security checks.

The CNIL emphasizes the need to train operators in the imperatives of privacy protection and recommends limiting the conservation of images to the time necessary for checks. The CNIL[13] also recommends that the visualization of images

---

12 Communication from the Commission to the European Parliament on the use of security scanners at EU airports, COM (2010) 311, $50.

13 But on this point, it is not followed.

is carried out in premises restricted to the public and is circulated to authorized persons.

7.1.1.3.1. Consent required

Searches and visits are carried out with the consent of the physical person being checked. In case of refusal, the person is subjected to another type of check, generally manual body searches, which is not without problems when it comes to privacy and human dignity. The body scanner cannot be used without free and informed consent.

7.1.1.3.2. Image analysis

The analysis of the images is subject to other advice dispensed by the CNIL which is as follows:

– anonymity: the analysis of the images is visualized by operators who do not know the identity of the physical persons and who are not able to simultaneously visualize the physical person and the image produced by the body scanner;

– non-identification: the image produced by the millimeter scanner must include a system that blurs or even prevents face recognition;

– respect for personal data: storage and recording of images is prohibited. Thus, identifying databases should not be used and privacy should not be threatened.

Should establishing airports be subject to a decree in the Council of State or a ministerial order?

7.1.1.3.3. The decree in Council of State

Until January 2011, the bill passed in first reading by the Assemblée nationale and the Sénat specified that a decree in the Council of State should determine the airports and destinations for which the use of control by imaging device using millimeter waves is authorized. The location of these airports was not irrelevant, since only one trial location existed in 2011 and relied on Aéroports de Paris. The decree in the Council of State, which has a higher value than a simple decree, brought legal security to the question of the location of the airports, which was initially restricted. The appropriateness of this recourse to the Council of State has been questioned.

7.1.1.3.4. The ministerial order

The ministerial order was proposed in an amendment by Jacques Gautier.

A joint order[14] of the Minister of Civil Aviation and the Minister of the Interior determined the airports in which the use of inspections by imaging devices using millimeter waves was authorized. The ministerial order adds an infra-legal value to the decree in Council of State. The guarantee in terms of individual liberties is therefore less far-reaching. On the contrary, the two ministers targeted by this amendment are indeed directly concerned: the Minister of Civil Aviation is in charge of the activities of air terminals and their installations, including millimeter wave body scanners; the Minister of the Interior is in charge of matters relating to national security, where the body scanner plays a role.

In an airport, identical screening and inspection stations are used, regardless of the destination. Hence, the author of the amendment, Jacques Gautier, said: "If one wanted to apply the text in its current wording and to base distribution according to the destinations, one would need to increase the quantities of equipment and people. I therefore propose that the reference to destinations be deleted, since filtering is carried out upstream anyway."

A debate took place on the proper basis for the decree in the Council of State or ministerial order with respect to the millimeter wave body scanner. Proponents of the Ministerial Order pointed out that the Order allows for simplification, which is justified "since it is simply a matter of listing airports"[15]; the necessary guarantees[16] are provided by law, that is, LOPPSI 2. Opponents of the ministerial order feared that the order would undermine individual liberties. This argument was presented not only by the usual opponents of the LOPPSI 2, the Greens and the French Communist Party, but by the Socialist Party. Jean-Pierre Miquel (SP), in particular, advocates, in matters of destinations, recourse to a jurisdiction, not to a minister – an agent of the executive who does not have the appropriate jurisdiction – since the location of a terminal falls within the scope of freedoms. "Everything that concerns public liberties must be the subject of a decision taken by the administrative or judicial courts."[17] For Jean-Pierre Miquel, the amendment reflected a deviation from civil liberties, and this is why the SP was opposed to the rectified Amendment 73. The Minister and the majority perceived in the introduction of the decree a desire for good administrative management. The decree was simpler than the decree in the Council of State and was consistent with its purpose, without infringing on public and individual liberties. The amendment was adopted and the ministerial order of the Minister of Civil Aviation and the Minister of the Interior replaced the decree in the Council of State.

---

14 Amendment no. 73 rectified, Sénat, January 19, 2011.

15 Jacques Gautier, Sénat, January 19, 2011.

16 Jean-Pierre Courtois, Sénat, January 19, 2011.

17 Jean-Pierre Miquel, Sénat, January 19, 2011.

Initially, the millimeter wave body scanner was used exclusively in Paris. The duration of the trial was an important issue for technicians, engineers, industrialists and users. The longer the duration of the experimentation, the more reliable the impact study, but too long a trial period was likely to lead to a generalization of the use of the body scanner, which was not perceived favorably by human rights associations.

The trial was planned for a period of three years: "The third to fifth paragraphs of Article L6342.2 of the Transport Code are applicable for a period of three years from the promulgation of this law." This means that the duration of the experiment was three years from the promulgation of the LOPPSI 2.

For the opponents of the body scanner, a period of three years corresponded to an almost irreversible commitment to using the millimeter wave body scanner in the long term. Two amendments were tabled before the Sénat.

Amendment no. 93 indicated that from the third to the fifth paragraph of Article L6342.2 of the Transportation Code, the applicability applied for a period of six months from the enactment of LOPPSI 2. The period of six months seemed much too short to the Minister and the Chairman of the Law Commission[18].

Amendment no. 27 indicated that from the third to the fifth paragraph of Article L6342.2 of the Transportation Code, the applicability applied for a period of one year from the enactment of LOPPSI 2[19].

The amendment was discussed. Jean-Pierre Courtois simply commented that a duration of one year seemed to him insufficient, but other actors intervened. The socialist party resolutely supported this amendment. The SP was not hostile to the body scanner, which is why a one-year experiment seemed to reconcile two requirements: the possibility of analyzing the tests and results over a suitable period of time from the point of view of the technicians and engineers, and the desire to avoid a commitment that it is too hasty and thus likely to lead to abuses of individual liberties. The Minister of the Interior at the time[20] was opposed to this amendment.

This opposition is based on two grounds: one relating to the situation prevailing in France, the other relating to the problems at the level of the European Union. For

---

18 Jean-Pierre Courtois, "Six mois, insuffisant", Sénat, January 19, 2011.

19 "We also propose shortening the length of the trial, which seems quite possible, since the trials are being carried out locally, which today makes it possible to reduce the duration envisaged in this text from three years to one year", Alain Anziani, Sénat, January 19, 2011.

20 Brice Hortefeux.

Hortefeux, in France, the millimeter wave scanner being tested at the Paris airports could not be measured in one year: the data would not be stable enough to be used, nor would it be capable of being analyzed and used because the operating time would be too short. If, despite everything, this amendment were accepted, France would be in a bad position compared to other European Union countries that were also experimenting with the use of the millimeter wave scanner at airports: "No reliable comparison with the data from other European Union countries can be made and used."[21] From the perspective of a European policy for civil aviation, or even body scanners, the deadline of one year did not seem to be able to be retained according to the minister.

Amendment no. 27 was not adopted, and it was thus the rather long three-year trial period which was promulgated. The data could be properly analyzed, compared and explained over a period of three years. However, there remained the issue of limits to freedoms, which was not taken into account.

7.1.1.3.5. Criticisms

Indeed, some criticisms were made.

No absolute guarantees of anonymity

This issue was raised by the European Data Protection Supervisor in his commentary to the Communication[22] from the Commission to the European Parliament and the Council on the use of security scanners at EU airports. In order to maintain the anonymity of natural persons using body scanners, two authorized persons work together: one of them brings the passenger into the scanner, while the other looks carefully at the display screen and carries out the check. The European Data Protection Supervisor stated in the above-mentioned communication that anonymity cannot be completely guaranteed. Even though no direct link is established between the authorized person who analyzes the images and the passenger who submits to the scanner, there is still the possibility of indirect identification, since the authorized person may be in contact with other agents who could identify the passenger. Actually, this is not at all impossible in the current context. Therefore, absolute anonymity cannot be proposed, and this is a fact to be remembered because anonymity is desired by the passenger.

Insufficient guarantees for privacy

The LOPPSI 2 states that for the body scanner, the traveler should be inspected by a person of the same gender. This acts as a guarantee against an individual

---

21 Brice Hortefeux, Sénat, January 19, 2011.
22 2010 311 final.

feeling that their most intimate parts have been palpated. Some human rights organizations have pointed out that the sexual orientation of the person entitled to checks should be taken into account as well as just their gender. A person's sexual orientation is sensitive data and should not be the cause of discrimination. If we add to this the problems that a transsexual person may face, we find ourselves in an inextricable situation.

Insufficiently guaranteed consent

Consent is required for the use of the body scanner. Hence, refusal is provided for in LOPPSI 2. This refusal is accompanied by an alternative: a traveler who does not want to use the millimeter wave body scanner "accepts" a check by metal detector and body search. A passenger cannot refuse every form of inspection; otherwise, he or she will be subject to sanctions. Incidentally, refusing any checks means that the person in question will be unable to take the flight they have booked, so can we really speak of free and informed consent? If the passenger has to choose between passing through a scanner and another investigative method, it must be determined whether this freedom of choice is real or whether passengers are forced, implicitly and not explicitly, to opt for the scanner. For example, if the refusal to submit to the inconveniences, real or supposed, of the body scanner means that you are unable to board your flight, the contract initially provided for is not executed, the choice does not exist and the question of consent is distorted: there is no possibility of materializing the agreement of will between the parties, as initially mentioned in a bilateral contract, since the transport service is no longer on offer.

If refusal of the scanner results in an additional and lengthy wait in order to reach the alternative – another inspection system – and if this additional wait results in a delay such that the passenger, although he has complied with an alternative method, is not able to board the plane for which he had made a reservation, the freedom of consent is partly vitiated. In fact, the contracting party may be opposed to the use of a body scanner, while insisting above all on the execution of the contract and its materialization, that is, boarding a flight to one's chosen destination in due time. In this case, the customer can reverse his refusal and accept the body scanner. Is this non-vitiated consent in this case? At the very least, there is room for doubt.

Despite these reservations, the experiment was carried out successfully. The millimeter wave scanner is used as a means of inspection in France, and as in many Western countries, it is in force in airports. It is obvious that the body scanner complements other security systems, including SIS[23], VIS, the Eurodac database and baggage control. The scanner supplements a system that is both complete and disparate in terms of control techniques.

---

23 Schengen personal data file.

7.1.2. *The body camera*

The body camera is a box the size of a packet of cigarettes, capable of videoing and possibly audio recording individuals. These cameras are at the disposal of police forces, placed in law enforcement vehicles or stapled to police uniforms during interventions.

The body camera was first used in the United States. Introduced in 2012 in Rialto, California, body cameras are believed to have contributed to an 88% drop in complaints against police officers. In the United States, the federal government believes that wearable cameras tend to ease tensions between the public and the police.

In 2013, in France, the Ministry of the Interior decided to experiment with these tools in Béziers, Narbonne and in priority security zones. Fabrice Cantele, head of the Biterroise police force, stated that the aim was to "film situations that deteriorate. This is additional evidence that can support legal proceedings"[24]. According to Jean-Michel Weiss[25]: "It is a tool that makes it possible to protect citizens. It also protects police officers when they are the victim of insults, disorderly behavior, threats or errors of judgement."

During this trial phase, the shelf life of the images was very limited. The files were systematically overwritten on return from the callouts unless the judicial police needed them for proceedings. In the Languedoc-Roussillon region of France, where body cameras have been tested several times in the absence of a legal framework, the example of the city of Narbonne was followed: a protocol for the use of body cameras was validated by the prefecture and the public prosecutor's office, following their instructions. Municipal by-laws, which set the framework for the system, were adopted at the end of February 2015.

The introduction of body cameras was decided, before the October 2015 Inter-ministerial Committee, by the Inter-ministerial Committee for Equality and Citizenship on March 6, 2015. At that time, a regulatory framework was planned. However, the Council of State informed the government that the use of cameras implied the intervention of a law, not a decree.

Indeed, the entire legal basis of video surveillance, video protection and the capture of images and sounds is a legal matter. The use of body cameras differs from video protection and the capture of images and sounds, but is based on the legislative instrument.

---

24 *Midi Libre*, 9/12/2015.

25 Secretary General of the Autonomous Federation of Municipal Police 34-30 (FADPM 34-30).

The Council of State and the CNIL have been assiduously working on body cameras. The Council of State has insisted a lot on the indispensable nature of the law for pedestrian cameras.

It was first considered for inclusion in the Equality and Citizenship Bill, which was discussed in the summer of 2016. It was then included in the bill strengthening the fight against organized crime and its financing, efficiency and guarantees of criminal procedure.

In the first version, body cameras featured in Part I, devoted to the fight against organized crime and terrorism through electronic communication tools. Then, in its opinion of January 28, 2016, the Council of State decided that the body camera system did not seem to have found its rightful place in Part I, which is specifically related to the fight against organized crime and terrorism. It proposed inserting the instrument in Part III, assigning it its own chapter.

The Council of State also expressed reservations about the impact study, which deals not only with body cameras but also with the reform of the Code of Criminal Procedure. It requested two corrective referrals, at the initiative of rapporteurs, but was not satisfied with the work conducted in this context; in particular, the data that allowed a better appreciation of the relevance of certain measures – comparative law studies, with references to foreign or European illustrations – appeared to be insufficient. The state of the law was even judged "deficient" by the Council of State on these points.

The CNIL established a chapter devoted to body cameras in its activity report[26].

7.1.2.1. The legislative framework

A legislative framework exists for cameras installed on public roads. The Code of Internal Security provides for purposes, locations of where to place the cameras, a maximum retention period for recordings, the rights of the persons concerned and investigation methods:

– the purposes envisaged are namely preventing attacks on the safety of persons and property, preventing acts of terrorism, rescuing people, protecting against fire and regulating road or rail transport flows;

– the places where cameras are allowed to film are the public highway and establishments open to the public when there is a risk of aggression or theft; it is forbidden to install cameras for the purpose of recording inside apartment buildings or in their entrances;

---

26 Progress Report 2015, 18–21.

– the maximum retention period for recordings is one month;

– the persons concerned by the recording have several rights: they have the right to information in a clear and permanent way on the existence of the video-protection system and the authority or person responsible, the right to access to the recordings in question and the right to verify or destroy the recording within the time period;

– the devices are controlled by prefectural authorization, which is adopted following an opinion issued by the departmental commission of video protection, and inspections by the CNIL during the implementation of the tools.

These methods, specific to video protection, are not easily transposed to embedded devices.

Cameras are capable of filming not only public roads and establishments open to the public, but also everything in their field of vision, whether public or private, in an undifferentiated manner[27], depending on the circumstances of the operation.

The registration of private areas and private homes infringes on the privacy of the persons concerned. Consequently, interference by public authorities, authorized by way of exemption, implies that essential guarantees must be envisaged so that the principle of proportionality applicable to the respect of privacy and the protection of personal data is firmly established.

The obligation to provide information is not easy to ensure and assume for body cameras either. It is essential to determine that the persons filmed are fully aware of the recording to which they have been subject; the right of access is not self-evident; however, these are the main guarantees in terms of the fundamental freedoms of the persons concerned.

Body cameras, including those that have been tested and used by law enforcement agencies, are often equipped with microphones that record the words spoken by those being filmed. Clearly, these various aspects are not covered by the Internal Security Code.

A specific framework was called for by the CNIL. This is a necessary legislature since the law aims to guarantee fundamental freedoms, both individual and collective, which naturally includes the privacy of private life. In 1995[28], the legislator, in a different economic and political context, intervened to set the rules of video surveillance, in order to associate the imperative of public order, the respect of

---

27 The positioning of fixed cameras is clearly defined.
28 Law 95-73 of January 21, 1995.

privacy and the search for the perpetrators of offences, under the guidance of the Constitutional Council.

7.1.2.2. *Purposes*

For body cameras, according to the CNIL, there is a mandatory legal precedent: to ascertain and define the purposes of the devices. Body cameras, called mobile cameras in the final text of the law of June 3, 2016, do not give rise to a permanent and continuous use. Their purpose is to avoid incidents that might occur during interventions by police and gendarmerie officers, and to circumscribe the components of such incidents, if they do occur, by authorizing the use of recordings as evidence when proceedings are initiated against either the officers or the person filmed. It is therefore a question of physically and legally securing the interventions that are carried out by police officers and the national gendarmerie.

Complementary purposes will be taken into account, including the use of recordings for pedagogical or training purposes. In addition, the law has another precedent: to determine the categories of persons entitled to use the devices.

Finally, the law will be required to specify the places in which recordings may be made and the categories of data that may be collected. Thus, it will be possible to make audio recordings that were not provided for in the Internal Security Code, if this is indispensable to the objective pursued. Special confidentiality measures are required to accompany the installation and use of the audio–video recording.

The precise perimeter of installation of the mobile cameras is indicated: particular attention is paid to the layout of the places where the interventions of the police and the national gendarmerie are likely to allow these recordings, which also have an audio element. Technically, on the basis of the purposes assigned to the mobile cameras, it is conceivable that the majority of interventions may be concerned, without distinction between the public or private nature of the place in question. However, the CNIL insists on the need to take into account the principle of proportionality and legal guarantees when it comes to application, especially if "this data capture is authorized in private homes in the context of interventions by security forces"[29].

The modalities of legal guarantees tend to preserve freedoms when installing mobile cameras.

Specific rules are reserved for recordings made in private homes, where only compelling circumstances would allow recourse to this type of recording.

---

29 Les caméras-piétons. Bilan d'activité, CNIL, 20.

Since the sole purpose of the recordings is to provide evidence in the event of an offense or negligence, only the opening of legal, administrative or disciplinary proceedings making it desirable to consult these recordings would allow the exploitation of these videos or audio-videos.

The use of recordings for educational purposes implies the removal of any element allowing the direct or indirect identification of the persons filmed. This last point refers to the European regulation[30] of the Parliament and Council which applies since April 27, 2016. Face blurring and efforts to distort the sound will be implemented.

The individuals being recorded can only be recorded for the purpose of specific information. The use of specific visual cues will allow the person being filmed to realize that he or she is being recorded. Furthermore, the public will be able to access audio and video recordings under the same conditions as those provided for video protection.

7.1.2.3. *The security requirement*

In the regulation of April 27, 2016, Article 32 is related to security: the regulation encourages anonymization and encryption practices, and the provision of information by operators and access providers.

As far as mobile cameras are concerned, security measures must guarantee that recordings cannot be viewed before the launch of proceedings. They must allow consultations of these recordings to be traced, as well as their integrity.

The CNIL studies on mobile cameras were transmitted to the Ministry of the Interior. The latter admitted that a legislative framework was needed in this area and implied guarantees in the area of personal data, which conditions the acceptability of mobile cameras by civil society.

The Penal Reform Law of 2016 sought to implement security imperatives and guarantees of individual liberties.

The capture of images and sounds by police and gendarmerie officers equipped with individual cameras was authorized for officers equipped with these devices when an incident occurs or is likely to occur.

Image capturing can intervene in all public or private places where authorized personnel also appear, including in the private homes of persons where permitted.

---

30 By-law 2016/279 published May 14, 2016.

The purpose of the devices is to prevent incidents that could occur during the course of these interventions and to contribute to the repression of the offences sought during these interventions, by collecting evidence that will be used in criminal, administrative or disciplinary proceedings. Consequently, this links in theory the administrative police and the judicial police to disciplinary proceedings.

Mobile cameras should make it possible to reduce violence against public officials and subsequent challenges by public persons. In the Assemblée nationale, an amendment was passed allowing the cameras to be used as soon as a person concerned by an intervention by law enforcement agencies requests them. In the Sénat, this possibility disappeared. As Senator Philippe Paul pointed out[31]: "It seems indeed difficult to define the conditions under which the request for triggering will be considered legitimate: should any request, even if expressed in a violent manner, be granted? Moreover, if the camera does not work, will the legal proceedings that may result from the callout be null and void?"

However, the law offers guarantees, notably visibility and compliance with the imperatives of freedom. In terms of visibility, the cameras are worn so as to be plainly visible, have a visible signal that makes the recording known and must produce, except in specific circumstances, the information of the persons recorded. Staff members with mobile cameras cannot have direct access to the recordings they make. Unless used in judicial, administrative or disciplinary proceedings, recordings will be erased after six months.

7.1.2.3.1. Compliance with the imperatives of freedom[32]

The Council of State considers the use of mobile cameras is justified by a public interest motive[33] and that the implementation is proportionate to the objectives. The individuals filmed are informed that their image is being recorded; agents equipped with cameras are unable to access the images themselves. A Council of State decree must be issued after consulting the CNIL in order to organize data processing.

Before the Sénat, the question of the shelf life, which is six months, was raised, instead of one for video protection. This difference did not seem unusual to Minister Bernard Cazeneuve, but parliamentarians were not convinced and reduced the retention period from six months to one month. The final text of June 3, 2016 saw a return to six months.

---

31 Les républicains, Sénat, January 31, 2016.

32 See four so-called "natural" rights in Article 2 of the 1789 Declaration of the Rights of Man and of the Citizen: liberty, property, security and resistance to oppression.

33 Prevention of public order violations and their possible repression.

Generally speaking, the principle of proportionality seems to have been fairly well taken into account. This is all the more necessary because, in a world where insecurity, and above all the fear of insecurity, is constantly growing, the State injects itself with a virus, thus taking the risk of "mimicry of a counter-violence that feeds others and ends up contaminating the entire system"[34].

For municipal police officers, this text provided for the possibility of recourse, but only on an experimental basis, until June 2018.

This trial did not start swiftly because of the wait for a decree, which was finally published in December 2016. The trial with municipal police officers was launched in July 2017.

Authorizations were granted to the municipal police forces of 391 cities. Subsequently, the legislator decided to definitively authorize municipal police officers to use the mobile cameras. Since the promulgation of the law of August 3, 2018, municipal police officers have been subject to the same authorization regime as their colleagues in the national police force and the gendarmerie: they can film an intervention in any place, public or private; recording is not permanent; a "specific visual signal" must indicate that the camera is recording; the data subjects are informed when the camera is activated; employees do not have direct access to the recording they have made; and deletion takes place within six months.

The law stipulated that the terms and conditions of application would be specified by a decree in the Council of State. The decree was delayed and municipal police officers had to suspend the use of their body cameras.

The implementing decree was finally signed. The Minister of the Interior confirmed its publication in the Official Gazette on March 1, 2019. Since then, a number of municipalities have begun to equip themselves with body cameras for use in missions by municipal police officers. Mobile cameras are a useful tool for ensuring the safety and security of citizens and the State.

7.1.3. *UAVs: a dual use – military and civilian*

The UAV, or unmanned aerial vehicle, has played an increasingly important role in the 21st century – first in the military sector, and subsequently in the civil and commercial sectors.

---

34 Monod, J.-C. (2007). *Penser l'ennemi, affronter l'exception. Réflexions critiques sur la pensée de Carl Schmitt*. La Découverte, Paris, 173–174.

7.1.3.1. *In the United States*

UAVs were initially developed primarily in the United States, the world's leading military power, which has used drones in Pakistan and Afghanistan. The drone can kill without endangering the lives of military personnel.

The International Civil Aviation Organization uses the term RPAS[35].

Advances in computing and technology have transformed some UAVs into platforms used in intelligence and electronic warfare.

Second, civil and commercial uses have multiplied, not only in the United States, but in most developed countries and particularly in Europe. In the spring of 2014, the European Commission announced proposals to develop the regulation of civil UAVs in Europe: "Many people, including myself, are concerned about the security, safety and privacy issues raised by these devices."[36]

In 2014, the Commission planned to carry out an impact assessment, and the European Aviation Safety Agency[37] began developing new safety standards adapted to civil UAVs, with a view to "phasing in RPAS" in airspace from 2016.

In the United States, since March 2016, it has been mandatory to register a UAV with the Federal Aviation Administration in order to be allowed to fly on US soil. Owners of UAVs weighing between 250 grams and 25 kilograms are required to register their aircraft. Failure to register leads to fines and, in some cases, criminal prosecution.

In Canada, Transport Canada is responsible for the safety of civil aircraft. The required safety is the same as for manned aircraft; a flight operations certificate is required to fly UAVs.

7.1.3.2. *In Japan*

In Japan, the Civil Aviation Bureau announced in 2015 that "AU/UAVs should not fly near or over airports, should not fly more than 150 meters above the ground or water surface, should not fly over urban and suburban areas, and should not fly in the vicinity of buildings or important facilities in the country, including nuclear facilities".

---

35 Remotely Piloted Aircraft System.
36 Silm Kallas, Vice-President of the Commission in charge of Transport.
37 EASA.

7.1.3.3. *In France*

France, which is involved in several types of operations, particularly in Africa, has understood the importance of observation and surveillance. The military planning law of December 18, 2013 emphasized observation and surveillance, while envisaging the implementation of a combat UAV program. As for surveillance UAVs, tactical UAVs are used to provide permanent and accurate intelligence; these are SDTIs (interim tactical UAV systems), which are now obsolete and have been replaced, in cooperation with the United Kingdom in 2019. As for MALE UAVs, they are part of the "knowledge and anticipation" function; several MALE UAVs have been acquired in recent years. France intends to begin using the US MQ-9 Reaper systems via the Foreign Military Sale[38] procedure, with an interest in the French and European industry. Combat UAVs, meanwhile, are intended to replace combat aircraft, since they save soldiers' lives. The option for combat UAVs is European.

7.1.3.4. *Drones and armies in the United States*

It is necessary to focus on the situation in the United States since drones, in their military function, first appeared in the United States. UAVs were initially designed to limit military losses and to replace combat aircraft[39]. Kellan Howell's analyses in the *Washington Times* are illuminating in this regard[40]. Military drones began to be used shortly before the end of the Vietnam War. Military uses are bound to develop at an increased pace: it is in the interest of armies to reduce the risk incurred for decades by the military and to prevent civilians from bearing the collateral damage. Ultimately, in 2030, the US military should use 30,000 of these unmanned aerial vehicles, according to current estimates. In reality, with drones we are witnessing a phenomenon quite similar to that which accompanied the rise of the Internet in the United States as well, and particularly in California. However, the United States has reacted faster with drones than it did with the Internet. In the privacy sector, UAVs are a primary source for digitizing personal data: thanks to the technologies that UAVs are equipped with[41], they contribute to the digital materialization of the data that underlies the physical data. Indeed, the images and other information collected and connected by UAVs are then processed on a computer and are likely to be stored on a machine or, in other circumstances, projected onto the network. As the use of UAVs increases, so does the amount of data collected. And this collection is facilitated by the aerial approach, which allows a very broad scan of the zones that these aircraft fly over.

---

38 FMS.

39 Wolf, N. (2012). The coming drone attack on America. *The Guardian*, December 21.

40 See, in particular: Howell, K. (2013). *Washington Times*, November 7.

41 Capture of images, sounds and thermal data.

7.1.3.5. *Commercial use of UAVs*

The commercial use of UAVs is growing exponentially. Amazon delivers its packages using these small robots called drones, while journalists use drones for complex photo shoots.

The police and intelligence services are planning to use drones in surveillance. By 2014, the border police would have drone devices to limit illegal immigration. Nevertheless, some states are trying to limit the use of surveillance UAVs so that they are not abused: 18 states have declared themselves in favor of a limitation.

Like UAVs, video surveillance is also on the agenda. There are many intelligent video surveillance projects. Among those worth noting are Trapwire and INDECT, which use surveillance cameras and also UAVs equipped, most of the time, with facial recognition technology, which makes it possible to identify a physical person according to his or her height, age, gender and skin color. The drone can appear as a technology that facilitates video surveillance on public roads. The camera is not fixed; it can capture several areas. It is a form of mobile video surveillance. The acceptance of surveillance by UAVs raises the same questions as video protection in legal and sociological terms. It is necessary to take into account the possible factors of acceptance of video protection in order to transpose them onto an on-board video system.

In the United States, privacy groups in the United States have campaigned for the illustration and defense of the First and Fourth Amendments, except at the time of the Patriot Act. The EPIC[42] and the EFF[43] work tirelessly to this end and have emphasized the difficult relationship between privacy and UAVs. With the advent of UAVs, the EFF has insisted on the need for transparency for citizens. Senator Dianne Feinstein, who usually defends the NSA's role in the intelligence community[44] and supported the reformed FISA law, expressed concern that the use of UAVs is increasing and could become systematic.

"I saw with my own eyes their ability to monitor. There was a demonstration in front of my house, so I went to the window to look and see who was there, staring at me." Dianne Feinstein gave a deposition in December 2013 and gave a thoughtful testimony: "Obviously the pilot was surprised, because the drone swung around and crashed. But was he equipped with a camera? Could an ill-intentioned person have

---

42 Electronic Privacy Information Center; Washington, DC.

43 Electronic Frontier Foundation.

44 Dianne Feinstein chaired the Senate Intelligence Committee in the United States and supported the US intervention in Iraq.

installed a firearm on this drone?" The Senator argued that police must seek a warrant before using a drone and also carry out a fact-finding mission when citizens are under surveillance through these devices.

A similar concern is shared by Google's former executive chairman, Eric Schmidt. The latter expressed relative concern and called for the regulation of civilian UAVs. Indeed, Schmidt fears a situation where neighbors would be likely to spy on each other via drones; he also fears the use of drones by delinquents and criminals, including terrorists. "How would you react if your neighbor bought a surveillance drone and flew it out of his yard and over your property all day long?"[45]

The American police has also made its reservations known. According to the EFF, "drones are capable of intercepting messages on the Wi-Fi network, of simultaneously tracking sixty-five people or identifying the brand of a milk carton at an altitude of more than ten thousand meters"[46].

Actors in the electronics, police, and political arenas in the United States fearfully envision a fairly immediate future where drones would be able to monitor the comings and goings of any individual.

US citizens' complaints about UAVs have tended to increase, which is logical since Americans are the largest users of UAVs for civilian use. As early as 2014, the Capitol Hill Seattle Blog reported that a complaint had been filed by a Seattle resident. "This afternoon, a foreigner flew a drone over my garden and next to my house. I ended up looking out the third floor window and saw a drone hovering a few feet away. My husband went to talk to his landlord equipped with a remote control, who was on the opposite sidewalk," she said. "He asked him to fly his drone somewhere else, but the man replied that flying his drone next to our windows was legal."

The complainant stated that the drone was equipped with a camera. The respondent justified his behavior by arguing that he was using his drone for scientific research. This exception would have been admissible if the defendant had been able to prove that he had a license and that he was using the UAV for purposes provided for under US law, which was not the case. Other complaints were subsequently filed.

As of October 19, 2013, the Special Rapporteur on extrajudicial, summary or arbitrary executions and the Special Rapporteur on the promotion and protection of

---

45 www.cnetfrance.fr; geeko.lesoir.be.
46 www.monde-diplomatique.fr/2013/12/PFLIMLIN/49974.

human rights and fundamental freedoms and counterterrorism published a report on the use of drones in the context of counterterrorism. According to the report, there may be doubts about so-called "low-level" targets. There is disagreement here between the rigorous position of the ICRC[47] and the defenders of the American position that a member of a terrorist organization can be targeted at any time. The exception introduced by the Supreme Court[48] must be interpreted strictly: the necessity of self-defense must "be immediate, irresistible and must not leave the choice of means or the time for deliberation"[49].

In France, as early as 2012, the CNIL commented on the ethical and legal frameworks to be put in place for UAVs and surveillance. Civilian UAVs can be used by voyeuristic neighbors. Indeed, depending on mobile camera sensors, camera, microphone, sound or thermal sensor or geolocation device, videos or photos taken using UAVs are often capable of distinguishing facial features and body forms. Thus, we enter the realm of personal data.

Is it possible to equate image capture by a drone with video protection? For CCTV/video-protection systems used on the public highway[50], only public authorities are authorized to film the area, and for specific purposes – in particular, the prevention of attacks on the safety of people and property or the prevention of acts of terrorism. The persons authorized to consult the images resulting from these devices must have prefectural authorization. Based on the reasoning of a lawyer, Betty Sfez, as drones equipped with cameras are similar to surveillance systems, it is possible to question the application of the video surveillance/video-protection regime.

However, the transposition of these rules is eminently complex. Who can use a drone filming a public highway and who is authorized to view the images captured by the drone?

When a drone is filming a public highway, how can the people being filmed be informed that such a system has been set up and oppose the image being recorded? Doctrine and jurisprudence are yet to find the answers to these questions.

---

47 International Committee of the Red Cross.

48 Carolina case law.

49 See Report by Christopher Heyns: une attaque de drones ne peut être légale que si elle satisfait l'ensemble "des régimes juridiques internationaux applicables" (droit d'usage de la force interétatique, droit international humanitaire).

50 Foest, D. La vidéosurveillance dans les lieux publics et ouverts au public: dispositif et application de la loi du 21 janvier 1995. DESS thesis, mention du Droit du numérique et des nouvelles techniques, Université Paris XI, under the direction of Professor Arlette Heyman-Doat.

On the legal level, two decrees dated December 17, 2015 regulate UAV law. The 2015 decrees abolish the notion of aircraft category to take into account their take-off weight.

7.1.3.6. *The law of October 24, 2016*

The law of October 24, 2016 codified in Article L 6214-1 of the French Transportation Code made electronic registration mandatory if the mass of UAVs is greater than or equal to a threshold set by regulation, which may not be greater than 800 g. A decree dated October 11, 2018 retained this 800 g mass. In 2019, the registration of UAVs weighing more than 25 kilos was made mandatory.

7.2. Standards in relation to terrorism

Anti-terrorism laws and digital development are growing in parallel. Digital technology appeared in the last two decades of the 20th century but has played a key role since the beginning of the 21st century, with broadband and very high-speed broadband giving rise to a priority installation program at the EU level.

At the same time, anti-terrorist laws are increasingly being passed in Western countries. Since the Patriot Act, which limited individual freedoms and the secrecy of correspondence in the United States, laws limiting privacy have been passed in many nation-states.

In France, it is worth mentioning the framework law of 2002[51], the law of March 9, 2004[52], the anti-terrorism law of 2006[53], the Lopssi 2 of March 14, 2011[54], the law of November 13, 2014[55], and the law of October 30, 2017 reinforcing internal security and the fight against terrorism[56].

Geopolitically speaking, France has changed a lot over the last two decades. It has reintegrated NATO's integrated command bodies[57], having left them in 1966, has participated in military operations in Afghanistan, Mali, the Central African Republic and, in 2014, in air strikes in Iraq. In this context, France, which boasted of its independence while respecting the fundamental principles of the Atlantic

---

51 Framework law 2002-1094 of August 29, 2002.

52 Law 2004-204 on the adaptation of justice to crime of March 9, 2004.

53 Law 2006-64 of January 23, 2006.

54 Law 2011-267 of March 14, 2011 of orientation and programming for internal security.

55 Law 2014-1353 of November 13, 2014.

56 Law 2017-1510 of October 30, 2017 strengthening internal security and the fight against terrorism.

57 Decision taken in 2007, which became effective in April 2009.

Alliance at the time of Charles de Gaulle, has become an ally of the United States and played an active role in the geomilitary field on behalf of NATO and the UN Security Council. In most of these instances, the fight against terrorism is cited as the primary or secondary motive for French military efforts.

On the legal level, if the notion of terrorism is assimilated to a concept of transition, it is part of a vision of the international order that is divided between a traditional, interstate option and a supra-state, universalist option[58].

7.2.1. *The law of 2014*

In the summer of 2014, new measures were considered and anti-terrorism legislation was drafted. It was decided that the procedure chosen would be that of accelerated voting, which limits the examination by the Assemblée nationale and the Sénat to a single reading. This procedure was justified by the threatening nature of terrorist intentions against France and also by the broad and diversified commitment of the French army.

7.2.1.1. *Exemptions to freedom of expression*

Freedom of the press and the 1881 Act raise questions about the use of these exemptions in relation to section 10 of the 2014 anti-terrorism bill. The Anti-Terrorism Bill provides for the suppression of terrorist propaganda. This raises questions about the status of the 1881 press law. Several amendments have been tabled, without much success. They have the merit of highlighting the contradictions of the bill with regard to the 1881 law. An amendment (no. 141) was presented to the Assemblée nationale by Laure de la Raudière[59]. It suggested deleting two paragraphs (4 and 5) to ensure that the repression of terrorism did not cease to depend on the 1881 law[60]. The amendment was rejected.

Another amendment (no. 36) was presented by the ecologist group with a request for an open vote. It applied to article 4 of the anti-terrorist law, which deals with "terrorist propaganda". As de la Raudière pointed out, the purpose of this article is to remove the offenses of "provocation of acts of terrorism" and "apology for acts of terrorism" from the procedural regime of the 1881 law, so that these

---

58 Laurens, H. (2009). Conclusions. In *Terrorismes, histoire et droit*, Delmas-Marty, M., Laurens, H. (eds). CNRS.

59 UMP congresswoman.

60 "Terrorist propaganda is, in my opinion, from a legal point of view, an abuse of freedom of expression and must be judged as such", Laure de la Raudière, Assemblée nationale, second session of September 17, 2014.

offenses can be integrated into the Penal Code. The amendment stipulates that the crime of "glorifying acts of terrorism" should continue to be subject to the 1881 Press Act, while the crime of "provoking acts of terrorism" should be introduced into the Penal Code. On this subject, it is appropriate to refer to the ideas of Julie Alix[61] as well as Isabelle Attard[62], who draws a distinction between apology and provocation. These two concepts have almost nothing in common: the rapporteur stipulated that apology for terrorism is "the expression of an opinion, certainly potentially odious, but which does not directly incite someone to commit a crime". Moreover, Article 4 makes non-public provocation an offence, although it does not incriminate non-public apology. The 1881 law, despite its seniority, protects both individual and collective liberties. Although heir to the Third Republic, the origin of this law goes back to the Enlightenment, before the Revolution, when the Encyclopedia, on a philosophical level, and the pamphlets, in terms of what we today call civil society, disseminated ideas that contributed to the collapse and disintegration of the "old regime". Hence, it is appropriate that the 1881 law, which protects freedom of expression, should apply to apology and not to provocation. Environmentalists fear a programmed disintegration of the 1881 law[63]. Amendments have already taken place and have undermined this law, which is essential for freedoms[64].

In an open ballot, out of 17 votes cast, four voted in favor of the amendment and nine against the amendment, which was defeated.

7.2.1.2. The Internet: an aggravating factor

The offences established by Article 4, both apology and provocation, are aggravated insofar as the medium used is the Internet. A debate is under way on the appropriateness of this aggravating circumstance.

This is not the first time that an offence has been aggravated when the medium used is prohibited. This happened, for example, in the case of moral harassment.

Two amendments are intended to prevent the introduction of this "aggravating cause"[65]. First, this is the case with amendment 9, defended by Isabelle Attard. The number of offences for which the medium of the Internet is an aggravating

---

61 Alix, J. (2010). *Terrorisme et droit pénal, étude critique des incriminations terroristes.* Dalloz.

62 Member of Parliament, ecologist, researcher.

63 Julie Attard uses the term "unraveling".

64 "Do not create a new crime of opinion … which is a dangerous tool in the hands of a democratic government and an atomic weapon in the hands of an authoritarian government", Isabelle Attard, Assemblée nationale, second session of September 17, 2014.

65 Amendments no. 9 and no. 131.

circumstance is tending to increase over time. A confusion is being established between the possible uses of the tool and the actual audience: while it is true that some Internet content is very accessible, the audience and the impact of this content can often be more limited than with the medium of a newspaper. Moreover, online content is much easier and quicker to remove than a newspaper article. For a press article, a newspaper must be withdrawn from sale (following a conviction, for example) to limit its circulation, which very rarely happens, whereas withdrawing content from the Web can be accomplished in a very short period of time and is more easily pronounced by a court of law.

Finally, on the basis of the text under review, the sentence pronounced could be seven years' imprisonment, which exceeds the other convictions for this crime.

Nicolas Huicq[66] intervened in the debate to emphasize the characteristics of the Internet. Technically, this space knows no spatio-temporal boundaries. It works on instantaneity. It is very difficult, if not impossible, to block foreign sites. Parliamentarian Huicq referred to geopolitics and cybersecurity: "If it were possible to exercise such control, the Baltic countries would not have experienced attacks any more than Iran did from the Israel Defense Forces in the sphere of electronic warfare."[67]

Amendment 131 seeks to delete paragraph five of Article 4 and deals with aggravating circumstances relating to the Internet[68]. Christian Paul[69] noted that the Internet allows the permanent and repeated dissemination of images that may be used to serve a terrorist cause, especially through links pointing to a certain amount of content. The question that arises is whether aggravating circumstances will be effective in the fight against terrorism. The latter does not only target the jihadist movement, but protean movements. Aggravating circumstances have not been foreseen for the book, in the context of printing, nor for television, which is watched by millions of people. In this case, why take this initiative for digital networks and the Internet? "If it were demonstrated that, for a few dozen sites, since most of the activity takes place on social networks, it would be worthwhile to provide for aggravating circumstances and that there were no other solutions, such as increasing

---

66 UMP deputy.

67 Nicolas Huicq, Assemblée nationale, second session of September 17, 2014.

68 On the Internet, the deputy agrees on the scope of the law, which is restricted: most of the sites in question are located abroad; only five are in France: "The provisions will be inapplicable, since the publishers will arrange for the data not to be hosted in France or will use data encryption techniques", Lionel Tardy, a right-wing deputy, Assemblée nationale, second session of September 17, 2014.

69 Socialist congressman.

criminal sanctions, we could perhaps move in this direction. But this is not the case".[70] As a result, the introduction of aggravating circumstances is dangerous and contributes to the "exfiltration"[71] of the 1881 Act. Indeed, the aggravating circumstances are not adapted to the characteristics of digital networks. "Aggravating circumstances" constitute a risk for democracy and are not adapted to the stakes raised by terrorism. The amendment was therefore not adopted.

Another amendment[72], more modest, but along the same lines as the previous one, was presented and defended by Danielle Auroi[73]. It did not call into question the "aggravating" circumstances but proposed to reduce the amount of the penalty for non-public statements. Indeed, to justify the aggravation of penalties for the apology and provocation of terrorism on the Internet, the rapporteur stated: "This aggravating circumstance of commission by means of the Internet is justified by the particularly extensive and rapid publicity that this communication tool makes it possible to give to the messages conveyed." The argument of extensive advertising was no longer valid if the comments were not public. The amendment therefore moved towards removing the aggravation of the penalty when the provocation was not public, even though the facts were committed by using a telecommunications service to the public online. This reasoning was not accepted by the rapporteur, Sébastien Piettasanta. He tried to show that non-public provocation on the Internet exists, that it is likely to gather an important audience via private forums, and that the multiplier effect of this would be powerful. The rapporteur was therefore against softening the penalty. For the government, Myriam El Khomri considered the case of social networks which can have a negative effect in terms of non-public provocation. Amendment no. 10 was rejected.

Another amendment[74] envisaged a new type of incrimination in the context of provocation. Meyer Hahib[75] called for emblems or flags to be covered by provocation in the same way as words. The amendment was fairly favorably received, but rejected, because flags – to the extent that they are accompanied by explicit utterances, which is almost always the case – fall under Article 4. The proposed offence would be weaker than apology for terrorism, since the person incriminated would only risk one year's imprisonment, whereas apology is punishable by five years' imprisonment. Hahib had the support of the UMP

70 Christian Paul, Assemblée nationale, second session of September 17, 2014.

71 Term used by Marie-Françoise Bechtel, MRC-PS deputy.

72 Amendment no. 10.

73 Member of Parliament for the Environment.

74 Amendment no. 125.

75 UDI deputy "*Français hors de France*" (French outside France).

group, which called for an open vote. Among the 30 votes cast, nine voted in favor of the amendment and 21 voted against.

Another amendment, no. 11, returned to the freedom of expression and the political character of the opinions disseminated with regard to apology and provocation. It was important not to provide for an immediate trial for the apology of terrorism, by inserting a paragraph which, after the word "political", added the words "crime of apology of terrorism" to Article 397-6 of the Code of Criminal Procedure. Actually, Article 397-6 of the Code of Criminal Procedure in fact provides for the exclusion of press and political offenses from the scope of the procedures of summons by report and immediate appearance. However, the offense of apology for terrorist acts may seem to fall into these two categories. Apology for terrorism is an opinion that does not directly incite the commission of an offense. The impact study and the report justify Article 4 by the need to judge the apology of terrorist acts by immediate summons. However, it is not appropriate for a newspaper publisher or the author of a political statement to be tried immediately. The amendment was nevertheless rejected.

Two additional amendments shed some light on the bill.

The first amendment sought to strengthen repression by making it a crime to consult a site[76]: this was about creating a specific offense around the habitual consultation of sites that glorify terrorism or incite terrorist action. Internet users would be placed in police custody, and in this context, it would be possible to assess the dangerousness of these persons. A two-tier filter would be put in place so as not to disproportionately infringe on freedom of communication and opinion. A distinction would be made between simple consultation and routine consultation. Persons consulting these sites for professional reasons, such as intelligence missions or scientific research, could not be incriminated. This amendment took over from a bill[77] that was not put on the agenda. The rapporteur expressed the unfavorable opinion of the commission, which did not wish the consultation of sites to be incriminated. Nevertheless, the commission's work tended to admit that routine consultation is part of the list of material facts that, in conjunction with others, prove terrorist action, yet the amendment was rejected.

The second additional amendment is amendment no. 59 as corrected. This was an amendment proposed by Eric Ciotti[78], which provided for an alternative to prison

---

76 Amendment no. 58.
77 Co-signed by three UMP deputies: Philippe Goujon, Guillaume Larrivé and Eric Ciotti.
78 UMP deputy.

for minors[79]. This alternative is already provided for racial crimes. The CRIF and the Holocaust Memorial provide training for these crimes. The rapporteur acknowledged that there are "in juvenile criminal law, courses of civic training, which may be similar to this type of punishment". However, the amendment was rejected.

Before the Sénat, the Law Commission, contrary to what happened before the Assemblée nationale, considered that only the offenses of apology for terrorism and provocation to terrorism committed on the Internet should be assimilated to terrorist offenses and included in the Penal Code; the specific regime of the 1881 law should continue to apply to the commission of the same offenses on traditional media. In public session, the Sénat retained this wording[80]. A difference thus appeared to exist between the digital medium of the Internet and the medium of the press as it was already understood in 1881, when the law protecting the press was passed.

7.2.1.3. Administrative blocking of sites

The administrative blocking of sites is the other essential aspect relating to the relationship between digital technology and the anti-terrorist law: it also raises the question of freedom of expression via the Internet with regard to the fight against terrorism.

7.2.1.3.1. The imperative of freedom of expression and opinion

Recent history points to a certain mistrust of administrative measures. The administrative block was adopted in the framework of the LOPPSI 2 for child pornography sites, with reference to the Convention on Cybercrime[81]. It led to a referral to the Constitutional Council, which did not follow it up. The provisions never came into force for lack of an implementing decree.

Some deputies and senators argued that the fight against terrorism does not justify the blocking of sites, let alone an administrative blockade. According to Lionel Tardy, "administrative blocking is a device that can be dangerous for those who have nothing to do with terrorism, and totally counterproductive in the fight against those who are involved in it"[82].

---

79 That is, a training program to "de-indoctrinate" minors.
80 It rejected the Government's amendment no. 74, Sénat session of October 15, 2014.
81 November 23, 2001, text signed and ratified by France.
82 Lionel Tardy, Assemblée nationale, second session of September 17, 2014.

7.2.1.3.2. Technical security

The implementing decree of February 5, 2015[83] relates, as envisaged, to the administrative blocking of terrorist and child pornography sites. Collaboration was institutionalized with the *Office central de lutte contre la criminalité liée aux technologies de l'information et de la communication* (Central Office for the Fight against Crime, Information and Communication Technologies). Even with this implementing decree, technical security issues were far from being resolved. Internet service providers would be given a list of sites to be blocked by the intelligence services, if they have not managed to obtain the removal of content from the host or publisher. According to Lionel Tardy, "in addition to the risk of blocking sites that should not be blocked, the devices envisaged in this bill are very easily circumvented, whether by the site owners or by visitors". This risk was highlighted as early as 2011 in the report on network neutrality by Corinne Erhel and Laure de La Raudière. Some encryption practices "present security risks far greater than the defense of interests protected, ineffectively, by blocking or filtering", wrote these MPs[84], "unless you want to ban all secure sites, particularly in the banking or Internet sales, you can do nothing against data encryption, which is the only guarantee of secure transactions".

The director of the French National Agency for Information Systems Security expressed his reservations at a symposium held on September 10, 2014. These reservations were of a technical nature. Thus, the deadline for implementing the blocking must be taken into consideration. In addition, is it advisable to use blocking by host name and domain name or through URL filtering? The application decree referred to both domain names and host names. It is also important that the chosen solutions do not block legal content not covered by the law. According to Marie-Anne Chapdelaine[85], "whether we are talking about IP blocking, by router or by domain name or by DPI, each method has its own constraints and specificities, all of which can be potentially circumvented"[86].

Most stakeholders, represented in particular by the National Digital Council and the Commission for Reflection on Rights and Freedoms in the Digital Age (created by the Assemblée nationale in 2013) shared these concerns. Anonymization

---

83 Decree no. 2015-125 of February 5, 2015 relating to the blocking of sites provoking acts of terrorism or apology for terrorism and sites broadcasting images and representations of minors of a pornographic nature.

84 Corinne Erhel and Laure de la Raudière, Rapport sur la neutralité des réseaux, Assemblée nationale, April 13, 2011.

85 Member of parliament for the socialist party.

86 Marie-Anne Chapdelaine, Assemblée nationale, second sitting of September 17, 2014.

techniques[87] are fairly easy to use and lead to circumvention. Blocking devices are likely to lead to overblocking on sites that are not targeted by the blocking measure, which can pose a danger to the resilience of the network. Moreover, if there are four main operators, other, smaller operators will find it difficult to apply such a measure.

Withdrawal of Article 9

The deletion of Article 9 was requested by several deputies, including Lionel Tardy. It was naturally refused by the Law Commission. The latter adopted, to improve the bills, an amendment proposed by the rapporteur Sébastien Pietrasanta: the monitoring of the list of sites to be blocked is to be ensured by a "qualified" person. This person will not be a magistrate, but a person appointed by the CNIL for a period of three years with a non-renewability clause to guarantee his independence[88]. Also taking into account the principle of subsidiarity, the government believed that there was no threat to freedoms with Article 9.

On the technical question and the small number of sites that would be affected by the implementation of Article 9, Minister Cazeneuve did not deny that few French sites would be involved. However, he did call for cooperation between the countries of the European Union so that a single anti-terrorist body could apply the measures envisaged in France in the various member states of the European Union.

7.2.1.3.3. The use of a judicial judge

This was the subject of two amendments, no. 123 and no. 130, and the debate was relaunched by amendment no. 77.

Amendment 123 was presented by Isabelle Attard. She wanted the blocking measure to be decided by the judicial judge. She encouraged the use of the mechanism put in place to block illegal sites that offer online gambling, via the *Autorité de régulation des jeux en ligne* (Online Gambling Regulatory Authority) (ARJEL)).

Amendment 130 was presented by Christian Paul. He also proposed that recourse be made to the judicial judge for blocking. The question that arose was whether the blocking corresponds to a preventive administrative police measure, which can be appealed to the administrative judge, or whether it is a judicial decision, after a complaint has been lodged. Minister Cazeneuve noted that it is impossible for a Minister of the Interior to file a complaint. He is likely to intervene under Article 809 of the Code of Criminal Procedure, when he has an interest to act. Emergency

---

87 Recommended by the regulatory authorities in the field of personal data.

88 The CNIL in fact chose a magistrate honorary adviser to the Court of Cassation from among its members.

administrative police measures are a reliable means of prevention. These amendments were defeated.

With amendment 77, Lionel Tardy mentioned the administrative blocking and, again, the judicial judge. Like Christian Paul, he reaffirmed that going through a judicial judge is "an inescapable principle". He mentioned the opinion of the director of the ANSSI which expressed reservations on the technical level and in particular blocking at the URL level, implemented through DPI[89]. Minister Cazeneuve referred to the positions of the Constitutional Council. The latter validated the concept of administrative blocking in its decision no. 2011-625 of March 10, 2011: "The decision of the administrative authority may be contested at any time and by any interested party before the competent court, if necessary, in summary proceedings." Amendment 77 was rejected.

Devices for reporting illegal content: a crime of opinion?

Two identical amendments, 16 and 76, were proposed, both aimed at deleting paragraph two. This paragraph stipulates that hosters and ISPs are required to set up mechanisms for reporting illegal terrorism-related content. The Constitutional Council had already noted "the frequent difficulty of assessing the legality of content". This is particularly true for what is deemed to be an apology for terrorism. On this subject, Lionel Tardy declared: "It is not the role of intermediaries, whether they are hosts or ISPs, to assess the content of sites ... The National Digital Council has issued a very strong opinion on this subject ... the qualification of the notions of commission of terrorist acts or their apology is open to subjective interpretations and carries a real risk of drifting towards a crime of opinion." Moreover, instead of developing the internet-signal.gouv.fr reporting platform, operators were frequently called on, thus acting as a lobby which could bias the debate.

A qualified person appointed by the Defender of the Rights, and not by the CNIL

Danielle Auroi[90], in amendment no. 3, requested that the qualified person be appointed not by the CNIL, but by the Defender of the Rights, who would have a broader vocation than the CNIL in terms of freedoms and would be independent, given their irrevocability, their long mandate of six years, and their incompatibility with other elective or professional functions. The amendment was withdrawn insofar as it seemed to run contrary to the Constitution which, in Article 71-1, stipulates that "the institutional act defines the remit and form of the intervention of the rights defender". As the law under discussion is not an institutional act, it could not modify its competences.

---

89 Deep Packet Inspection.

90 Member of Parliament for the Environment.

Auroi managed nevertheless to get an amendment on the qualified person adopted: amendment no. 4. This amendment provides for the annual submission of an activity report by the competent person. In this way, specific information will be provided on the number of requests for withdrawals and the contents actually withdrawn. The application to draw up a report appears in the application decree of February 5, 2015.

7.2.1.3.4. The administrative blocking and the apology for and provocation of terrorism

Amendment no. 39 returned to the possibility of allowing the administrative blocking of sites that glorify and incite terrorism. This question was addressed by UMP, Socialist and Green party deputies as well as being defended by Auroi: "Blocking websites does not allow their content to be removed and can easily be circumvented by various technical means that are simple and already widely known. The systematic blocking of content that glorifies or incites terrorism would make the phenomenon less visible, better encrypted and therefore even more difficult to control."[91]

In addition, the possible incitements to apologize for and provoke terrorism would appear on social networks and blocking them would prove very difficult. The amendment was rejected.

Access from the premises of the police or gendarmerie to a computer system for the purpose of a search of a person's data[92]

Two amendments, no. 97 and no. 129, were tabled but not retained: amendment 97 sought to guarantee the rights of persons searched, in particular "protected professions", lawyers, doctors and judges. Amendment 129 emphasized the need to take into account data storage practices, in particular through cloud computing and the reference to Article 57 of the Code of Criminal Procedure, according to which the investigator cannot consult or enter data without the presence of the person concerned, a third party designated by him or, failing that, two witnesses. The rapporteur argued that the search of remotely stored data is carried out under the conditions mentioned in the Code of Criminal Procedure.

7.2.1.3.5. The cost of these measures for operators

This cost is heavy to bear, according to the operators whose point of view was relayed by some deputies and senators.

---

91 Danielle Auroi, Assemblée nationale, first session of September 18, 2014.
92 Article 10 of the bill.

The compensation of costs incurred by the operator in the application of the new measures is an obligation under the Constitution. The compensation must have an indisputable basis. The decree that would be devoted to this subject implies that justifications for the elements corresponding to the additional costs must be provided for in law.

Before the Sénat, the time limit available to the publisher or content host to remove disputed content was increased to 48 hours. The mixed Joint Committee favored the text adopted by the Assemblée nationale[93] on the prohibition of referencing sites by enforcement, and the deadline was reduced to 24 hours. In addition, the CMP approved the ban on the listing of sites upon enforcement.

After the adoption of the anti-terrorism law, there were no referrals to the Constitutional Council. In fact, it takes sixty members of parliament from the same chamber to refer it to the Constitutional Council. However, only the ecologist parliamentarians had abstained by the time the law was finally adopted. On the contrary, constitutional control has been carried out in certain countries of the European Union with regard to certain anti-terrorist laws[94].

7.2.2. *The law strengthening internal security and the fight against terrorism*

After the 2015 attacks in France, the government informed the ECHR that, in light of the situation, certain provisions of the European Convention for the Protection of Human Rights and Individual Freedoms would no longer be honored, including the declaration of a state of emergency[95].

A state of emergency is a form of state of exception that allows administrative authorities (Minister of the Interior, prefects) to impose measures that restrict freedoms, such as prohibiting the circulation of firearms for certain categories. The most significant measures are house arrest, closure of certain places, prohibition of demonstrations, and day and night administrative searches. The judicial authority is thus relieved of some of its prerogatives. Unlike the state of siege, it does not apply to the armed forces.

---

93 Amendment no. 13.

94 Roudier, K. (2012). Le contrôle de constitutionnalité de la législation anti-terroriste; étude comparée des expériences espagnole, française, italienne. Prix de thèse du Conseil constitutionnel 2012, *Nouveaux cahiers du conseil constitutionnel,* 37, October.

95 In force since the attacks of November 13, 2015.

An extension of the state of emergency was approved, but the state of emergency could not be extended indefinitely. The bill put an end to the state of emergency but introduced into the French legal corpus measures that had previously applied during the state of emergency. This led to the passage of the law of October 30, 2017, strengthening internal security and the fight against terrorism[96], under the government of Édouard Philippe, championed by Interior Minister Gérard Collomb.

The rapporteur[97] and former Keeper of the Seals Michel Mercier proposed a time limit for the application of certain provisions of December 31, 2021. All the provisions were involved in administrative control or surveillance, namely, the subpoena in the municipality, the preventive use of electronic tags and the administrative search. The provision that was supposed to authorize the Minister of the Interior to declare all of its telephone numbers and electronic communication identifiers was deleted from the text because Michel Mercier believed that these measures would have been "a strong infringement of constitutional freedoms: respect for privacy, secrecy of correspondence and the rights of defense".

Those under house arrest would be subject to three checks per week, instead of one per day in the initial bill, to ensure that the ordinary system is not more severe than the state of emergency.

The renewal of summonses, decided for periods of three or six months, would be authorized by a judicial judge who is the judge of liberties and detention; there would no longer be any question of unlimited renewal by the prefect. However, there was an update with respect to the state of emergency: the creation of "protective perimeters" around a place or event subject to a terrorist risk. This measure makes it possible, within these perimeters of protection, to carry out checks on individuals and body searches of people going to these places or events. Opponents of the law have pointed out that this new infringement on privacy is unacceptable. The law was applicable until December 31, 2020 and subject to monitoring by parliament[98].

Protective perimeters were established by the administrative authority by means of a reasoned order; access and movement of persons were regulated[99] with the aim of securing a place or event exposed to the risk of terrorism.

The administrative authority may also close places of worship in order to prevent the commission of terrorist acts if the words expressed in such places of worship, the

---

96 Law no. 2017-1510.

97 UDI senator.

98 Article 5 of the law.

99 Article L226-1 of the Internal Security Code.

ideas or theories disseminated therein or the activities that take place there incite the commission of terrorist acts or condone such terrorist acts. The closure may not exceed six months[100].

Individual administrative control and surveillance measures may be taken by the Minister of the Interior after informing the public prosecutor in Paris and the territorially competent public prosecutor, if there are serious reasons to believe that the behavior of the person concerned constitutes a particularly serious threat to security and public order. These measures are as follows:

– prohibition to move outside a determined geographical perimeter, no smaller than the territory of the commune. The delimitation of this perimeter does not obliterate the normal and habitual pursuit of family activities and professions, but may extend to the territories of other communes or departments other than the habitual place of residence;

– the person concerned is required to report periodically to the police or gendarmerie units;

– declare his place of residence and any changes to the place of residence.

These obligations are decided for a maximum period of three months from the notification of the decision of the Minister of the Interior, when the conditions provided for are still met. Beyond a cumulative period of six months, each renewal is subject to the existence of new or additional elements. The total cumulative duration of these obligations does not exceed 12 months[101].

Visits and seizures are also provided for by law. Upon reasoned referral by the administrative authority, the liberty and custody judge of the Paris Regional Court, by a written and reasoned order, having obtained the opinion of the Public Prosecutor of the Republic of Paris, may authorize the visit to a place and the seizure of documents, objects or data, for the sole purpose of preventing the commission of terrorist acts. This can be ordered if there are serious reasons to believe that a place is frequented by a person whose behavior is a particularly serious threat to public safety and order, who, moreover, habitually enters into relations with persons or organizations that incite, facilitate or participate in acts of terrorism. The order also applies to those who support or disseminate information about terrorist acts, when this dissemination is accompanied by ostensible adherence to the ideological cause that disturbs public order, or adheres to themes that incite the commission of acts of terrorism or condone terrorist acts.

---

100 Articles L227-1 and L227-2 of the Internal Security Code. In fact, very few places of worship have been closed since the law came into force.
101 Articles L228-1 et seq. of the Internal Security Code.

The visit takes place between 6 a.m. and 9 p.m. in the evening, unless express, written, reasoned authorization is granted by the liberty and detention judge of the High Court of Paris, and is subsequently based on the urgency or the needs of the operation.

The person in question must be in a position to provide information on the objects, documents and data present at the location of the visit which relate to the initial purpose of preventing the commission of terrorist acts. If "there are serious reasons to believe that his/her behavior constitutes a threat of a particularly serious nature to public security and order", the person in question may be detained on the spot by a judicial police officer for the time strictly necessary to conduct operations, provided that the liberty and detention judge of the High Court of Paris is informed of this first.

If the visit makes it possible to determine that the person in question possesses documents, objects or data that post a grave threat to security and public order, the documents may be seized in order to prevent the commission of terrorist acts. The data contained in any computer system or terminal equipment present at the place of the visit may also be seized, by either copying or by seizing the device if copying cannot be done or completed during the visit[102].

Finally, around borders, ports and airports, the identity of a person can be verified by judicial police officers, for the investigation and prevention of offences related to cross-border crime, to verify compliance with the obligations of holding, carrying and presenting ID and documents provided for by law[103].

Between November 1, 2017 and January 17, 2020 there were settled: 509 protected zones, seven closures of places of worship, 236 individual administrative control and surveillance measures, 150 visits and 854 seizures.

Of the 74 individual administrative control and surveillance measures taken as of November 30, 2018, three concern persons who have been under a state of emergency for more than 600 days and eight for more than a year, first under the state of emergency and then under the act to strengthen internal security and the fight against terrorism[104].

---

102 Articles L229-1 et seq. of the Internal Security Code.

103 Article 78-2 of the Code of Criminal Procedure.

104 See Pascual, J. (2017). Premier bilan de la loi de sécurité intérieure. *Le Monde,* December 20.

Protected zones are aimed at securing an event, although some cases have raised questions of legality[105].

The law takes up the idea of the state of emergency. The *New York Times* has stated that the law legalizes "the state of emergency decreed by François Hollande on a permanent basis"[106] and the texts have "contributed little to the fight against terrorism, any more than the existing laws, while really threatening the rights of citizens". For Dominique Rousseau, professor of constitutional law[107], this legislation "makes us accustomed to living under a state of emergency".

The text was not referred to the Constitutional Council before its promulgation. It was seized of four priority constitutionality issues on measures to prevent acts of terrorism. Its decisions of February 16 and March 29, 2018 declared the essential elements to be in conformity with the Constitution. However, the conditions for appeals to the administrative judge and the seizure of documents or objects during searches with effect from October 1, 2018 were censured.

The 2018–2022 Programming and Reform Law for Justice brought changes intended to draw the conclusions of these censures[108].

In November 2020, Parliament debated a law on "global security" that would encourage the use of surveillance drones in missions entrusted to the police, introduce blurring of police officers and gendarmes filmed during police interventions, and allow municipal police to participate in securing sports, recreational and cultural events.

Thus, between increased means and security purposes, the old balance between security requirements and the protection of freedoms is increasingly being challenged. Is there still a spirit of freedom, to use the title of Luis Bunuel's film?

---

105 Daubresse, M.-P., Rapport fait au nom de la commission des lois constitutionnelles, de législation, du suffrage universel, par la mission de contrôle et de suivi du 30 octobre 2017 renforçant la sécurité intérieure et la lutte contre le terrorisme, December 19, 2018.

106 Blavignat, Y. (2017). Le New York Times étrille le projet de loi antiterroriste de Macron. *Le Figaro,* June 13.

107 Raulin, N. (2017). Dominique Rousseau: "Emmanuel Macron se mêle de tout, comme ses prédécesseurs". *Libération*, August 3.

108 Article 65 of Law No. 2019-222 of March 23, 2019 on 2018–2022 programming and justice reform.

8

Security and Democracy

Between intelligent machines and security requirements, is there a place for this spirit of freedom, supported by the fundamental rights that forged a new conception of democracy after World War II, and in particular, freedom of opinion, freedom of expression and freedom of communication? This is the question we have to answer.

> Democracy is a form of government that involves a plurality of opinions, and the claim to be in possession of the facts does not match with democracy. It is necessary to accept that there are different opinions and not just one truth, which the government would do well to apply[1].

The protection of diversity of opinion is one of those fundamental freedoms guaranteed by the Universal Declaration of Human Rights (1948), the European Convention for the Protection of Human Rights and Fundamental Freedoms of the Council of Europe (1950), the UN International Covenant on Civil Rights (1966) and the European Charter of Fundamental Rights (2000).

But since the beginning of the 21st century, social networks and the GAFA economy have made information faster. Hence, the mass media have focused on the not so recent problem of "misinformation", which is the subject of new provisions.

French law has long contained provisions aimed at stopping the spread of false information. The law of July 29, 1881 on the freedom of the press[2], which punishes knowingly erroneous, defamatory, insulting or provocative statements, was made applicable to online public communication services by article 6 of the law of

---

1 Jean-Claude Monod, May 22, 2018 at a conference on "fake news", headquarters of the Centre national de la recherche scientifique.

2 Chapters IV and V.

June 21, 2004 on confidence in the digital economy. The electoral code guarantees the proper conduct of election campaigns by combating the dissemination of fake news and commercial advertising for election propaganda purposes (article L52.1). The summary procedure is likely to put an end to damages resulting from the content of an online public communication service; it is a matter of stopping the dissemination of false information that would infringe on the privacy or the protection of personal data.

However, the dissemination of false information during election periods is largely amplified by digital platforms and social networks, the economic model of which values content that generates controversy after controversy.

In the United States, during the election campaigns for Donald Trump and Hilary Clinton, it appears that Facebook relayed "fake news" which, according to the American media, came from Russia with the aim of destabilizing the American political world. Facebook does not wish to regulate the news that circulates on its network, whether fake or otherwise. This regulation does not correspond to its role, which is assimilated to a liberal interpretation of the First Amendment of the American Constitution, relating in particular to the free circulation of information and freedom of the press.

France, however, has had a different conception of freedom of the press since the law of 1881. This corresponds to legislation concerning false news and hate speech.

8.1. Fake news

Two laws, one an ordinary bill and the other an institutional bill, were adopted on "false information"[3]. The concept of fake news was not defined in the original text because it is based on the definition contained in the 1881 law on freedom of the press.

It is worth mentioning the lengthy work on the definition of "false information". First adopted by the Law Commission, misinformation is "any allegation or imputation of a fact without verifiable elements that make it likely"[4].

The amendment clarifies that opinions and satirical articles will be excluded from the scope of the Act. Indeed, caricature and satire are part of the freedom of the

---

3 Bill "relating to the fight against the manipulation of information". Some deputies and senators have regretted that the reform is carried out through an institutional bill that does not provide scope for an impact study.

4 Amendment AC16.

press, even though the application of these forms of freedom has often given rise to diverse jurisprudential interpretations. "The fight against misinformation will be limited to cases in which it is established that the dissemination of such information is done in bad faith", writes Naïma Moutchou[5]. The Cultural Affairs Commission has defined false information as "any allegation or imputation of a fact that lacks verifiable elements of such a nature as to make it plausible". The rapporteur then had a new wording approved, as follows: "Any allegation or imputation of a fact, inaccurate or misleading, constitutes false information." And the notion of "bad faith" was replaced by the notion of "deliberate misrepresentation".

8.1.1. *The definition*

In the second reading before the Assemblée nationale, the rapporteur proposed a new definition – which was adopted – of misinformation: "Inaccurate or misleading allegations or imputations of a fact likely to alter the truthfulness of the forthcoming ballot are deliberately, artificially and massively disseminated by means of an online public telecommunication service." This definition would have the merit of being more operational.

The LREM rapporteur of the bill, Bruno Studer, rewrote articles 4, 5, 6 and 9 in the first reading, when the text was initially being examined, and these rewriting amendments were adopted before the study of the multiple amendments proposed by the other deputies. However, the deputies quickly adopted an amendment aimed at strengthening "the importance of developing a critical assessment of the information circulating online" in civic education courses and an amendment that encourages "platforms, news agencies, online publishers, advertisers and representative organizations of journalists" to meet regularly "in order to exchange and conclude agreements allowing for greater synergy in terms of transparency and cooperation". The Council of State delivered its opinion, which was very well argued, on April 19, 2018.

While the approach of the new laws was not without reservations, the MPs supplemented suggestions and criticisms with contrasting approaches.

8.1.2. *Obligations*

8.1.2.1. *Transparency*

Emphasis was placed on the transparency needed for platforms that are not negligible in size, but which may limit the freedom to provide information society

---

5 LREM deputy of the Val d'Oise.

services. This derogation from a non-negligible freedom is justified by an overriding reason of general interest, related to the straightforward information that citizens should have during electoral periods. This argument is based on the case law of the Court of Justice of the European Communities, with the Cassis de Dijon judgment[6], the Commission v. France judgment[7] and the ARD judgment[8]. It is also based on the criterion of the sincerity of the ballot, confirmed by the Constitutional Council. The compelling reason is thus satisfied. Indeed, the provision does not pursue an economic objective. And the provision is proportionate to the aim pursued.

The laws amplify the requirements previously imposed on the platforms by article L111-7 of the consumer code: the platforms must reveal not only the existence of an intermediation relationship, but also the identity of the third party that wishes to promote certain informational content. The platforms will have to set up a system that allows users to report false information and be more transparent about their algorithm. Platforms that exceed a certain volume of connections per day will have to have a legal representative in France. Another LRM amendment, supported by the government, intends to oblige platform operators to make their algorithms public.

Finally, platforms must display not only the identity of the person paying for the promotion of information content, but also the identity of the person on behalf of whom they are acting. The additional information is not the result of a search imposed on the platforms, but of a declarative precision provided by the person who tends to promote the content in question: this way, the platforms would reveal the identity of the person acquiring the content.

8.1.2.2. Ballots

The protection of information is limited to national and European ballots. It is a question of being diligent in providing information concerning the identity of the actors who can influence the order and the way in which information is presented via the Internet and the financial means used to this end. Let us not forget that advertising for electoral propaganda purposes, including the purchase of commercial links in order to obtain more favorable SEO[9], is prohibited in the three months preceding the election[10] and requires that commercial communications that are part

---

6 February 20, 1979, No. 120/78, on the circulation of goods.

7 October 22, 1998, Commission v. France, C 184/96, relating to the freedom to provide services and reasonable consumer protection.

8 October 28, 1999, ARD v. Pro Sieben Media AG, C 6/98, on the excesses of TV advertising.

9 Conseil d'État 2009, Élections municipales de Fuveau, No. 317637, T.

10 Article L52.1 of the Electoral Code.

of the information society and the person for whom they are designed be identifiable[11].

However, the Council of State gave its opinion and suggested modifications. First, it stated that the term "information content" is not sufficiently precise; the law, especially in this context, implies precision. Consequently, only information content relating to "a debate of general interest" should be retained. The notion of a debate of general interest is valued highly by the Council of Europe. The ECHR has brought it into play in the confrontations between freedom of expression and protection of privacy.

Moreover, it stated that the reference to the status of natural and legal persons should be deleted, as it does not allow the identification of "the reference", especially when this reference applies to a legal person.

The law focuses on the summary procedure created for election periods. According to article L163-2 of the Electoral Code, from 2020 a new summary procedure, which could only be used during the electoral periods preceding national and European elections, would be brought before a high court – the tribunal de grande instance – for information likely to alter the truthfulness of the ballot. Initially, there was talk of bringing the entire summary procedure before the Tribunal de grande instance de Paris, which attracted some criticism (particularly, with regard to the consequences in terms of appeals); an amendment envisaged making the summary procedure possible in the various constituencies, and the Assemblée nationale would subsequently return to the uniqueness of the summary procedure before the 17th criminal division of the Paris tribunal de grande instance. The judge would rule within 48 hours, and could, at the request of the Public Prosecutor's Office or any person with an interest in the case, impose prescriptions on hosts and Internet service providers[12]. This is likely to happen too late, due to the ever-increasing speed of propagation of false news. The focus on "artificial and massive" dissemination of false information does not open the way to the fight against the dissemination of false information that would result from unfortunate attempts to reach a certain truth. Nevertheless, this new form of summary proceedings has advantages for the candidates in the elections, who would be able to take advantage of a judicial decision to respond in a timely manner in the public debate to unfounded attacks against them.

Only false information which the judge in charge of the summary proceedings considers to be transmitted and disseminated with the deliberate intention to cause

---

11 Article 6 of Directive 2000/31/EC.

12 Background: liability of hosting providers, Internet service providers in the law of June 21, 2004 for confidence in the digital economy, transposing the directive of the June 8, 2000.

harm is covered by the provision. The notion of "deliberate intention" replaces the notion of "bad faith". And the Council of State considers that this new method of summary proceedings does not disproportionately infringe on freedom of expression[13]. However, there may sometimes be a lack of proportionality, for example, when "removing a site disseminating this false information from an index", whereas only the links leading to the pages disseminating this information should be removed from the search results. Likewise, the law should not "prevent access to the e-mail addresses of online public communication services disseminating such false information". Moreover, the question of the time limit for the summary proceedings arises[14]. The Council of State would like this deadline to be set at 48 hours and for the order to be issued as a first and last resort.

The text stipulates that the CSA[15], *Conseil Supérieur de l'Audiovisuel*, is able to conclude an agreement when the refusal is necessary for public order or if the nature of the programming envisaged disregards the other provisions. Moreover, the CSA seems to follow the precedent of its case law, which has recognized that the CSA could refuse to conclude an agreement for a reason of public order[16] and has censured an agreement concluded by the CSA because the programs of the service concerned contravened the purpose of public order[17]. In summary, the CSA must not enter into an agreement with a service that would disregard legislative principles, including those set out in articles 1 to 5 of the law of September 30, 1986.

The law authorizes the CSA to refuse to enter into an agreement with a legal person that would be under the control or influence of a foreign state and could act to destabilize its institutions, in particular through the dissemination of fake news. However, the criterion based on the influence exercised on a legal person by a foreign state seems new and uncertain in terms of its basis and scope. The second criterion can only be retained if it establishes that the legal person is under the influence of a foreign state.

Moreover, this provision applies only to legal persons whose services would be likely to harm the fundamental interests of the Nation. The reference to the fundamental interests of the Nation refers to a concept defined in particular in articles L811-3 of the Internal Security Code and 410-1 of the Criminal Code. These

---

13 Article 11 of the Declaration of the Rights of Man and of the Citizen of 1789 and Article 10 of the European Convention for the Protection of Human Rights and Fundamental Freedoms.

14 Article L163-2 that article 1 of the proposed law no. 799 proposed for insertion in the Electoral Code.

15 The French Audiovisual Board.

16 Conseil d'État, February 11, 2004, Société Médya TV, No. 249175, Rec.

17 Conseil d'État, July 11, 2012, Media place partners, No. 351253, T.

interests have constitutional rank[18], but the undertaking to destabilize the nation's institutions is a new concept which is difficult to circumscribe.

The CSA, in order to justify its refusal, may take into account considerations of content already proposed by the applicant, his subsidiaries and the legal entity that controls it or its subsidiaries. The CSA must be able to mobilize a set of indices outside the scope of the programming envisaged by this service. Thus defined, the principle of the provision does not disregard any constitutional or conventional requirement. Indeed, the Constitutional Council recognizes that it is open to the legislator to subject the private audiovisual communication sector to a regime of administrative authorization. The prevention of breaches of public order is one of the objectives of constitutional value to be reconciled with freedom of expression and communication[19]. The envisaged provision does not seem irreconcilable with those of Directive 2010/13/EU. The European Court of Justice recognizes in this matter the possibility for Member States to provide for additional rules in relation to public policy[20]. Finally, freedom of expression is not absolute and may be restricted where the restriction is necessary and proportionate. The Council of State points out that the services that may be covered by the provision will not meet the condition specified by the ECHR, which tends to subordinate the protection of journalists' freedom of expression to good faith and the provision of reliable and accurate information in accordance with journalistic ethics[21].

During the periods preceding national elections and referendums, the CSA has the power to suspend, until the end of voting operations, the dissemination by any electronic communication process of a service of a legal entity controlled or under the influence of a foreign state, which would be able to alter the indispensable sincerity of the ballot. This is a new special police power for the CSA. This power implies of course the strict application of the principle of proportionality. However, the decisions of the CSA will have to be motivated and subject to a prior controversial procedure. Before the Assemblée nationale, some representatives of the people argue that the CSA is not a sufficiently independent body so as to conduct an effective control mission.

The Council of State was particularly interested in the provisions that surround it. First, the President of the CSA may refer a matter to the President of the Administrative Jurisdiction Division of the Council of State to stop the broadcasting, not only by a satellite operator but also by a service distributor, of a television service under French jurisdiction. The purpose of this extension is to apply the

---

18 Decision No. 2016-590 QPC of October 21, 2016.

19 Decision no. 2016-738 DC of November 10, 2016.

20 CJUE, September 22, 2011, Mesopotamia Broadcast A/S METV, c-244 and 245/10.

21 ECHR GC, 10, 12, 2077, Stoll v. Switzerland, no. 69698/01.

specific summary proceedings. This article sets out a new hypothesis of referral to the president of the Administrative Jurisdiction Division of the Council of State in order to stop the dissemination of any electronic communication process in relation to the characteristics mentioned in point 24. The Council of State suggests replacing the words "the company with which it has concluded the agreement" with the words "the company studying the service in question": the office does not confine itself solely to the companies covered by the agreement, but to services that do not have any agreement with or authorization from the national authorities.

8.1.2.2.1. Access providers and hosts

Certain provisions of the law of June 21, 2004 aimed at instilling confidence in the digital economy[22] have been modified. Access providers and hosting providers are required to cooperate to combat the dissemination of misinformation. This obligation is broken down into three measures: to set up a system that allows anyone to report the content in question; to inform the competent public authorities quickly of any false information activity that is reported; and to make public the resources devoted to the fight against the dissemination of false information.

Before the modifications were introduced, the initial purpose of the 2004 law was, as far as hosts and access providers were concerned, to combat "the glorification of crimes against humanity, hate speech and child pornography". The scope of application has been extended four times, but the offences which necessitated cooperation related to the dissemination of violent content or speech and resulted in quite serious criminal offences. The extension provided for in this case does not constitute an offence. Thus, a great power of appreciation is given to technical intermediaries, and these providers may be tempted to retain a broad definition of misinformation so as not to fail in meeting their obligations – to the detriment of freedom of expression. The usefulness of transmitting this information to the competent public authorities is questionable, since "false information" is not criminally reprehensible. Moreover, the obligation of cooperation is not sufficient to call into question the responsibility of the hosts[23] because of the content containing false information that they would store.

Indeed, the question of the liability of technical service providers was examined by the Constitutional Council back when the law of June 21, 2004 was adopted: the aim was to determine the scope of application of this liability, with some legal experts being in favor of strict liability. Other legal experts, following debates within the Internet Rights Forum, sought on the contrary to limit the scope of application of

---

22 Article 6 of the law of June 21, 2004.

23 The law of June 21, 2004 gave rise to heated discussions on the liability of hosting and access providers.

the liability of technical intermediaries, in a concern for the respect of freedom of expression and freedom of communication.

In a reservation of interpretation made in its decision no. 2004-496 DC[24], the Constitutional Council ruled that the liability of hosts and access providers could only be engaged if the intermediaries did not withdraw blatantly unlawful information, denounced as such by a third party. However, the dissemination of false information is not necessarily illegal, and if an offence is nevertheless constituted, the offence is not demonstrably unlawful.

Hence, the Council of State advises that only the obligation imposed on Internet service providers and hosts to make public the resources they devote to the fight against the dissemination of false information should be retained in this article. This is a desirable transparency measure that is all the more relevant as it is capable of strengthening the self-regulation of the actors concerned.

The laws also emphasize a new mission assigned to the national education system: to make children and adolescents aware of the need to develop a critical mind when it comes to the dissemination of information, within the framework of modern technologies: young people, and even children, approach the sphere of information much more through social networks than through television. This consists of civic education, facilitated by teachers and perhaps journalists.

Many amendments have been tabled and maintain only fragile links with the body of the law: the neutrality of the Internet was reaffirmed as a consequence of the American position of hostility towards this neutrality, and the creation of an ethics body for journalists. These amendments have been rejected, as well as other amendments of lesser interest.

Objections have been raised against these laws and are based on the defense of freedom of expression: the law could, in some cases, lead to a certain amount of self-censorship[25]. And in the current geopolitical context, it could be directed against the organizations of a single foreign state: Russia.

In fact, based on the concept of "national security", which originated in the Americas[26] but was introduced into French law in the law of July 10, 1991 on the interception of telecommunications[27], it plays an increasingly important role in

---

24 As of June 10, 2004.

25 This explains in part the Sénat's rejection, on August 26, 2018, of the texts adopted by the Assemblée nationale on first reading.

26 United States and National Security Doctrine in Latin America.

27 See security interceptions.

French law, as evidenced in particular by the law on intelligence, where, incidentally, foreign policy is becoming increasingly important as grounds for interception. France rejoined NATO's integrated military bodies in 2008 and this had consequences for the French normative landscape. Commercial sanctions measures have been adopted in recent years by most Western states against Russia. In particular, there is distrust towards the Russian media.

As of April 4, 2018, the Minister of Foreign Affairs Jean-Yves Le Dryan notably likened Russia and its media[28] to mouthpieces for propaganda, with reference to the law against false information. The control powers of the CSA are not the ideal way of defending against threats to the freedom to circulate opinions that are not just the most commonly accepted ones[29].

8.1.2.2.2. Normative adoption

The Sénat rejected the text with a reservation without examining it in July 2018. The meeting of the mixed Joint Committee was a failure. In a second reading,[30] the Assemblée nationale adopted a new version of the text which was subject to rare modifications on October 10, 2018. The text was then examined by the Sénat on October 17, 2018. The Law Commission decided to submit a motion to the Sénat to add the preliminary question to the proposal for an institutional law. On November 5, 2018, the text was rejected and arguments were notably opposed to the summary proceedings.

In the wake of this rejection, the Minister of Culture Franck Riester worked on the legislative dossier previously defended by Françoise Nyssen. The text was definitively adopted by the Assemblée nationale on November 20, 2018. In addition to these laws, the government launched a project on the ethics of information led by Emmanuel Hoog[31].

The Constitutional Council was referred to by 60 deputies and 60 senators on November 23, 2018 and in two decisions made public on December 20, 2018, it declared the texts to be in conformity with the Constitution.

---

28 Russia Day or "Sputnik".

29 According to the European Convention for the Protection of Human Rights and Fundamental Freedoms, freedom of expression implies the possibility of expressing minority opinions, even those that attract the disapproval of a large majority, with exceptions such as racist or revisionist theories that are not allowed in the Council of Europe and the European Union.

30 Franck Riester succeeded Françoise Nyssen at the Ministry of Culture.

31 Formerly Managing Director of Agence France Presse.

Two reservations are worth noting. The first relates to the referral to the summary proceedings judge: the Constitutional Council indicates that the procedure cannot be used against "opinions, parodies, partial inaccuracies or exaggerations"[32]. Moreover, the proof of inaccuracy shall be immediate and easy. The dissemination of false information corresponds to the three conditions set by the legislator: it must be artificial or automated, massive and deliberate.

The second reservation concerns the CSA, which can suspend a broadcasting agreement for a radio or television service "concluded with a legal person controlled by or under the influence of a foreign State". This suspension is not possible where the information that is broadcast is vague or misleading, as there is a risk that the scrutiny may not always be fair. Most of the provisions of the two laws were not questioned, but some commentators, such as Roseline Letteron[33], believed that these reservations would likely render the text inapplicable.

Scientists, for their part, remained doubtful: "We are seized by a malaise. Doubt and mistrust go hand in hand with the scientific position – this is why we need to produce evidence – but we sense that we are held hostage by supporters of ideologies that are not in search of truth," notes Jean-Gabriel Ganascia[34]. The debate remains open.

In the United States, misinformation is regularly reported, but it seems that many people enjoy it or even seek it out.

According to an article published in the *Boston Globe* on January 17, 2020, the start-up NewsGuard, which specializes in the fight against misinformation, conducted a study on misinformation. According to the results, sites that spread misinformation have gained popularity in the United States. About 10% of the top 10 most popular articles in December 2019 came from such sites, a 20% increase over the previous month.

This sudden increase is largely explained by the impeachment procedure that was launched, with the failure to impeach Donald Trump. A number of the Internet users, in particular Republicans, most likely resorted to these sites at the time that the impeachment procedure was launched.

"We think this is happening at a time when the political news is getting tense. As things become more polarized, there is an increased incentive for people to create

32 See ECHR, January 9, 2018, Damien Meslot v. France.
33 Letteron, R. (2018). Les réserves du Conseil constitutionnel. *Liberté, Libertés chéries*, December 22/*Les crises*, rubrique Médias, December 29, 2018.
34 President of the Ethics Committee of the CNRS, Conference on "fake news", May 22, 2018 at the Centre national de la recherche scientifique.

misinformation and a growing interest in these stories," commented Steven Brill, co-CEO of NewsGuard.

It would appear that this phenomenon is unique to the United States. Indeed, studies have also been carried out, including by NewsGuard in Germany, France, Italy and the United Kingdom. However, sites that spread false information are consulted less than in the United States. Nevertheless, the ripple effect of social networks facilitates the sharing of false information.

Some social networks use algorithms to combat misinformation, but this has not made the misinformation go away. Facebook, for example, has integrated a form of artificial intelligence that is able to detect deep fakes, a type of fake video. In spite of these measures, American Internet users appreciate false information. In order to determine whether sites are hosting false information, NewsGuard bases its analysis on these key criteria:

– presence of fake or visibly distorted information;

– uncorrected glaring errors;

– articles, the sources of which are not apparent;

– hidden or insufficiently clear political orientation;

– unknown site owners.

In spite of the dissemination of this false information, American legislation protects its authors pursuant to the First Amendment of the American Constitution. Facebook has taken the initiative in sending warnings that receive false information. Should the "spirit of freedom" rely on legislation? One might be inclined to think so.

On the contrary, the example of the new French legislation on misinformation encourages conformism.

Legislation on false information can be supplemented, in Germany and in France, by legislation on hate speech. However, it is not so straightforward.

Freedom of expression is guaranteed in France by a text with constitutional value, the Declaration of the Rights of Man and of the Citizen, of August 26, 1789[35], and by the Universal Declaration of Human Rights[36].

---

35 Article 11: "The free communication of thoughts and opinions is one of the most precious rights of man; every citizen may speak, write and express freely except to answer to the abuse of this freedom in cases determined by law."

36 "Every individual has the right to freedom of opinion and expression, which implies the right to not be persecuted for his or her opinions and to seek, receive and respond, regardless of boundaries, to information and ideas by any means of expression".

8.2. Hate speech

Abuses of this freedom of expression are becoming increasingly frequent, since the preferred means of expression in this area are digital. The danger posed by this abuse to the freedom of expression seems to be more and more pressing, as it goes through social networks, hosts and access providers.

Hence, the French law of June 21, 2004, which translates the directive of June 8, 2000 on electronic commerce into the French legal corpus, has been amended by a law on hate speech on the Internet, devoted to the fight against racism, anti-semitism, xenophobia and homophobia. The latter is based on the opinion of the Council of State of May 26, 2019.

This law came after the German NetzDG law, adopted in June 2017, which entered into force on January 1, 2018 and obliges exchange platforms[37] to delete messages inciting hatred and violence within 24 hours after a user has alerted them to proven facts and within seven days for more complex cases. Fines for refusal to comply can reach 50 million euros.

This law incurred the irony of the satirical newspaper *Titanic*. The newspaper's Twitter account was blocked for 48 hours. "With this case of censorship with *Titanic*, what we feared with this law actually happened", said Frank Überall, president of the German Journalists Association[38]. A balance is not always easy to find.

This fight and an evolution of the responsibility of hosting and access providers are intended to interest the whole of the European Union[39]. Actually, it should not be forgotten that some countries of the European Union, such as the Scandinavian countries, are more attached than others to freedom of expression.

8.2.1. *The report*

The law is inspired by the report "Strengthening the fight against racism and anti-Semitism on the Internet" requested by Prime Minister Édouard Philippe from a

---

37 See YouTube, Facebook and Twitter.

38 DJV.

39 President Emmanuel Macron declared on March 7, 2018: "This year, we hope to be able to lead a battle at the European level to legislate to force operators to withdraw all such content as soon as possible and to build the legal framework for the liability of platforms and all these message broadcasters."

European perspective, with the desire for the French government to position itself in the vanguard of this European project.

The report was drawn up by Karim Amellal, author and teacher, Laetitia Avia, Member of Parliament for Paris, and Gil Taïeb, President of the Representative Council of Jewish Institutions in France. Following the report, Avia was encouraged to develop a draft law on hate speech disseminated on the Internet, intended to complement the 1881 Press Law and amend the LCEN of June 21, 2004.

This bill is part of an international framework, along with the Convention on Cybercrime of November 23, 2001[40], which also includes, under number 189, the additional protocol[41] on racist and xenophobic remarks, within the European framework of the European Convention for the Protection of Human Rights and Fundamental Freedoms (ECHR)[42], and the European Charter of Fundamental Rights, adopted on December 7, 2000[43].

In France, the LCEN applies to the liability of hosts and access providers, after a period of contrasting case law[44]. The host is a professional who allows Internet users to have web pages that can be put on online sites. The law of June 21, 2004 opted, after much discussion, for a limited liability regime defined in article 6.1.2 of the LCEN. This specific regime applies to "natural or legal persons who provide, even free of charge, communication services to the public online, and store signs, writing, images, sounds or messages of any nature provided by recipients of these services". They are not liable for information stored at the request of a recipient of these services in the event that one of the two following conditions is met: either they were not actually aware of its illicit nature or of facts and circumstances that reveal this nature, or from the moment that they became aware of it, they acted promptly to remove this data or prevent access. This exemption from liability does not apply if the recipient of the service acts under the authority or control of a service provider.

A broad interpretation of "demonstrably unlawful" has the effect of extending the host's scope of liability. It is worth quoting the judgment of December 12, 2007

---

40 French ratification took place in 2006.

41 2003.

42 Text of November 4, 1950, entered into force on September 3, 1953, ratified by France on September 3, 1974.

43 The Charter has had the same value as a treaty since December 2009 and the entry into force of the Lisbon Treaty.

44 Paris Court of Appeal decision of February 10, 1999, Estelle Lefébure v. Valentin Lacambre.

relating to Bloogers, Google Inc.'s platform at that time[45]. Google Inc. saw the same reasoning applied in two decisions of the Paris Tribunal de Grande Instance of October 19, 2007 and February 20, 2008[46].

The most favorable situation for the sites is when the judges recognize them as hosts while allowing them to benefit fully from the limited liability regime provided by the LCEN. The sites qualified as hosts have not been found liable because, in accordance with the limitation provisions set forth in the LCEN, either the notification made by the victims of the illicit content was not in conformity with the LCEN or the sites reacted promptly.

8.2.2. *The proposed new mechanism*

The principles of simplicity, accessibility, visibility and availability are adopted by platforms, search engines and access providers. Reporting procedures are well defined: procedures are only carried out online; the various items make it possible to specify the nature of the alleged infringement; associations and authorities have privileged access; a single button is created, with an easily identifiable logo; and the Internet user is informed as his report is processed.

The platform has 24 hours to withdraw racist, anti-semitic, xenophobic or homophobic comments. When the content is not strictly illicit, the platforms will, however, have seven days to examine it. The Internet user can then appeal against the response. In the event of non-compliance, the platforms expose themselves to a fine corresponding to 4% of worldwide turnover, as provided for in the GDPR in the event of non-compliance with the protection of personal data.

8.2.2.1. *Setting up a blocking procedure*

The transposition of the ARJEL[47] and AMF[48] device to online hate speech is as follows: the administrative authority, depending on the CSA, asks the judicial authority to block access providers to hate sites and content, on the basis of an order on request.

---

45 Having dismissed the quality of publisher, the judge declared: "The host, while not responsible for the content it hosts, must, when data, the content of which is declared illegal is denounced, not leave it to the discretion of the judges, but assess whether such content is demonstrably illegal and, in this case, delete or make such data inaccessible."

46 Paris Tribunal de Grande Instance of February 5, 2008, Free v. SNE.

47 Procedure for illegal online gambling.

48 Autorité des marchés financiers.

As for the modification of the 1881 law, the cases of referral to the judge in charge of summary proceedings were broadened to include criminal sanctions, with the possibility of referring cases to the judge in charge of summary proceedings of the Tribunal de grande instance de Paris. Thus, there will be formal notice addressed to publishers of illicit online sites, copy of the formal notice to hosting providers, and possibly a referral to the President of the tribunal de grande instance de Paris, in the form of summary proceedings.

With respect to filtering online advertising on hate sites, advertisers have until now been able to display ads on sites with hate content. Hate content is more revenue-generating than non-hate content, and social networks have a vested financial interest in hate messages: a shocking statement, including an extreme or hateful message, feeds platforms' business models. An Internet user seeking recognition could therefore accept hateful content without being personally convinced of it.

The report "Strengthening the fight against racism and anti-Semitism on the Internet" suggests providing for the publication of a list of the media used for their advertisements in order to limit this dissemination and the financing of hate sites: Decree no. 2017-159 of February 9, 2017 relating to digital advertising services, in force since January 1, 2018, obliges vendors selling advertising space to provide this list to their advertisers. The European Commission suggests that the platforms, in cooperation with the advertising industry, demonetize the sites[49]. It is also possible to encourage so-called "responsible" advertising investment by companies, to prevent the publication on toxic sites of pornographic comments or images, false information and anti-semitic comments (as the French government's information service has done since January 1, 2019).

As for the difficult cooperation with online platforms, it was not very effective in bringing authors out of anonymity. In the presence of a racist or anti-semitic insult on the Internet, the public prosecutor could not rely on the platform where the remarks were made to identify the author, even though article 6 of the LCEN provides for a notice. The low level of convictions for these crimes does not encourage victims to file a complaint.

In terms of facilitating the filing of complaints, the 2018–2022 programming and justice reform bill provides for[50] the possibility of filing a complaint for offences committed online, and extending the online filing of complaints to offences covered by the 1881 law, when they are carried out via a public communication tool.

---

49 As part of the *Follow the money* initiative.
50 In article 27.

A summary penalty order is ideally the procedure used for hate speech. The order involves the expeditious processing of cases since it is not based on the controversial principle and does not require a hearing. The summary penalty order signed by the president of the court is a simplified procedure that determines the amount of the fine and an additional penalty, in a specialized chamber at the High Courts. This chamber, with magistrates specifically trained in the resolution of these cases, should allow justice to be achieved more harmoniously.

The Assemblée nationale created a prosecutor's office specializing in online hate: the latter would initially be in charge of all judicial investigations relating to messages posted on the Internet and some of the non-public insults.

The platforms point out that they deploy powerful algorithms to detect illegal content. According to Twitter, "more than 70 changes to its products, policies and operations were counted in 2018" and Twitter has increased its "hate action rates" 10-fold.

The text also aims to provide a better response to the problem of "mirror sites" that appear with the data set of a previous platform when access may have been blocked. Nevertheless, many MPs, from various political parties, considered the role given to the GAFA to be exorbitant. They narrowly failed to create a criminal offense of abusive withdrawal. Avia pushed through two amendments that she said limited the risk of censorship by requiring social networks to "prevent the risk of unwarranted withdrawals".

A lively debate centered around interoperability: a user of one social network can exchange and interact with users of another social network. This initiative was rejected by the rapporteur Avia. The platforms and social networks concerned were called "content accelerators".

To this end, an online hate observatory could be entrusted with a monthly barometer and the publication of an annual report on key trends in hate speech as it appears on the Internet, particularly on social networks. The Observatory would maintain civil relations with the regulatory authority, while retaining its autonomy.

To raise the awareness of civil society, associations are able to report content to the platforms[51] and initiate legal proceedings with regard to this societal law. They can also encourage civil society actors, particularly Internet users, to combat hate speech. Thus, the *Seriously*[52] project concocted by Renaissance Numérique put a form online whose purpose was to thwart targeted messages. It is the youngest

---

51 Trusted flaggers.
52 http://Seriously.ong.

demographic who are the largely concerned, since 80% of children between 11 and 17 years old go online every day and most of them are loyal to social networks. An online presence on the platforms where violent discourse has most often appeared would therefore be useful. This initiative would be inspired by the "Promeneurs du Net"[53] supported by the ministry in charge of youth.

Another prevention would be to make zones of respect appear on social networks and virtual chat rooms. The Respect Zone association could label websites. Training initiatives for teaching staff could serve as intermediaries with the younger demographic. This set of actions could, if not prevent, at least limit hate speech.

8.2.2.2. *The law and the U-turn by Parliament*

From now on, racist, anti-semitic, anti-religious, and homophobic content, child pornography and direct provocation of terrorist acts will be questioned.

This concerns the 24-hour withdrawal of hateful content, a penal measure that the senators considered unaccomplished in legal terms, contrary to European law[54] and not really respecting freedom of expression. The Assemblée nationale's amendment targets "terrorist" comments and the withdrawal must be done in 1 hour, which was criticized even more.

In the event of non-compliance with the withdrawal obligation, the platforms are liable to fines of up to 1.25 million euros. Operators must acknowledge receipt of the notification and inform the users who initiated the publication of the content of the date and time of the notification, the follow-up given to the notification and the reasons for their decisions within 24 hours if they make the content inaccessible or stop referencing it, or, failing this, within seven days of receipt of the notification.

Illegal content is replaced by a message indicating that it has been removed. Deleted illegal content is kept for a maximum period of one year for the purposes of research and for the judicial authority's observation.

The CSA (French Audiovisual Board) is tasked with regulation. It proposes recommendations that platforms must comply with. It has the power to issue formal notices and pronounce a financial sanction that cannot exceed 4% of the total annual worldwide turnover of the previous fiscal year. The sanction takes into account the seriousness of the breaches and, where applicable, their recurrence.

---

53 Originated in Sweden.

54 The European Commission has noted a generalized filtering, in contradiction with the directive of June 8, 2000 on e-commerce.

Many were critical of this. Most are hostile to the role of platforms. You entrust censorship to Google, Facebook, Twitter, (which is essentially) private censorship, says François Ruffin[55]. Two associations of Jewish resistance fighters[56] wrote on this subject to Premier Édouard Philippe: "On the pretext of the sluggishness of the judicial system, instead of, as it should be, transferring to a specific independent public authority the task of deciding on the withdrawal of hate speech, the text under discussion delegates the deletion of such speech to the Internet platforms themselves." Laure de la Raudière returned to freedom of expression: "I share the objective ... to fight against online hate, but I want to reiterate my concern that the platforms will become judges of freedom of expression."[57] A letter signed shortly before the final vote by the *Association des avocats conseils d'entreprises*, Change.org, the *Conseil national des barreaux*, the *Conseil National du numérique*, the *Fondation Internet nouvelle génération*, *Internet sans frontières*, Internet society France, *La Quadrature du Net*, the *Ligue des droits de l'homme*, *Renaissance numérique* and the *Syndicat des avocats de France* speaks for itself: "By circumventing the prerogatives of the judicial judge, the text of the law undermines the guarantees that nowadays allow us to preserve the balance of our fundamental rights and freedoms ... with regard to the provisions of the text, platform operators will be encouraged to opt for over-censorship."

On June 18, 2020, the Constitutional Council ruled against the Avia law: it disapproved of the fact that private individuals could decide on the hateful nature of statements within 24 hours, in a way that was disproportionate to the requirement of freedom of expression. Moreover, with regard to statements inciting terrorism, it is impossible to bring a case before a judge within one hour. The government noted the decision and committed to reworking the text.

On June 19, 2020, the Constitutional Council abolished the offence of concealing stolen goods in support of terrorism, which had been enshrined by the Court of Cassation in January 2020. At the European level, the Commission had urged France to postpone the adoption of the Avia law. Hence, these recent texts on misinformation and hate speech paint a picture of a society that seeks above all security and risks committing abuses by wanting to prevent abuses.

With the pandemic of 2020, the emergency measures taken in the public health sector seem likely to undermine individual and collective freedoms. This is notably the case in China, with the tracking of patients on smartphones. In France, according

---

55 France insoumise.

56 "La Mémoire des Résistants juifs de la MOI" and "L'Union des Juifs pour la résistance et l'entraide".

57 Laure de la Raudière, UDI, Assemblée nationale, session of January 15, 2020.

to the CNIL, tracking would comply with the GDPR, but the suspicion of liberticide is strong.

Is the spirit of freedom there? It is not certain, and one must suspend the answer whether there will be conformity with the law as well as with Cartesian logic.

Conclusion

Security, Technologies and the Spirit of Freedom

We have demonstrated that in an era of constantly changing technologies, innovation is an ever more pressing issue for the various players involved.

Currently, security and technologies are coming up against artificial intelligence. According to the encyclopedia *Larousse*, artificial intelligence (AI) is defined as "the theories and techniques used to create machines capable of simulating intelligence". It is not an autonomous discipline; it draws on mathematics, computer science and neurobiology. It uses very complex algorithms and will find many applications in the 2020s and 2030s in various sectors of industry and services.

In his article "Computing Machinery and Intelligence"[1], Alan Turing wonders when a machine might be considered conscious[2].

Artificial intelligence has developed in several stages:

– in the 1980s, machine learning became a reality; learning algorithms were created. The general public saw, in May 1997, the Deep Blue computer beat the world chess champion Garry Kasparov;

– in the 2000s, the Internet and Big Data allowed computers to analyze masses of data;

– around 2015, artificial intelligence would begin to be able to truly understand situations, make decisions and improve its deductive capacity. To achieve such results, investments increased 10-fold between 2010 and 2017[3].

---

1 Turing, A. (1950). *Mind*, October.
2 See lecture "Intelligent machinery, a heretical theory", given at Society 51 in Manchester.
3 5 billion euros in 2017.

Some applications are military in nature. On January 27, 2010, the US Air Force collaborated with the industry to achieve advanced intelligence information gathering designed to help the US military defeat its enemies; the US Air Force is currently using ontological reasoning[4] to strike adversaries at the most vulnerable point. In addition, more than a thousand of the latest generation F22 and F35 bombers and fighters are equipped with AI.

Other numerous applications concern the Internet. In January 2018, artificial intelligence models were established by Microsoft and Alibaba. In February 2019, the research institute OpenAI created an AI program capable of generating texts that can give the impression of originality.

In France, on January 20, 2017, Axelle Lemaire intended to promote science and industry through an AI project. For its part, the same year (2017), the CNIL published its report "Comment permettre à l'Homme de garder la main?" (How can we make sure humans stay in control?) which made recommendations on the ethics of artificial intelligence[5]. In September 2017, Cédric Villani, first vice-president of the *Office parlementaire d'évaluation des choix scientifiques et technologiques* (Parliamentary Office for the Evaluation of Scientific and Technological Choices)[6] was tasked with launching a consultation[7] on artificial intelligence. The French legislation would involve the entry into force of AI and the movement of autonomous vehicles; the State's algorithms are open, but it is necessary to oppose decision-making in the absence of human intervention. AI is a new vector of suppression and job creation.

Strong artificial intelligence implies that the machine animated by AI is able to conform to intelligent behavior, as well as to be conscious. Most scientists do not oppose the creation of intelligence on a material medium other than biological, which is possible with quantum algorithms.

Whether it is a strong or weak intelligence, artificial intelligence finds outlets in finance with projects such as those of Bridgewater Associates, which manages funds, the military field with drones, decision support[8], and medicine, with expert

---

4 A form of artificial intelligence.

5 CNIL, December 2017.

6 OPECST.

7 Report of March 28, 2018.

8 An arms race with AI support is underway.

systems for diagnostic assistance, police intelligence, law, public transportation[9], robotics and art.

Some scientists will note that it is possible to envisage a hypothesis where machines with an artificial intelligence substitute at least partially for humans, just as humans have dominated animal species. The astrophysicist Stephen Hawking wondered in November 2017 at the Web Summit technological fair in Lisbon: "Will we be helped by artificial intelligence or set aside or even destroyed by it?"[10]

According to Moshe Vardi[11], artificial intelligence could lead to mass unemployment. AI would not only be used in homes as a domestic robot, or computer developer, or journalists' collaborator, or designer; machines would be more powerful than humans in almost all tasks. This risk is taken seriously on a legal level: the European Parliament has asked a commission to study the possibility that a robot may be given a legal personality, different from the one given to natural and legal persons. On December 18, 2018, the European Union's High Level Expert Group on Artificial Intelligence will publish a document on ethical guidelines for artificial intelligence.

As far as the ecosystem is concerned, it was noted that the consumption of scarce resources, servers and energy was very important.

The societal aspect is not negligible. On September 28, 2016, the largest industrial players in artificial intelligence created a partnership for artificial intelligence for the benefit of citizens and society. In 2017, Google DeepMind put the examination of ethical issues in the artificial intelligence sector on its agenda[12]. On July 18, 2018, more than 2,000 researchers, engineers and artificial intelligence industry leaders signed an open letter[13] pledging to "never participate in or support the development, manufacture, trade or use of autonomous lethal weapons" and that "the decision to take a human life should never be delegated to a machine".

9 See UrbanLoop system, in Nancy.

10 "Selon Stephen Hawking, l'intelligence artificielle est un danger pour l'humanité-Web Développement Durable", www.webdeveloppementdurable.com.

11 American computer expert.

12 Intelligence artificielle: Google DeepMind se dote d'une unité de recherche sur l'éthique. *Le Monde*, October 4, 2017.

13 Lethal Autonomous Weapons Piedge [Online]. Available at: futureoflite.org.

Critical analysis of artificial intelligence has its conceptual roots in the previous approach to techniques and technology, with Lewis Mumford (USA)[14], Jacques Ellul (France)[15] and Günther Anders (Germany)[16].

The activists of the Technologos group have revived the theses of Jacques Ellul[17], considering that the State does not have the power to regulate the empowerment of the technical process. This is partly in line with the words of Irving John Good: "Suppose there is a machine that surpasses in intelligence everything a man is capable of, however brilliant he may be. Since the design of such machines is part of intellectual activity, this machine could in turn create machines better than itself; this would undoubtedly result in a chain reaction of intelligence development, while human intelligence would almost remain in place. As a result, the ultra-intelligent machine will be the last invention that man will need to make, provided that the said machine is docile enough to constantly obey it."[18]

In an era of debate for the animal species, between speciesism and anti-speciesism, a difficult relationship between human beings and artificial intelligence has evolved. If artificial intelligence gains a privileged place on the planet, not only human rights will be called into question, but also security as it is currently understood. Nevertheless, it is obvious that whoever the social actors are, security will remain a priority that has to and will have to be combined with artificial intelligence. Whether the spirit of freedom is disappearing remains to be seen, and this is a possibility to be explored in the years to come.

---

14 Mumford, L. (1974). *Le Mythe de la machine*, two volumes, 1967–1970. Fayard.

15 Ellul, J. (2008). *La Technique ou l'enjeu du siècle*, 3rd edition, 1954. Economica.

16 Anders, G. (1956/1980). *L'obsolescence de l'homme*, vol. 1, vol. 2. Fario.

17 Ellul, J. (2004). *L'illusion politique*, 3rd edition, 1965. La Table ronde.

18 Good, I.J. (1966). Speculations Concerning the First Ultraintelligent Machine. In *Advances in Computers*, vol. 6, 31–88.

References

Alix, J. (2010). *Terrorisme et droit pénal, étude critique des incriminations*. Dalloz, Paris.

Chemillier-Gendreau, M. (2013). *De la guerre à la communauté universelle*. Fayard, Paris.

Delmas-Marty, M. (2013). *Libertés et sûreté dans un monde dangereux*. Le Seuil, Paris.

Ellul, J. (2012). *Le système technicien*. Le Cherche-Midi, Paris.

Foucault, M. (1975). *Surveiller et punir*. Gallimard, Paris.

Gavroy, R. (2016). Les drones et le droit au respect de la vie privée. Thesis, Université catholique de Louvain, Ottignies-Louvain-la-Neuve.

Granger, M.-A. (2011). *Constitution et sécurité intérieure, essai de modélisation juridique*. LGDJ, Paris.

Guerrier, C. (2000). *Les écoutes téléphoniques*. CNRS, Paris.

Huchet, L. (2016). Researcher at Nantes University.

Latour, B. (2000). La fin des moyens. *Réseaux, communication, technologie, société*, 18(100), 39.

Lucotte, M. (2019) Professor at Montréal University.

Maljean-Dubois, S. (2017). Circulation de normes et réseaux d'acteurs dans la gouvernance internationale de l'environnement [Online]. Available at: https://halshs.archives-ouvertes.fr/halshs-01668013/document.

Mattelart, A. and Vitalis, A. (2014). *Le profilage des populations*. La Découverte, Paris.

Roché, S. (1993). *Le sentiment d'insécurité*. PUF, Paris.

Solzhenitsyn, A. (2009). *In the First Circle*. Harper Perennial, New York.

References

Index

S, V

Other titles from

in

Innovation, Entrepreneurship and Management

2021

ARCADE Jacques
Strategic Engineering (Innovation and Technology Set – Volume 11)

BOBILLIER CHAUMON Marc-Eric
Digital Transformations in the Challenge of Activity and Work:
Understanding and Supporting Technological Changes
(Technological Changes and Human Resources Set – Volume 3)

BUCLET Nicolas
Territorial Ecology and Socio-ecological Transition
(Smart Innovation Set – Volume 34)

DIMOTIKALIS Yannis, KARAGRIGORIOU Alex, PARPOULA Christina,
SKIADIS Christos H
Applied Modeling Techniques and Data Analysis 1: Computational Data
Analysis Methods and Tools (Big Data, Artificial Intelligence and Data
Analysis Set - Volume 7)
Applied Modeling Techniques and Data Analysis 2: Financial,
Demographic, Stochastic and Statistical Models and Methods (Big Data,
Artificial Intelligence and Data Analysis Set – Volume 8)

DISPAS Christophe, KAYANAKIS Georges, SERVEL Nicolas,
STRIUKOVA Ludmila
Innovation and Financial Markets
(Innovation between Risk and Reward Set – Volume 7)

GOGLIN Christian
Emotions and Values in Equity Crowdfunding Investment Choices 2:
Modeling and Empirical Study

HELLER David
Performance of Valuation Methods in Financial Transactions (Modern
Finance, Management Innovation and Economic Growth Set – Volume 4)

UZUNIDIS Dimitri, KASMI Fedoua, ADATTO Laurent
Innovation Economics, Engineering and Management Handbook 1: Main
Themes
Innovation Economics, Engineering and Management Handbook 2: Special
Themes

2020

ACH Yves-Alain, RMADI-SAÏD Sandra
Financial Information and Brand Value: Reflections, Challenges and
Limitations

ANDREOSSO-O'CALLAGHAN Bernadette, DZEVER Sam, JAUSSAUD Jacques,
TAYLOR Robert
Sustainable Development and Energy Transition in Europe and Asia
(Innovation and Technology Set – Volume 9)

BEN SLIMANE Sonia, M'HENNI Hatem
Entrepreneurship and Development: Realities and Future Prospects
(Smart Innovation Set – Volume 30)

CHOUTEAU Marianne, FOREST Joëlle, NGUYEN Céline
Innovation for Society: The P.S.I. Approach
(Smart Innovation Set – Volume 28)

2019

AMENDOLA Mario, GAFFARD Jean-Luc
Disorder and Public Concern Around Globalization

BARBAROUX Pierre
Disruptive Technology and Defence Innovation Ecosystems
(Innovation in Engineering and Technology Set – Volume 5)

DOU Henri, JUILLET Alain, CLERC Philippe
Strategic Intelligence for the Future 1: A New Strategic and Operational
Approach
Strategic Intelligence for the Future 2: A New Information Function
Approach

FRIKHA Azza
Measurement in Marketing: Operationalization of Latent Constructs

FRIMOUSSE Soufyane
Innovation and Agility in the Digital Age
(Human Resources Management Set – Volume 2)

GAY Claudine, SZOSTAK Bérangère L.
Innovation and Creativity in SMEs: Challenges, Evolutions and Prospects
(Smart Innovation Set – Volume 21)

GORIA Stéphane, HUMBERT Pierre, ROUSSEL Benoît
Information, Knowledge and Agile Creativity
(Smart Innovation Set – Volume 22)

HELLER David
Investment Decision-making Using Optional Models
(Economic Growth Set – Volume 2)

HELLER David, DE CHADIRAC Sylvain, HALAOUI Lana, JOUVET Camille
The Emergence of Start-ups
(Economic Growth Set – Volume 1)

HÉRAUD Jean-Alain, KERR Fiona, BURGER-HELMCHEN Thierry
Creative Management of Complex Systems
(Smart Innovation Set – Volume 19)

SAULAIS Pierre, ERMINE Jean-Louis
Knowledge Management in Innovative Companies 1: Understanding and Deploying a KM Plan within a Learning Organization
(Smart Innovation Set – Volume 23)

SERVAJEAN-HILST Romaric
Co-innovation Dynamics: The Management of Client-Supplier Interactions for Open Innovation
(Smart Innovation Set – Volume 20)

SKIADAS Christos H., BOZEMAN James R.
Data Analysis and Applications 1: Clustering and Regression, Modeling-estimating, Forecasting and Data Mining
(Big Data, Artificial Intelligence and Data Analysis Set – Volume 2)
Data Analysis and Applications 2: Utilization of Results in Europe and Other Topics
(Big Data, Artificial Intelligence and Data Analysis Set – Volume 3)

UZUNIDIS Dimitri
Systemic Innovation: Entrepreneurial Strategies and Market Dynamics

VIGEZZI Michel
World Industrialization: Shared Inventions, Competitive Innovations and Social Dynamics
(Smart Innovation Set – Volume 24)

2018

BURKHARDT Kirsten
Private Equity Firms: Their Role in the Formation of Strategic Alliances

CALLENS Stéphane
Creative Globalization
(Smart Innovation Set – Volume 16)

CASADELLA Vanessa
Innovation Systems in Emerging Economies: MINT – Mexico, Indonesia, Nigeria, Turkey
(Smart Innovation Set – Volume 18)

CHALENÇON Ludivine
Location Strategies and Value Creation of International
Mergers and Acquisitions

CHAUVEL Danièle, BORZILLO Stefano
The Innovative Company: An Ill-defined Object
(Innovation between Risk and Reward Set – Volume 1)

CORSI Patrick
Going Past Limits To Growth

D'ANDRIA Aude, GABARRET Inés
Building 21st Century Entrepreneurship
(Innovation and Technology Set – Volume 2)

DAIDJ Nabyla
Cooperation, Coopetition and Innovation
(Innovation and Technology Set – Volume 3)

FERNEZ-WALCH Sandrine
The Multiple Facets of Innovation Project Management
(Innovation between Risk and Reward Set – Volume 4)

FOREST Joëlle
Creative Rationality and Innovation
(Smart Innovation Set – Volume 14)

GUILHON Bernard
Innovation and Production Ecosystems
(Innovation between Risk and Reward Set – Volume 2)

HAMMOUDI Abdelhakim, DAIDJ Nabyla
Game Theory Approach to Managerial Strategies and Value Creation
(Diverse and Global Perspectives on Value Creation Set – Volume 3)

LALLEMENT Rémi
Intellectual Property and Innovation Protection: New Practices
and New Policy Issues
(Innovation between Risk and Reward Set – Volume 3)

UZUNIDIS Dimitri, SAULAIS Pierre
Innovation Engines: Entrepreneurs and Enterprises in a Turbulent World
(Innovation in Engineering and Technology Set – Volume 1)

2016

BARBAROUX Pierre, ATTOUR Amel, SCHENK Eric
Knowledge Management and Innovation
(Smart Innovation Set – Volume 6)

BEN BOUHENI Faten, AMMI Chantal, LEVY Aldo
Banking Governance, Performance And Risk-Taking: Conventional Banks Vs Islamic Banks

BOUTILLIER Sophie, CARRÉ Denis, LEVRATTO Nadine
Entrepreneurial Ecosystems (Smart Innovation Set – Volume 2)

BOUTILLIER Sophie, UZUNIDIS Dimitri
The Entrepreneur (Smart Innovation Set – Volume 8)

BOUVARD Patricia, SUZANNE Hervé
Collective Intelligence Development in Business

GALLAUD Delphine, LAPERCHE Blandine
Circular Economy, Industrial Ecology and Short Supply Chains
(Smart Innovation Set – Volume 4)

GUERRIER Claudine
Security and Privacy in the Digital Era
(Innovation and Technology Set – Volume 1)

MEGHOUAR Hicham
Corporate Takeover Targets

MONINO Jean-Louis, SEDKAOUI Soraya
Big Data, Open Data and Data Development
(Smart Innovation Set – Volume 3)

MOREL Laure, LE ROUX Serge
Fab Labs: Innovative User
(Smart Innovation Set – Volume 5)

PICARD Fabienne, TANGUY Corinne
Innovations and Techno-ecological Transition
(Smart Innovation Set – Volume 7)

2015

CASADELLA Vanessa, LIU Zeting, DIMITRI Uzunidis
Innovation Capabilities and Economic Development in Open Economies
(Smart Innovation Set – Volume 1)

CORSI Patrick, MORIN Dominique
Sequencing Apple's DNA

CORSI Patrick, NEAU Erwan
Innovation Capability Maturity Model

FAIVRE-TAVIGNOT Bénédicte
Social Business and Base of the Pyramid

GODÉ Cécile
Team Coordination in Extreme Environments

MAILLARD Pierre
Competitive Quality and Innovation

MASSOTTE Pierre, CORSI Patrick
Operationalizing Sustainability

MASSOTTE Pierre, CORSI Patrick
Sustainability Calling

2014

DUBÉ Jean, LEGROS Diègo
Spatial Econometrics Using Microdata

LESCA Humbert, LESCA Nicolas
Strategic Decisions and Weak Signals

2013

HABART-CORLOSQUET Marine, JANSSEN Jacques, MANCA Raimondo
VaR Methodology for Non-Gaussian Finance

2012

DAL PONT Jean-Pierre
Process Engineering and Industrial Management

MAILLARD Pierre
Competitive Quality Strategies

POMEROL Jean-Charles
Decision-Making and Action

SZYLAR Christian
UCITS Handbook

2011

LESCA Nicolas
Environmental Scanning and Sustainable Development

LESCA Nicolas, LESCA Humbert
Weak Signals for Strategic Intelligence: Anticipation Tool for Managers

MERCIER-LAURENT Eunika
Innovation Ecosystems

2010

SZYLAR Christian
Risk Management under UCITS III/IV

2009

COHEN Corine
Business Intelligence

ZANINETTI Jean-Marc
Sustainable Development in the USA

2008

CORSI Patrick, DULIEU Mike
The Marketing of Technology Intensive Products and Services

DZEVER Sam, JAUSSAUD Jacques, ANDREOSSO Bernadette
Evolving Corporate Structures and Cultures in Asia: Impact of Globalization

2007

AMMI Chantal
Global Consumer Behavior

2006

BOUGHZALA Imed, ERMINE Jean-Louis
Trends in Enterprise Knowledge Management

CORSI Patrick *et al.*
Innovation Engineering: the Power of Intangible Networks